NELSON
Primary Maths
for Caribbean Schools

2nd edition

ERROL FURLONGE
Consultant editor Peter Clarke

JUNIOR BOOK 4 & 5

Text © Errol Furlonge, 1997, 2005

The right of Errol Furlonge to be identified as author of this work has been asserted by him in accordance with the Copyright, Designs and Patents Act 1988.

All rights reserved. No part of this publication may be reproduced or transmitted in any form or by any means, electronic or mechanical, including photocopy, recording or any information storage and retrieval system, without permission in writing from the publisher or under licence from the Copyright Licensing Agency Limited, of Saffron House, 6-10 Kirby Street, London, EC1N 8TS.

Any person who commits any unauthorised act in relation to this publication may be liable to criminal prosecution and civil claims for damages.

First published in 1997 by:
Stanley Thornes (Publishing) Ltd

Second edition published in 2005 by:
Nelson Thornes Ltd
Delta Place
27 Bath Road
CHELTENHAM
GL53 7TH
United Kingdom

11 12 13 / 10 9 8 7 6 5

A catalogue record for this book is available from the British Library

ISBN 978 0 7487 9630 4

Page make-up and Illustration by IFA Design Limited, Plymouth, Devon, UK.

Printed in China by 1010 Printing International Ltd

Contents

Junior Book 4

Unit 1: Numbers to 1 000 000 — 1
- Review of numbers to 1000 — 1
- Word problems using a calculator — 3
- Reviewing place value in 4-digit numbers — 4
- Ordering 4-digit numbers — 5
- Rounding numbers – review — 6
- Approximation — 8
- From 4-digit numbers to 6-digit numbers — 9
- Place value in 6-digit numbers — 10
- One million — 11
- Place value for numbers with more than six digits — 13
- Large numbers in expanded form — 14
- Rounding large numbers — 16
- Assessment 1 — 20

Unit 2: Multiplication and division — 21
- Review of multiplication — 21
- Multiplying 3-digit numbers — 23
- Multiplying 4-digit numbers — 24
- Multiplication in money problems — 25
- Reviewing division by 1-digit divisors — 26
- Division by 2-digit divisors — 27

Unit 3: Solid shapes and symmetry — 29
- Solids: prisms and pyramids — 29
- Solids and their faces — 30
- Properties of solids — 31
- Nets — 32
- Symmetry — 34
- Assessment 2 — 35

Unit 4: Squares, square roots and factors — 36
- Squares — 36
- Square roots — 38
- Factors — 40
- Rectangle numbers — 41
- Prime numbers — 42
- Prime factors — 43
- Powers of numbers — 45
- Lowest common multiple (L.C.M.) — 46
- Highest common factor (H.C.F.) — 48

Unit 5: Equivalent fractions — 50
- Equivalent fractions — 50
- Ordering fractions — 52
- Creating equivalent fractions — 55
- Comparing fractions — 56
- Rewriting fractions with smaller denominators — 58
- Word problems — 60
- Assessment 3 — 61

Unit 6: Mixed numbers and improper fractions — 62
- Addition and subtraction of simple fractions — 64
- Addition of mixed numbers — 66
- Subtraction of mixed numbers — 68

Unit 7: Multiplication and division of fractions — 72
- Multiplying a fraction by a whole number — 72
- Multiplying a whole number by a fraction — 73

iii

Fractional parts of concrete quantities	74
Word problems	75
Division by a fraction	76

Unit 8: Angles — 77

Clockwise and anti-clockwise turns	77
Comparing angles	78
Lines and angles	79
Measuring angles	80
Right angles	82
Identifying right angles	84
Measurement of angles	86
Assessment 4	88

Unit 9: Decimals — 89

Revision of tenths	89
Addition of decimals	90
Subtraction of decimals	91
Word problems	92
Decimal numbers – hundredths	93
Converting fractions to decimals	96
Thousands to hundredths – the place value chart	97
Decimal numbers in expanded form – thousands to hundredths	98
Ordering decimal numbers	99
Place value – millions to hundredths	100
Decimal numbers in expanded form – hundred thousands to hundredths	101
Approximation to the nearest tenth	102
Assessment 5	103

Unit 10: Addition and subtraction of decimals — 104

Adding decimal numbers in hundredths	104
Regrouping hundredths in adding	105
Regrouping tenths in adding	106
Subtraction of hundredths	107
Regrouping hundredths in subtraction	108
Regrouping tenths in subtraction	109
Decimal numbers in linear measurement	110
Problem solving	112

Unit 11: Percentages — 114

Fractions as percentages	114
The whole – 100%	115
Percentages and fractions	116
Finding percentages	118
Finding percentages of quantities	119
Discounts	121
Assessment 6	122

Unit 12: Unitary method, wages and interest — 123

Unitary method	123
Wages and salaries	126
Percentages and interest	127

Unit 13: Measurement of length/Circumference — 129

Centimetres and millimetres	129
Metres and millimetres	131
Kilometres and metres	132
Approximation to the nearest hundredth	135
Approximation in lengths	136

The circle	137
Measuring circumference	139
Finding the diameter and radius	141
Assessment 7	142

Unit 14: Area and volume — 143
Area of a right-angled triangle	143
Area of any triangle	145
Area of borders and paths	146
Surface area of cuboids	148
Word problems	150
Volume of a cuboid	151
Assessment 8	152

Unit 15: Mass and weight — 153
Kilograms and grams	153
Approximation in weight	154
Adding kilograms and grams	155
Subtracting kilograms and grams	156
Multiplying kilograms and grams	157
Dividing kilograms and grams	158
Word problems	159

Unit 16: Time — 160
Reviewing five-minute intervals in time	160
Reading the time to one-minute intervals	161
Word problems	162
Assessment 9	164

Unit 17: Handling data — 165
Average or mean	165
Mode	166
The pie chart	167
End-of-year test – Standard 4	171

Junior Book 5

Unit 18: Angles/Triangles/Polygons — 175
Measuring angles	175
Using a paper protractor	176
Using the protractor	178
Obtuse and acute angles	179
Reviewing angles	180
More about angles	181
Perpendicular and parallel lines	183
Drawing squares and rectangles	184
Triangles and their angles	185
Drawing right-angled triangles	186
Scalene triangles	188
Drawing other triangles	189
Polygons	191
Special quadrilaterals	192
Nets	193
Assessment 10	194

Unit 19: Multiplication and division of fractions — 195
Multiplying a fraction by a fraction	195
Multiplying a mixed number by a fraction	197
Division of fractions by whole numbers	199
Division of a fraction by a fraction	201

Unit 20: Multiplication and division of decimals — 203
Fractions and decimal numbers	203
Multiplying tenths by whole numbers	204
Multiplying hundredths by whole numbers	205
Multiplying two decimal numbers	205
Finding a rule for multiplying decimals	207

Estimating products of decimal numbers	210
Word problems	211
Changing money	212
Multiplying decimals by multiples of 10	213
Dividing decimal numbers by whole numbers	214
Expressing a fraction as a decimal	216
Dividing two decimal numbers	218
Assessment 11	219

Unit 21: Transformations/Symmetry — 220
Translation	220
Flips and reflections	221
Rotation	222
More transformations	223
Symmetry	224

Unit 22: Percentages — 225
Fractions, decimals and per cent	225
Percentages of quantities	227
Finding percentages	230

Unit 23: Discount/Profit and loss/Interest — 231
Discount	231
Profit and loss	233
Percentages and taxes	235
Interest on loans and hire purchase	236
Word problems	238
Assessment 12	239

Unit 24: Unequal sharing — 240

Unit 25: Circumference and pi — 243
Perimeter of compound shapes	246
Word problems	247

Unit 26: Area of triangles/Compound shapes/Circles — 248
Area of triangles	248
Area of an obtuse-angled triangle	249
Area of compound shapes	250
Word problems	252
The parallelogram	252
The rhombus	254
Area of a parallelogram	255
The trapezium	256
Area of a circle	257
Assessment 13	259

Unit 27: Volume and capacity — 261
Litres and millilitres	261
Reviewing volume	264
Volume and capacity	266
Volume of a cylinder	268

Unit 28: Time — 270
Minutes and seconds	270
Speed	273
Finding distance and time	274
Assessment 14	276

Unit 29: Statistics — 277
Mean and mode	277
The pictograph	278
The bar graph	279
The pie chart revisited	280

Specimen paper — 282

Acknowledgements

The author acknowledges the assistance and co-operation of all the practising teachers who responded to the questionnaire relating to the use of the series, and those who willingly discussed and advised on the contents of the course.

1 Numbers to 1 000 000

Review of numbers to 1000

Using a calculator

You will need: a calculator.

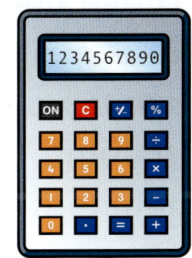

1. Use only these keys $+$, $-$, $=$, 9 and 4 to make all the numbers from 1 to 20.

   For example:
   $$9 + 9 + 9 + 9 - 4 - 4 - 4 - 4 = 20$$

2. Instead of 9 and 4 use 7 and 2 to make the numbers 1 to 20.

Cover the grid

A game for two players.

You will need: 2 calculators, 10 counters in one colour, 10 counters in a different colour.

Rules

- Take it in turns to play.
- Choose any pair of numbers from the list opposite.
- You can use either the $+$ or the $-$ key.
- Is your answer on the grid?
- If so, cover it with a counter.
- The winner is the first to get four counters in a row vertically, horizontally or diagonally.

| 64 | 37 | 29 | 95 | 48 | 81 | 52 | 68 | 73 |

112	8	110	143	31
35	176	120	44	132
93	101	66	27	121
47	159	52	85	124
168	149	141	125	19

1

UNIT 1 Numbers to 1 000 000

These calculations are to give you practice using a calculator. You must first work out the answer to each calculation in the usual way and then check your answers using a calculator.
In some of the calculations you have to work out the missing numbers.

1.
```
    119
   2734
 +   56
 _____
```

2.
```
   4317
    594
 + 2172
 _____
```

3.
```
     88
   7351
 + 1002
 _____
```

4.
```
    246
   3153
 + 2418
 _____
```

5.
```
   1392
    604
   2119
 + 4240
 _____
```

6.
```
    432
   5144
   3018
 +  576
 _____
```

7.
```
   2045
    976
    480
 + 3184
 _____
```

8.
```
   7013
   2645
    784
 +  596
 _____
```

9.
```
   2☐80
    5☐8
 + 473☐
 _____
   ☐072
```

10.
```
   516☐
   12☐4
 +  ☐99
 _____
   ☐109
```

11.
```
   4☐2
   3☐09
 +  54☐
 _____
   ☐811
```

12.
```
     46
    209
 + ☐☐☐☐
 _____
   2142
```

13.
```
   4218
 - 1064
 _____
```

14.
```
   5912
 - 1934
 _____
```

15.
```
   6010
 - 2314
 _____
```

16.
```
   7120
 - 3075
 _____
```

17.
```
   4328
 - 1529
 _____
```

18.
```
   60☐9
 - 182☐
 _____
   4☐95
```

19.
```
   1000
 -  437
 _____
```

20.
```
   6212
 - ☐☐☐☐
 _____
   2317
```

Numbers to 1 000 000   **UNIT 1**

Word problems using a calculator

1. The number of people who attended a Test Match in Trinidad is shown in the table below.

Friday	Saturday	Sunday	Monday	Tuesday
9375	9690	5421	8218	6054

   Use the information above to answer these word problems.
   - (a) What was the total attendance on the five days?
   - (b) What was the largest attendance on any one day?
   - (c) What was the difference between the smallest and largest attendance?
   - (d) Approximately how many thousand people attended on Saturday?
   - (e) About how many thousand people attended the five days?

2. A shopping list was made up of the following items.

   5 kg of rice at $2.45 per kg
   10 kg of flour at $2.85 per kg
   4 litres of cooking oil $7.50 per litre
   6 kg of potatoes at $3.25 per kg
   8 litres of milk at $4.75 per litre

   - (a) What was the cost of each item?
   - (b) What was the total cost of the items?
   - (c) How much change would you get from $200?

3. A football field measures 100 m by 60 m. How many metres does a footballer run in training if he runs around the field eight times?

Now check your answers using a calculator.

3

UNIT 1   Numbers to 1 000 000

Reviewing place value in 4-digit numbers

Remember: the number frame for 4-digit numbers begins with thousands.

Example

4321 is
and in expanded form is
or

thousands	hundreds	tens	units
4	3	2	1
4000 +	300 +	20 +	1
4 × 1000 +	3 × 100 +	2 × 10 +	1 × 1

The number 4321 is read four thousand, three hundred and twenty-one.

Write these numbers in words.

1. 230
2. 4201
3. 3550
4. 4404
5. 1072
6. 2700
7. 5060
8. 3033

Write these numbers:

9. five thousand, six hundred and twenty-three
10. eight thousand, one hundred and four
11. seven thousand and eighty-one
12. nine thousand and seven
13. six thousand and sixty
14. six thousand, six hundred and sixty

Write these numbers in expanded form.

15. 1432
16. 2341
17. 3142
18. 4321

What is the value of the red digit in each of the following:

19. 1234
20. 3142
21. 2413
22. 4123
23. 1101
24. 1011
25. 1110
26. 1001

Numbers to 1 000 000   **UNIT 1**

Ordering 4-digit numbers

Copy this number line.

The arrow shows approximately where 2200 is on the number line.

Show these numbers on your number line.

1. 2490
2. 2400
3. 3550
4. 2980
5. 3310
6. 3740
7. 3820
8. 4115

> We can compare numbers by comparing the digits, beginning from the left; the greater the value of the digit, the larger is the number.
>
> **Example** 2134 < 2213 and 3412 > 3214
>
> Our number line below shows this.
>
>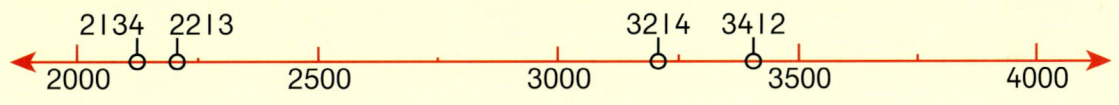

Write the correct sign, > or <, between the following pairs of numbers to make true statements.

9. 1405 ☐ 1516
10. 2372 ☐ 2306
11. 3553 ☐ 3520
12. 4610 ☐ 4160
13. 4001 ☐ 4100
14. 4820 ☐ 4280

Write each set of numbers in order, starting with the smallest.

15. 6026   2415   4922   3155   6242
16. 2790   3289   1669   2410   1999
17. 5540   4140   6001   5318   4870

UNIT 1 Numbers to 1 000 000

Rounding numbers – review

Remember: when we write numbers to the nearest ten, hundred or thousand, we say we **round** the numbers.

Sometimes we round upwards, sometimes downwards.
Look at the number lines below.

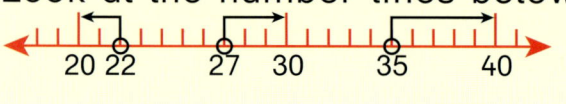 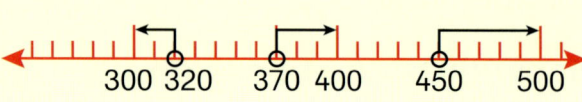

22 becomes 20 to the nearest 10
27 becomes 30 to the nearest 10
35, the mid-way number between 30 and 40, moves upwards and becomes 40

320 becomes 300 to the nearest 100
370 becomes 400 to the nearest 100
450, the number midway between 400 and 500, moves upwards and becomes 500

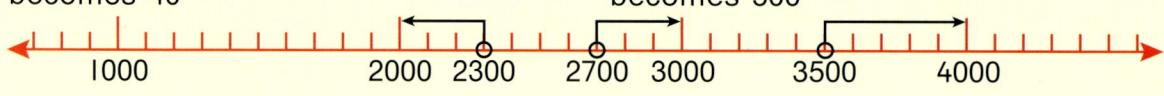

The number line above shows:
2300 becomes 2000 and 2700 becomes 3000 to the nearest 1000.
3500, the number midway between 3000 and 4000, moves upwards to 4000.

Notice how important the digit **immediately to the right** of the tens, hundreds, or thousands digit is when we are rounding to tens or hundreds or thousands.

Round these numbers to the nearest 10.
1. 33   **2.** 47   **3.** 55   **4.** 91   **5.** 99

Round these numbers to the nearest 100.
6. 125   **7.** 379   **8.** 550   **9.** 910   **10.** 990

Round these numbers to the nearest 1000.
11. 2416   **12.** 6730   **13.** 5550   **14.** 9100   **15.** 9900
16. 1997   **17.** 1097   **18.** 1500   **19.** 1050   **20.** 1100

Numbers to 1 000 000   **UNIT 1**

> **Remember:** we can write 4-digit numbers as:
> thousands plus a remainder,
> or, hundreds plus a remainder, or, tens plus a remainder.

Doing this helps us to round 4-digit numbers to the nearest thousand, or hundred, or ten, correctly and quickly.

Look at the place value chart below.

thousands	hundreds	tens	units
2	3	4	6
3	7	5	2
1	4	3	8

2 thousands plus 346 is
$\boxed{2}$ 000 to the nearest thousand
37 hundreds plus 52 is
$\boxed{38}$ 00 to the nearest hundred
143 tens plus 8 is
$\boxed{144}$ 0 to the nearest ten

> **Remember:** when we are rounding to the nearest ten or hundred or thousand, if the digit **immediately to the right** of the tens, or hundreds, or thousands digit is 5 or more than 5, we must round up; if less than 5 we must round down.

21. Copy and complete the table below. The first one is done for you.

Number	to the nearest 10	to the nearest 100	to the nearest 1000
2438	2440	2400	2000
4392			
1526			
6807			
5912			
3189			

UNIT 1 Numbers to 1 000 000

Approximation

Remember: rounding numbers helps us to estimate or give approximate answers to a calculation.
Rounding also helps us to check the answers to the problems.

Give approximate and exact answers to:

1.   1 3 1 4
         6 9 2
    + 2 9 2 0
    ───────

2.   2 9 0 5
    − 1 1 3 0
    ───────

3.   1 8 7 2
    ×   3
    ───────

4. 3) 5 7 3 0

Choose the correct answers from the numbers in the brackets in these calculations.

5. 1812 + 3109 + 1102 = (3023, 6023, 4023)
6. 5192 − 2851 = (3541, 1441, 2341)
7. 1120 × 4 = (5480, 4480, 6480)
8. 5720 ÷ 5 = (1144, 2044, 3144)

Choose the best estimate from 900, 1000, 1100 and 1200 for the answers to these calculations and then calculate the answers.

9. 342 + 660
10. 470 + 520
11. 512 + 410
12. 316 + 724
13. 395 + 690
14. 590 + 480
15. 1380 − 170
16. 1520 − 440
17. 2215 − 1090
18. 1637 − 1316
19. 1090 − 200
20. 1990 − 864

Now check your answers using a calculator.

8

Numbers to 1 000 000   UNIT 1

From 4-digit numbers to 6-digit numbers

> Complete this number pattern
> 1000, 2000, 3000, ____, ____, ____, ____, ____, ____, ____ *
> What number goes in the space marked *?
> How many digits does this number have?
>
> What is the largest 4-digit number?
> Count on from 9990, 9991, and so on to 9999.
> What is the next counting number after 9999?
> Use your calculator. The next counting number after 9999 is
> 9999 + 1 = *
> The number **ten thousand, written 10 000,** is the next counting number after 9999 and the smallest number with five digits.
>
> Continue this pattern of numbers
> 10 000   20 000   30 000 up to 90 000.
> What number will follow 90 000 in this pattern? Use your calculator to help you find the answer.
> How many digits does this number have?
> The number **one hundred thousand, written 100 000,** is the smallest number with six digits.

Write these numbers in words.

1. 15 000   2. 36 000   3. 20 000   4. 54 000   5. 125 000
6. 406 000   7. 150 000   8. 101 000   9. 909 000   10. 990 000

Write numerals for these.

11. twelve thousand   12. twenty-nine thousand
13. sixty thousand   14. one hundred and forty-six thousand
15. seven hundred and seventy thousand

UNIT 1 Numbers to 1 000 000

Place value in 6-digit numbers

This is how the place value chart looks with the numbers 1000, 10 000 and 100 000.

hundred thousands	ten thousands	thousands	hundreds	tens	units	number in words
		1	0	0	0	one thousand
	1	0	0	0	0	ten thousand
1	0	0	0	0	0	one hundred thousand

We can now put every digit in a 5-digit or 6-digit number in our new chart. This allows us to write our numbers in expanded form very easily.

	hundred thousands	ten thousands	thousands	hundreds	tens	units	number in words
432 187	4 4 × 100 000 400 000 +	3 3 × 10 000 30 000 +	2 2 × 1000 2000 +	1 1 × 100 100 +	8 8 × 10 80 +	7 7 × 1 7	four hundred and thirty-two thousand, one hundred and eighty-seven
12 058		1 1 × 10 000 10 000 +	2 2 × 1000 2000 +	0	5 5 × 10 50 +	8 8 × 1 8	twelve thousand and fifty-eight

Draw a chart like the one above. Put in the digits of the numbers below in the correct columns. Write the number in expanded form and also in words.

1. 15 463 **2.** 241 579 **3.** 20 492 **4.** 809 512
5. 416 028 **6.** 70 084 **7.** 220 202 **8.** 100 001

Numbers to 1 000 000   **UNIT 1**

Write numerals for the following numbers.

9. nineteen thousand, two hundred and forty-five
10. one hundred and twenty-three thousand, two hundred and fifty-six
11. two hundred and six thousand, five hundred and fifteen
12. five hundred and ten thousand, one hundred and one
13. seven hundred and twenty thousand and sixty-nine
14. six hundred thousand, six hundred and sixty
15. twenty thousand and five

One million

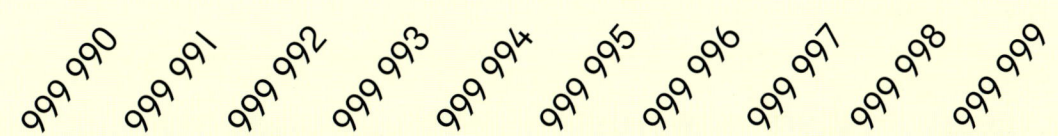

What is the largest 6-digit number?
What is the next counting number after 999 999?
Use your calculator. What is 999 999 + 1?
Your calculator should show the number 1 000 000.
The number 1 000 000 is one million.

Can you think of how large a million is?
Try to solve this problem with the help of your calculator.
   Most of us can count up to 100 in 1 minute.
   How far can you count in 5 minutes?
   What number will you get to in counting for 1 hour?
   Without resting or sleeping, what number will you reach after 24 hours?

UNIT 1   Numbers to 1 000 000

What number will you reach after 1 week?
Have you counted to 1 000 000 yet?

Here is another problem you and a friend can think about.

Suppose you were both putting corn grains into a barrel one at a time and in 1 minute each of you were able to put in 50 grains.
If you worked only for 12 hours a day, how many days will it take to put 1 000 000 grains in the barrel?

Counting on from 1 000 000

> Use your calculator to find the counting numbers from one million to one million and ten. How many digits are there in each of these numbers?

Write these numbers in words.

1. 2 000 000
2. 5 000 000
3. 9 000 000
4. 15 000 000
5. 24 000 000
6. 50 000 000
7. 142 000 000
8. 355 000 000
9. 600 000 000

Write numerals for these numbers.

10. six million
11. thirty-five million
12. forty million
13. one hundred and twelve million
14. two hundred and ten million
15. three hundred million

Numbers to 1 000 000   UNIT 1

Place value for numbers with more than six digits

How many digits do we need when writing hundreds of millions?
Here is our place value chart for numbers in millions.

hundred millions	ten millions	millions	hundred thousands	ten thousands	thousands	hundreds	tens	units
		3	4	5	6	7	8	9
	2	3	5	4	6	8	9	7
3	1	2	6	5	4	9	7	8

The chart above helps us to read the numbers.
The first is three million, four hundred and fifty-six thousand, seven hundred and eighty-nine.
Now write the other two numbers in words.

Write these numbers in words.

1. 2 135 418
2. 4 201 325
3. 6 120 340
4. 16 200 109
5. 10 015 116
6. 5 150 039
7. 1 124 001
8. 20 006 100
9. 9 210 101
10. 3 415 020
11. 5 029 209
12. 6 100 100

Observe that when we write large numbers we leave a space between the millions and thousands and between the thousands and hundreds digits.
We could also use commas:
    2 135 418 is the same as 2,135,418.

UNIT 1 Numbers to 1 000 000

Write numerals for these numbers.

13. four million, one hundred and twenty-three thousand, six hundred and seventeen
14. two million, four hundred and one thousand, two hundred and ninety
15. three million, fifty thousand, six hundred and six
16. fifteen million, one hundred and thirty thousand, two hundred and thirty-four
17. twenty-five million, ten thousand, five hundred and five
18. thirty million, one hundred thousand, two hundred and fifty-six
19. nine million, three hundred and thirty thousand, five hundred and twelve
20. six million, forty-five thousand, nine hundred and ninety

Large numbers in expanded form

Look at the place value chart below.
It shows the number 2 435 624

100 000 000	10 000 000	1 000 000	100 000	10 000	1000	100	10	1
		2	4	3	5	6	2	4
		2 × 1 000 000	4 × 100 000	3 × 10 000	5 × 1000	6 × 100	2 × 10	4 × 1

The number 2 435 624 in expanded form is written:

2 × 1 000 000 + 4 × 100 000 + 3 × 10 000 + 5 × 1000 + 6 × 100 + 2 × 10 + 4 × 1

Numbers to 1 000 000 UNIT 1

Make a place value chart for these numbers in columns from millions to ones, and then write them in expanded form.

1. 1 345 267   **2.** 215 106   **3.** 1 032 219   **4.** 2 205 052

5. 400 020   **6.** 1 040 204   **7.** 6 101 330   **8.** 1 500 505

Write these numbers as numerals and also in expanded form.

9. one million, two hundred and thirty-four thousand, five hundred and sixty-seven

10. two hundred and forty-three thousand, nine hundred and eighty-five

11. two million, one hundred and three thousand, four hundred and twenty

12. five hundred and five thousand, five hundred and five

13. one million, five hundred and forty thousand and fifty

14. three million, three hundred thousand and three

15. five million, five hundred thousand and fifty

Write the value of the red digits.

16. 5 321 046   **17.** 142 379   **18.** 1 528 463

19. 3 205 050   **20.** 623 065   **21.** 7 045 332

UNIT 1   Numbers to 1 000 000

Rounding large numbers

When we speak of the distance of the Earth from the Sun or the Moon, we think in millions of kilometres.

When we talk about the population of large countries, we think in millions (and in the case of smaller countries, thousands or hundreds of thousands).

When we consider the number of people who will watch the Olympics on television, we think in millions.

In all these cases we give approximate numbers and so we must round our numbers.

Follow the same steps as we did for 4-digit numbers.

HM	TM	M	HTh	TTh	Th	H	T	U	
		2	4	3	7	8	2		243 thousands plus 782 is 244 000 to the nearest thousand
		2	4	3	7	8	2		200 thousands plus 43 782 is 200 000 to the nearest hundred thousand
	1	8	9	3	3	3	5	2	18 million plus 933 352 is 19 000 000 to the nearest hundred thousand

16

Numbers to 1 000 000   UNIT 1

1. Copy and complete the table.

Number	to the nearest 1000	to the nearest 100 000	to the nearest million
1 524 610	1 525 000	1 500 000	2 000 000
4 205 136			
17 004 215			
6 513 600			
2 478 292			
1 809 910			
25 316 590			
4 781 499			
1 500 725			
10 039 655			
3 262 050			
9 831 272			
6 111 248			

UNIT 1   Numbers to 1 000 000

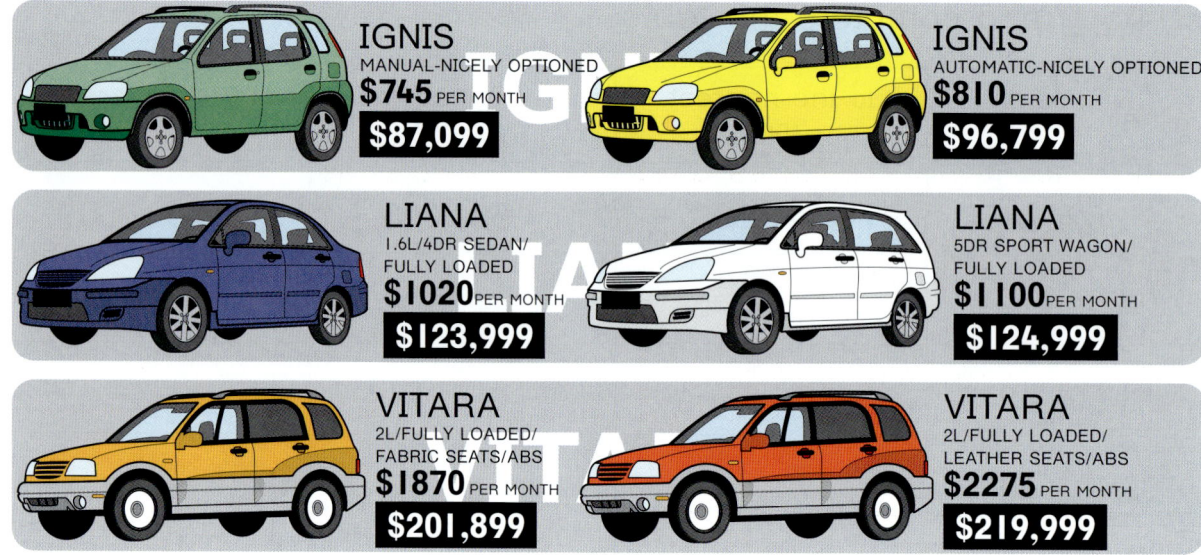

2. The price of each of the vehicles above is shown in the rectangle.

   (a) What is the price of the least expensive vehicle?
   (b) What is the price of the most expensive vehicle?
   (c) What is the difference in price between the most expensive and the least expensive vehicles?
   (d) List the prices of the vehicles in ascending order of magnitude.
   (e) Round off the prices listed in (d) to the nearest ten thousand dollars.

3. The summary below was taken from an electricity bill.

METER SUMMARY INFORMATION

Meter Number	Previous Date	Previous Reading	Present Date	Present Reading	Difference Days	Difference Units	Meter Multiplier	KWH** Consumption
126712	17-04-2004	72501	14-06-2004	73853	58	1352	1	1352

18

Numbers to 1 000 000   UNIT 1

Write in words:
  (a) the number of the meter,
  (b) the number of units used up to 17-04-2004,
  (c) the number of units used up to 14-06-2004,
  (d) the number of units used between 17-04-2004 and 14-06-2004.

4. The populations of the countries listed below were recorded in the 1990s and have been rounded to the nearest thousand.

Antigua and Barbuda	66 000	Jamaica	2 469 000
Barbados	259 000	St Kitts-Nevis	42 000
Bahamas	262 000	St Lucia	137 000
Dominica	72 000	St Vincent-Grenadines	109 000
Grenada	91 000	Trinidad and Tobago	1 286 000
Guyana	808 000		

Use the information in the table above to answer these questions.

  (a) Which country had the most people?
  (b) Which country had the fewest people?
  (c) Which country had just over $\frac{3}{4}$ million people?
  (d) Which country had just over $\frac{1}{4}$ million people?
  (e) What was the population of Jamaica to the nearest $\frac{1}{2}$ million?
  (f) What was the population of Trinidad and Tobago to the nearest one hundred thousand?
  (g) Rewrite the list of countries in order of size of population.

Assessment

Assessment 1

Write numerals for:
1. seven thousand, one hundred and sixty-three
2. twenty thousand, two hundred and two
3. three hundred and thirteen thousand, one hundred and thirty
4. four hundred and four thousand and forty
5. two million, three hundred and twenty-five thousand, four hundred and thirty-six
6. one million, ten thousand and ten

Write these numbers in words.
7. 15 024
8. 215 120
9. 105 036
10. 300 003
11. 10 210 140

Write these numerals in expanded form.
12. 1234
13. 20 350
14. 105 034
15. 1 020 305

What is the value of the red digit in each of these numbers?
16. 3142
17. 12 409
18. 110 032
19. 3 215 612

Round each of these numbers: (a) to the nearest thousand, (b) to the nearest hundred thousand.
20. 312 815
21. 461 352
22. 1 550 617

Write the correct sign, > or <, between the following pairs of numbers.
23. 2020 ☐ 2002
24. 3003 ☐ 3030
25. 1101 ☐ 1011

2 Multiplication and division

Review of multiplication

Copy and complete these calculations.

1. 243 × 10
2. 120 × 10
3. 264 × 20
4. 156 × 30
5. 312 × 40
6. 145 × 50
7. 324 × 60
8. 132 × 70
9. 216 × 80
10. 124 × 90

Now check your answers using a calculator.
Copy and complete these calculations.

11. 6 × 8 = ☐   (6 × 5) + (6 × 3) = ☐
12. 25 × 6 = ☐   (25 × 4) + (25 × 2) = ☐
13. 43 × 9 = ☐   (43 × 5) + (43 × 4) = ☐
14. 132 × 6 = ☐   (132 × 2) + (132 × 4) = ☐
15. 256 × 5 = ☐   (256 × 3) + (256 × 2) = ☐
16. 192 × 7 = ☐   (192 × 4) + (192 × 3) = ☐

Now check your answers using a calculator.
Copy and complete these calculations.

17. 24 × 16 = (24 × 10) + (24 × ☐) = ☐
18. 56 × 18 = (56 × 10) + (56 × ☐) = ☐
19. 36 × 15 = (36 × 10) + (36 × ☐) = ☐
20. 54 × 25 = (54 × 20) + (54 × ☐) = ☐
21. 68 × 32 = (68 × ☐) + (68 × 2) = ☐
22. 72 × 43 = (72 × ☐) + (72 × 3) = ☐
23. 48 × 54 = (48 × 50) + (48 × ☐) = ☐
24. 28 × 62 = (28 × ☐) + (28 × 2) = ☐

Now check your answers using a calculator.

UNIT 2   Multiplication and division

```
        36 × 15                              36 × 25
36 × 15 = (36 × 10) + (36 × 5)      36 × 25 = (36 × 20) + (36 × 5)

      3 6                                   3 6
   ×  1 5                                ×  2 5
      3 6 0    36 × 10                      7 2 0    36 × 20
   +  1 8 0    36 × 5                    +  1 8 0    36 × 5
      5 4 0    36 × 15                      9 0 0    36 × 25
```

Copy and complete these calculations.

25. 24 × 14   **26.** 32 × 15   **27.** 45 × 16   **28.** 54 × 18

29. 34 × 24   **30.** 23 × 25   **31.** 54 × 26   **32.** 45 × 28

33. 42 × 34   **34.** 32 × 35   **35.** 34 × 36   **36.** 56 × 38

37. 28 × 42   **38.** 34 × 53   **39.** 48 × 64   **40.** 65 × 52

Now check your answers using a calculator.

Work out the answers to these word problems. Show all your working.

41. What length of ribbon must I buy for 45 children if each child has to have a piece 24 cm long?

42. There are 36 plants in each row in a field of 32 rows. How many plants are there altogether?

43. A maxi taxi takes 42 passengers. How many passengers can travel in 18 maxi taxis?

44. A sack of potatoes weighs 25 kg. How many will 14 sacks weigh?

Multiplication and division   UNIT 2

Multiplying 3-digit numbers

```
         234 × 16                              234 × 26
234 × 16 = (234 × 10) + (234 × 6)    234 × 26 = (234 × 20) + (234 × 6)

        2 3 4                                 2 3 4
    ×     1 6                             ×     2 6
      2 3 4 0    234 × 10                   4 6 8 0    234 × 20
      1 4 0 4    234 × 6                    1 4 0 4    234 × 6
      3 7 4 4    234 × 16                   6 0 8 4    234 × 26
```

Copy and complete these calculations.

1. 234 × 14   2. 234 × 15   3. 234 × 18
4. 324 × 24   5. 324 × 25   6. 324 × 28
7. 432 × 34   8. 432 × 35   9. 432 × 38
10. 234 × 45   11. 324 × 56   12. 432 × 62

Now check your answers using a calculator.

Work out the answers to these word problems. Show all your working.

13. One hundred and forty-six people borrowed 12 books each from the library. How many books were borrowed?

14. A packet of sweets has 15 sweets in each packet. How many sweets are there altogether in 445 packets?

15. Soft drinks are sold in cases of 24.
    How many soft drinks will 125 cases contain?

UNIT 2 Multiplication and division

Multiplying 4-digit numbers

$$1342 \times 14$$
$$1342 \times 14 = (1342 \times 10) + (1342 \times 4)$$

```
    1 3 4 2
  ×     1 4
  ─────────
  1 3 4 2 0    1342 × 10
    5 3 6 8    1342 × 4
  ─────────
  1 8 7 8 8    1342 × 14
```

$$1342 \times 24$$
$$1342 \times 24 = (1342 \times 20) + (1342 \times 4)$$

```
    1 3 4 2
  ×     2 4
  ─────────
  2 6 8 4 0    1342 × 20
    5 3 6 8    1342 × 4
  ─────────
  3 2 2 0 8    1342 × 24
```

Copy and complete these calculations.

1. 1426 × 15
2. 1634 × 16
3. 1842 × 18
4. 2132 × 24
5. 2068 × 25
6. 2408 × 28
7. 1590 × 32
8. 1836 × 34
9. 3128 × 36
10. 1612 × 45
11. 2192 × 54
12. 1088 × 64

Now check your answers using a calculator.

Work out the answers to these word problems. Show all your working.

13. There are 1155 schools in the area. Each school is given 25 new tennis racquets. How many tennis racquets in total?

14. If I walk 9653 paces a day, how many paces will I walk in July (31 days)?

15. A school kitchen delivers 1756 meals every day. How many meals are delivered in 36 days?

Multiplication and division UNIT 2

Multiplication in money problems

Use your calculator to find out the following:

1. $2.15 × 10   **2.** $3.10 × 10   **3.** $4.00 × 10   **4.** $15.25 × 10

What do you notice about the answers to the problems above?

Now write answers to these.

5. $4.25 × 10   **6.** $2.50 × 10   **7.** $12.15 × 10   **8.** $21.50 × 10

$2.15 × 20 = $2.15 × 2 × 10 = $4.30 × 10 = $43.00

Use factors to work out these as quickly as you can.

9. $1.92 × 20   **10.** $2.24 × 30   **11.** $3.20 × 40   **12.** $4.00 × 50
13. $2.15 × 60   **14.** $3.45 × 70   **15.** $5.25 × 80   **16.** $6.00 × 90

Look at the problem $16.35 × 24

Remember that we can multiply by 20 and by 4 and add the results.

```
    $ 1 6 . 3 5
  ×         2 4
    3 2 7 . 0 0   = $16.35 × 20
        6 5 . 4 0 = $16.35 × 4
    $ 3 9 2 . 4 0 = $16.35 × 24
```

Copy and complete these calculations.

17. $15.24 × 18   **18.** $21.35 × 16   **19.** $14.40 × 15
20. $12.80 × 14   **21.** $19.36 × 24   **22.** $15.42 × 45
23. $16.33 × 26   **24.** $15.00 × 21   **25.** $17.08 × 35
26. $20.06 × 25   **27.** $20.10 × 32   **28.** $40.00 × 26
29. A colour marker cost $9.95. How much will 18 markers cost?

UNIT 2   **Multiplication and division**

Reviewing division by 1-digit divisors

$548 \div 4$

These are the steps we follow:

	1	3	7
4	5	4̸	8̸
	4	14	28
	1̸	12	28
		2̸	0

Steps
5 hundreds ÷ 4
1 hundred × 4 = 4 hundreds
5 hundreds − 4 hundreds = 1 hundred
1 hundred = 10 tens
10 + 4 = 14
14 tens ÷ 4
3 tens × 4 = 12 tens
14 tens − 12 tens = 2 tens
2 tens = 20 ones
20 + 8 = 28
28 ÷ 4 = 7
7 × 4 = 28

The steps written in the box are all done mentally and we write our workings out like this:

$$4\overline{)5^14^28}$$ quotient 137

When we have to divide by 2-digit numbers we need to write out our working as we have done at the top.

Copy and complete these calculations.
Show all your working as in the **top** example above.

1. $2\overline{)36}$ 2. $3\overline{)48}$ 3. $4\overline{)56}$ 4. $6\overline{)72}$

5. $3\overline{)132}$ 6. $5\overline{)345}$ 7. $6\overline{)276}$ 8. $7\overline{)392}$

9. $4\overline{)528}$ 10. $8\overline{)968}$ 11. $5\overline{)625}$ 12. $6\overline{)738}$

13. $3\overline{)216}$ 14. $6\overline{)212}$ 15. $8\overline{)357}$ 16. $9\overline{)559}$

Multiplication and division UNIT 2

Division by 2-digit divisors

Look at this calculation:

672 ÷ 21

```
        3 2
21 ) 6̶ 7̶ 2̶1̶
     67 42
     63 42
      4̶  0
```

Steps
We cannot divide 6 hundreds by 21.
6 hundreds = 60 tens   60 tens + 7 tens = 67 tens
67 ÷ 21 = 3 tens plus remainder (21 × 3 = 63)
67 tens − 63 tens = 4 tens   4 tens = 40 ones
40 + 2 = 42   42 ÷ 2 = 21 (21 × 2 = 42)
672 ÷ 21 = 32

Copy and complete these calculations.
Show all your working.

1. 165 ÷ 15
2. 224 ÷ 16
3. 198 ÷ 18
4. 253 ÷ 23
5. 384 ÷ 32
6. 528 ÷ 24
7. 615 ÷ 14
8. 546 ÷ 42
9. 663 ÷ 51
10. 233 ÷ 21
11. 713 ÷ 23
12. 882 ÷ 42
13. 308 ÷ 22
14. 504 ÷ 24
15. 561 ÷ 51
16. 992 ÷ 31
17. 704 ÷ 32
18. 759 ÷ 33

Look at this example now:

2546 ÷ 21

```
         1 2 1
21 ) 2̶ 5̶ 4̶ 6̶
     25 44 26
     21 42 21
      4̶  2̶  5
```

Steps
25 ÷ 21 = 1 plus remainder
21 × 1 = 21   25 − 21 = 4
4 hundreds = 40 tens
40 + 4 = 44   44 ÷ 21 = 2 plus remainder
21 × 2 = 42   44 − 42 = 2
2 tens = 20 ones   20 + 6 = 26
26 ÷ 21 = 1 plus remainder
21 × 1 = 21   26 − 21 = 5
2546 ÷ 21 = 121 r 5

UNIT 2 Multiplication and division

Copy and complete these calculations.
Show all your working.

19. 1845 ÷ 15	**20.** 3408 ÷ 16	**21.** 2556 ÷ 18
22. 4899 ÷ 23	**23.** 6496 ÷ 32	**24.** 3504 ÷ 24
25. 3086 ÷ 22	**26.** 7488 ÷ 24	**27.** 7310 ÷ 34
28. 6342 ÷ 21	**29.** 5382 ÷ 23	**30.** 7374 ÷ 31
31. 6025 ÷ 25	**32.** 4488 ÷ 34	**33.** 6846 ÷ 21
34. 4920 ÷ 41	**35.** 9702 ÷ 42	**36.** 6732 ÷ 51

Work out the answers to these word problems. Show all your working.

37. A sack of potatoes weighs 25 kg. How many sacks can be filled from a truck-load of 550 kg of potatoes?

38. A minibus can carry 42 passengers. How many buses will be required to transport 756 passengers?

39. In a hall which can seat 672 people each row of seating has 32 chairs. How many rows of chairs are there?

40. If I put 375 small tables in stacks of 15 how many stacks will I make?

41. Three thousand, five hundred and fifty books are to be distributed equally among 25 schools. How many books will each school receive?

42. A carton of eggs holds 24.
How many cartons will I need for 3456 eggs?

3 Solid shapes and symmetry

Solids: prisms and pyramids

Which of these solids are prisms and which are pyramids?
Name the solids that you recognise.

1.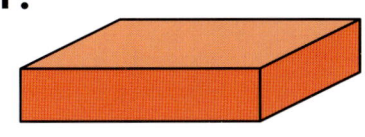

2.

3.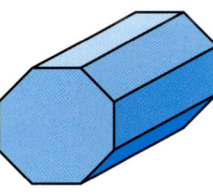

4.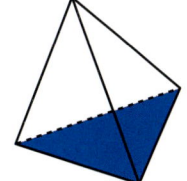

5.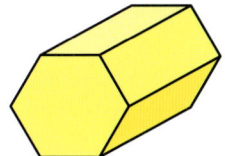

6.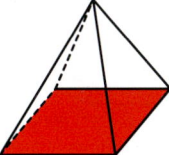

7.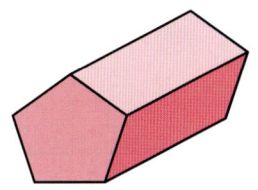

8.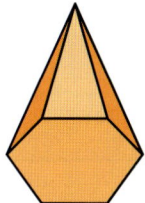

9.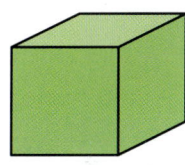

10. (a) What is the shape of the base of the square pyramid?
    (b) What is the shape of the other faces?

11. (a) What is the shape of the end faces of the triangular prism?
    (b) What is the shape of the other faces?

12. (a) What is the shape of the end faces of the rectangular prism?
    (b) What is the shape of the other faces?

13. (a) What is the shape of the base of the triangular pyramid?
    (b) What is the shape of the other faces?

UNIT 3   Solid shapes and symmetry

Solids and their faces

Copy these diagrams. Draw the faces for each solid.
Name the solids.

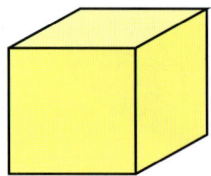

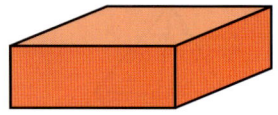

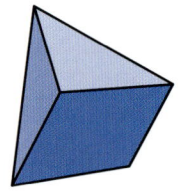

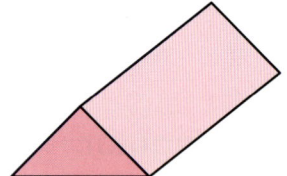

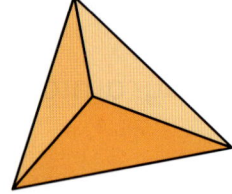

Solid shapes and symmetry   UNIT 3

Properties of solids

Copy and complete this table.

Solid	name of solid	shape of faces	number of faces	number of edges	number of vertices

UNIT 3   Solid shapes and symmetry

Nets

- Draw the solid which each net makes.
- Trace the nets onto squared paper.
- Cut out and make the solids.

You will need: squared paper, ruler and scissors.

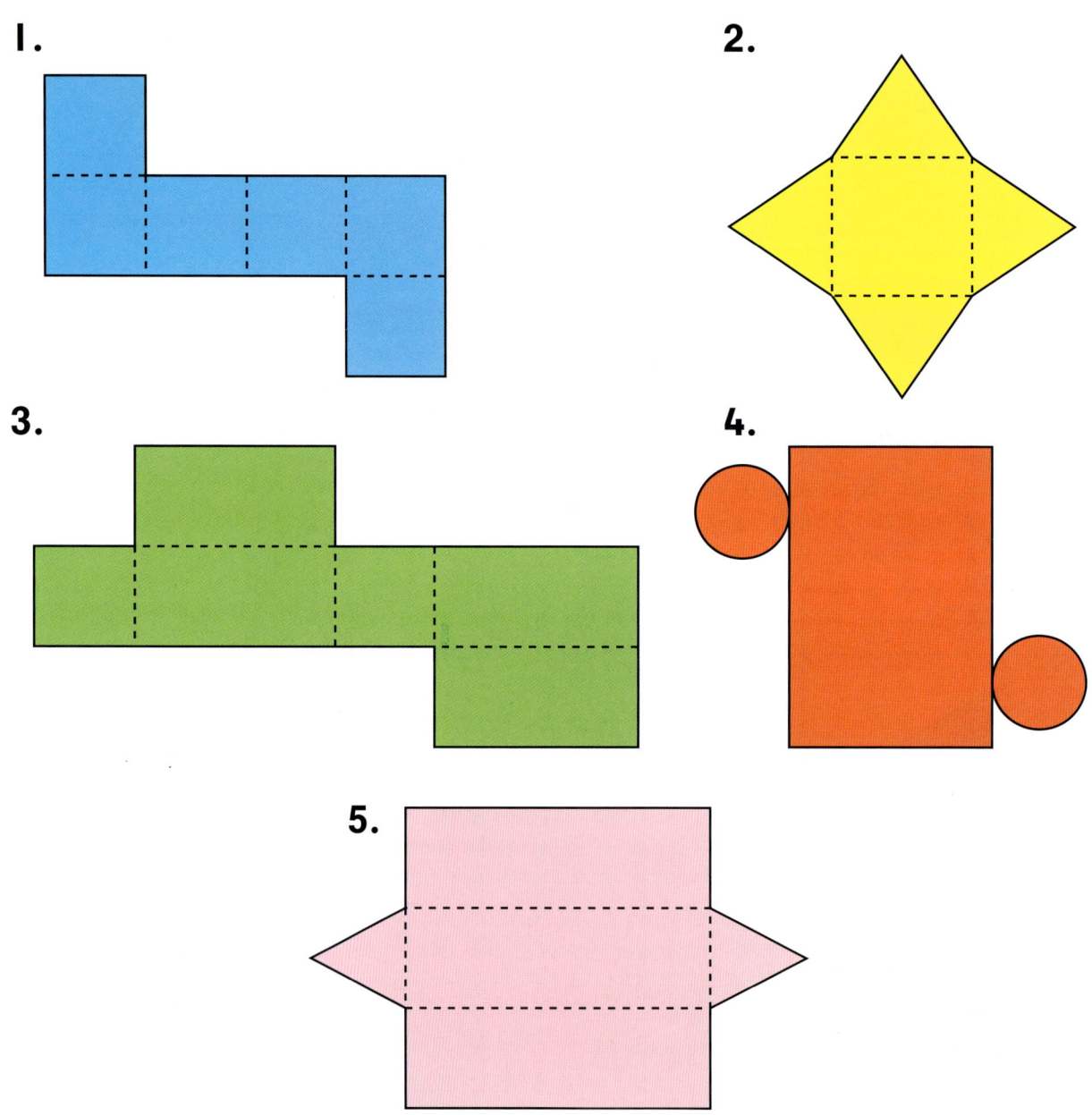

1.

2.

3.

4.

5.

Solid shapes and symmetry   UNIT 3

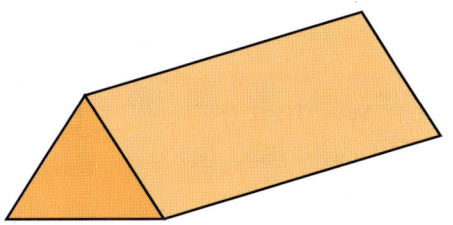

6. This triangular prism is 6 cm long. Its ends measure 3 cm × 3 cm × 3 cm. Draw the net for this prism.

7. Draw the net of a rectangular prism whose end faces measure 6 cm × 4 cm and which is 8 cm long.

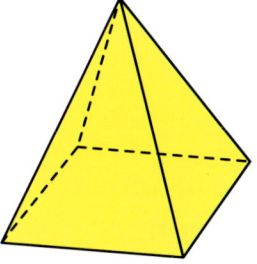

8. The base of this pyramid measures 6 cm × 6 cm. The edges of the triangular faces measure 8 cm.
Draw the net of the pyramid.

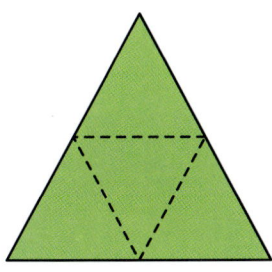

9. The edges of all these triangles measure 6 cm. Draw this net.

10. The end faces of a triangular prism measure 6 cm × 6 cm × 4 cm. Two of its other faces measure 8 cm × 6 cm and the third face measures 4 cm × 8 cm. Draw the net of this prism.

UNIT 3   Solid shapes and symmetry

Symmetry

> **Remember:** when we fold a circle along a diameter we divide the shape into identical halves; the diameter is a line of symmetry.

We say that the circle has **reflective symmetry**. If you place a mirror along a line of symmetry you will see the other half of the shape as an image or reflection in the mirror.

You will need: a mirror, paper and scissors.

Here are some letters of the alphabet.
- Use a mirror to find the lines of symmetry in each.
- Trace the letters and cut them out.
- Fold to check the lines of symmetry.

Assessment

Assessment 2

Find the products for the following:

1. 315 × 24   **2.** 2154 × 32   **3.** $12.50 × 15

4. A cinema ticket costs $10.25. How much should a group of 25 people pay to see a show?

5. A passenger bus can take 40 people sitting and 12 standing. How many people can travel in 15 buses?

Find the answers to the following:

6. 195 ÷ 15   **7.** 7584 ÷ 24   **8.** 5746 ÷ 26

9. Soft drinks are sold in cases of 24 bottles. How many cases are needed for 1536 bottles of drink?

10. A minibus can carry 25 students. How many buses are needed for an outing of 350 students?

11. A man is paid a daily wage of $60.00.
In addition he receives a meal allowance of $5.25 every day. How much money does the man get after 4 days?

12. Which solid shape does this net represent?

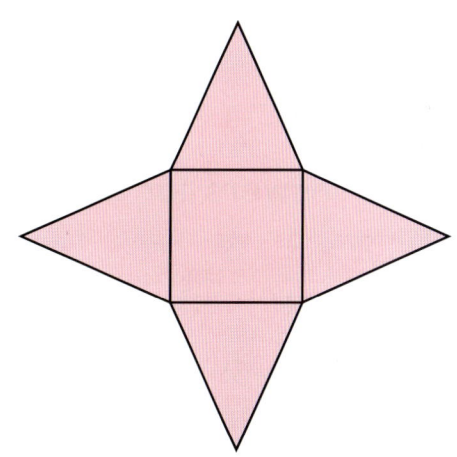

4 Squares, square roots and factors

Squares

> Some composite numbers form squares when they are shown as an array of rows and columns.
>
> For example, the numbers 4 and 9 shown as arrays on the right:
>
> The numbers 4 and 9 are called **square numbers**.
> We also say that 4 and 9 are squares of the numbers 2 and 3.
>
> 4 is the square of 2 and is written as $2^2 = 4$
> 9 is the square of 3 and is written as $3^2 = 9$
>
> 2^2 (which means 2×2) is read '2 squared'
> or '2 to the power 2'
> 3^2 (which means 3×3) is read '3 squared'
> or '3 to the power 2'

Draw arrays for the square numbers from 4^2 to 10^2.

1. $1^2 = 1 \times 1 = 1$
2. $2^2 = 2 \times 2 = 4$
3. $3^2 = 3 \times 3 = 9$
4. $4^2 = 4 \times 4 =$
5. $5^2 = 5 \times 5 =$
6. $6^2 = 6 \times 6 =$
7. $7^2 = 7 \times 7 =$
8. $8^2 = 8 \times 8 =$
9. $9^2 = 9 \times 9 =$
10. $10^2 = 10 \times 10 =$

Write answers for the following:

11. $2^2 + 3^2 =$
12. $3^2 + 4^2 =$
13. $6^2 + 10^2 =$
14. $10^2 + 9^2 =$
15. $10^2 - 7^2 =$
16. $9^2 - 6^2 =$
17. $8^2 - 5^2 =$
18. $5^2 - 2^2 =$

Squares, square roots and factors   UNIT 4

Look at the arrangement of these objects:

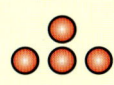 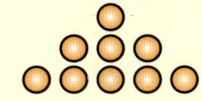 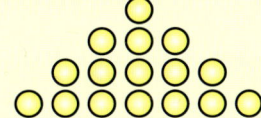

What is the shape of each arrangement?
Count the shapes in each arrangement by rows.

$1 + 3 = 4 = 2^2$
$1 + 3 + 5 = 9 = 3^2$
$1 + 3 + 5 + 7 = 16 = 4^2$

What do we call the numbers 1, 3, 5, 7, and so on?
Can you complete these statements:
The sum of the first two odd numbers is ☐.
The sum of the first three odd numbers is ☐.
The sum of the first four odd numbers is ☐.

Copy and complete the following statements.

19. $1 + 3 + 5 + 7 + 9 =$

20. $1 + 3 + 5 + 7 + 9 + 11 =$

21. $1 + 3 + 5 + 7 + 9 + 11 + 13 =$

22. $1 + 3 + 5 + 7 + 9 + 11 + 13 + 15 =$

23. $1 + 3 + 5 + 7 + 9 + 11 + 13 + 15 + 17 =$

Copy and complete the following:

24. $1^2 - 0 = 1 - 0 = 1$ **25.** $2^2 - 1^2 = 4 - 1 = 3$
26. $3^2 - 2^2 =$ **27.** $4^2 - 3^2 =$
28. $5^2 - 4^2 =$ **29.** $6^2 - 5^2 =$
30. $7^2 - 6^2 =$ **31.** $8^2 - 7^2 =$

UNIT 4   **Squares, square roots and factors**

Which set of numbers are we developing in this pattern? Without calculating the squares and subtracting, write the values of:

32. $12^2 - 11^2$ **33.** $14^2 - 13^2$ **34.** $15^2 - 14^2$ **35.** $19^2 - 18^2$
36. $21^2 - 20^2$ **37.** $25^2 - 24^2$ **38.** $50^2 - 49^2$ **39.** $91^2 - 90^2$

Now check your answers using a calculator.

Square roots

> **Remember:** $2^2 = 2 \times 2 = 4$
> and $3^2 = 3 \times 3 = 9$
> The number 2 is called the square root of 4.
> $\sqrt{4} = 2$ means the square root of 4 is 2,
> and $\sqrt{9} = 3$ means the square root of 9 is 3.

Copy and complete these statements: the first two are done for you.

1. $1^2 = 1 \times 1 = 1$; $\sqrt{1} = \sqrt{1 \times 1} = 1$
2. $2^2 = 2 \times 2 = 4$; $\sqrt{4} = \sqrt{2 \times 2} = 2$
3. $3^2 =$
4. $4^2 =$
5. $5^2 =$
6. $6^2 =$
7. $7^2 =$
8. $8^2 =$
9. $9^2 =$
10. $10^2 =$

Squares, square roots and factors   **UNIT 4**

Use your calculator to help you complete the following:

11. $11^2 = 11 \times 11 = 121$; $\sqrt{121} = \sqrt{11 \times 11} = 11$

12. $12^2 =$

13. $13^2 =$

14. $14^2 =$

15. $15^2 =$

16. $16^2 =$

17. $17^2 =$

18. $18^2 =$

19. $19^2 =$

20. $20^2 =$

21. $21^2 =$

22. $22^2 =$

23. $23^2 =$

24. $24^2 =$

25. $25^2 =$

UNIT 4 Squares, square roots and factors

Factors

> **Remember:** when we multiply numbers we get a **product** and the numbers we multiply are called **factors** of the product.

> **Example** 12 = 1 × 12, or 2 × 6, or 3 × 4
>
> 1, 2, 3, 4, 6 and 12 are all factors of 12

> **Remember:** we can also say that when we divide a number and the remainder is zero, then both the **divisor** (the number we divide by) and the **quotient** (the result when we divide) are factors of the number.
>
> 12 ÷ 2 = 6; and 2 and 6 are factors of 12
>
> 12 ÷ 3 = 4; and 3 and 4 are factors of 12
>
> 12 ÷ 12 = 1; and 12 and 1 are factors of 12

Write down all the factors of these numbers.

1. 18
2. 20
3. 24
4. 30
5. 32
6. 40
7. 48
8. 56
9. 60
10. 72
11. 84
12. 96

Squares, square roots and factors UNIT 4

Rectangle numbers

Remember: some numbers can be shown as a rectangular array of objects.

These numbers are called **rectangle numbers**.

6 and 8 are examples of rectangle numbers.

Some rectangle numbers can be arranged as different arrays. 12 is an example of such a number. We have a 6 × 2 and a 4 × 3 array.

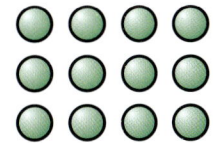

Use the answers to questions 1 to 12 on page 40 to solve the following problems.

How many different rectangles can you make having an area of:

1. 24 cm²   2. 40 cm²   3. 56 cm²

4. How many ways can you seat 72 guests at a dinner if you use more than two tables and there are the same number of guests at each table?

41

UNIT 4 Squares, square roots and factors

Prime numbers

Remember: rectangle numbers have at least two pairs of factors; one pair is the number itself and 1. Some numbers have only one pair of factors, the number itself and 1. These numbers are called **prime numbers**.

Use squared paper to draw a 1 to 100 square.

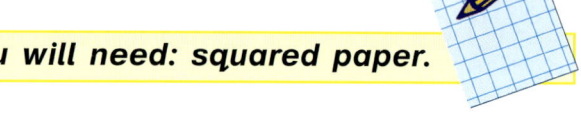
You will need: squared paper.

On your square:
- Cross out 1.
- Cross out all the multiples of 2 but not 2.
- Cross out all the multiples of 3 but not 3.
- Cross out all the multiples of 5 but not 5.
- Cross out all the multiples of 7 but not 7.

1	2	3	4	5	6	7	8	9	10
11	12	13	14	15	16	17	18	19	20
21	22	23	24	25	26	27	28	29	30
31	32	33	34	35	36	37	38	39	40
41	42	43	44	45	46	47	48	49	50
51	52	53	54	55	56	57	58	59	60
61	62	63	64	65	66	67	68	69	70
71	72	73	74	75	76	77	78	79	80
81	82	83	84	85	86	87	88	89	90
91	92	93	94	95	96	97	98	99	100

Write down all the numbers that have not been crossed out.
What are the factors of these numbers?
What do you call these numbers?

Squares, square roots and factors   UNIT 4

Prime factors

> Some factors of numbers are themselves prime numbers. A factor of a number which is a prime number is a **prime factor** of that number.
>
> **Examples**
> 6 has factors 1, 2, 3 and 6; 2 and 3 are the prime factors of 6.
> 12 has factors 1, 2, 3, 4, 6 and 12; only 2 and 3 are the prime factors of 12.

Which factors of the following numbers are the prime factors?

1. 18	**2.** 20	**3.** 24	**4.** 28
5. 30	**6.** 32	**7.** 33	**8.** 36
9. 40	**10.** 45	**11.** 48	**12.** 56
13. 60	**14.** 64	**15.** 70	**16.** 72

> A number which is not a prime number is a **composite number**. We can write any composite number as a product of its prime factors.
>
> **Examples**
> $6 = 2 \times 3$; $12 = 2 \times 6 = 2 \times 2 \times 3$; $18 = 2 \times 9 = 2 \times 3 \times 3$
> Sometimes, as in 12 and 18, we have to use a prime factor more than once.

Write these numbers as the product of their prime factors.

17. 8	**18.** 9	**19.** 15	**20.** 20
21. 24	**22.** 28	**23.** 30	**24.** 32
25. 36	**26.** 40	**27.** 45	**28.** 48

UNIT 4 Squares, square roots and factors

We can show the prime factors of numbers by using a **factor tree**.

Suppose we want to write 36 as the product of its prime factors. We can begin with any two factors of 36.

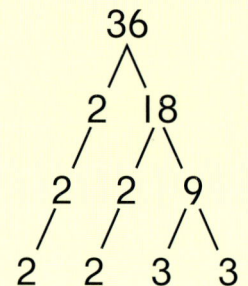 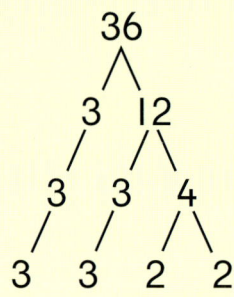 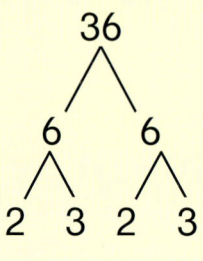 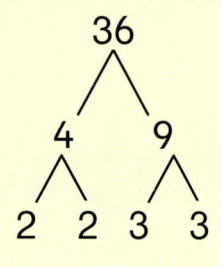

In every case we end up with the product 2 × 2 × 3 × 3 although we began with different pairs of factors.

Use factor trees to show the prime factors of these numbers.

29. 56   **30.** 72   **31.** 84

32. 90   **33.** 120   **34.** 144

35. 160   **36.** 192   **37.** 200

38. 210   **39.** 216   **40.** 240

41. 288   **42.** 320   **43.** 336

44. 360   **45.** 400   **46.** 42

Squares, square roots and factors   UNIT 4

Powers of numbers

Remember: 2^2 means $2 \times 2 = 4$, and we read 2^2 as '2 squared' or '2 to the power 2'

We can write numbers to powers higher than 2.
2^3 means $2 \times 2 \times 2 = 8$ and we read 2^3 as '2 cubed' or '2 to the power 3'.

Can you guess why we read 2^3 as '2 cubed'?
Here is a clue: 2^2 which we read '2 squared' can represent a square 2 units × 2 units.

The small number '3' in 2^3 and 3^3 which shows the power is called an **index**.

The plural of index is indices.

2 to the power 4 (which we write as 2^4) means
$2 \times 2 \times 2 \times 2 = 16$
2 to the power 5 (which we write as 2^5) means
$2 \times 2 \times 2 \times 2 \times 2 = 32$
2^1 means 2; 3^1 means 3, 4^1 means 4, and so on.

Write the meanings and values of the numbers below. The first one is done for you.

1. $2^6 = 2 \times 2 \times 2 \times 2 \times 2 \times 2 = 64$
2. $3^3 =$
3. $3^4 =$
4. $3^5 =$
5. $4^3 =$
6. $5^3 =$
7. $6^3 =$
8. $10^2 =$
9. $10^3 =$
10. $10^4 =$

UNIT 4 Squares, square roots and factors

Lowest common multiple (L.C.M.)

> **Remember:** multiples of a number are the products of the number and the other whole numbers.

Example 3, 6, 9, ... are multiples of 3, and 4, 8, 12, ... are multiples of 4.

Multiples of 2 are 2, 4, 6, 8, 10, 12, 14, 16, 18, ...
Multiples of 3 are 3, 6, 9, 12, 15, 18, 21, 24, 27, 30, ...
Multiples of 5 are 5, 10, 15, 20, 25, 30, 35, ...

The **lowest common multiple or L.C.M.** of 2 and 3 is 6.
The **lowest common multiple or L.C.M.** of 3 and 5 is 15.
The **lowest common multiple or L.C.M.** of 2 and 5 is 10.

Notice that the L.C.M. of two prime numbers is the product of the two numbers.

Look at the pairs of composite numbers: 6 and 8, 12 and 18.

Multiples of 6 are 6, 12, 18, 24, 30, 36	$6 = 2 \times 3$ and $8 = 2 \times 2 \times 2 = 2^3$
Multiples of 8 are 8, 16, 24, 32, 40, 48	Notice $24 = 2 \times 2 \times 2 \times 3 = 2^3 \times 3$
L.C.M. of 6 and 8 is 24	L.C.M. of 6 and 8 = $24 = 2^3 \times 3$
Multiples of 12 are 12, 24, 36, 48	$12 = 2 \times 2 \times 3 = 2^2 \times 3$ and
Multiples of 18 are 18, 36, 54, 72	$18 = 2 \times 3 \times 3 = 2 \times 3^2$ and
L.C.M. of 12 and 18 is 36	$36 = 2 \times 2 \times 3 \times 3 = 2^2 \times 3^2$
	L.C.M. of 12 and 18 = $36 = 2^2 \times 3^2$

In both cases the L.C.M. is the product of the highest powers of the different factors of each number.

Example
Find the L.C.M. of 15, 20 and 30
$15 = 3 \times 5$; $20 = 2 \times 2 \times 5 = 2^2 \times 5$; $30 = 2 \times 3 \times 5$
L.C.M. $= 2^2 \times 3 \times 5 = 60$.

Squares, square roots and factors   UNIT 4

Use prime factors to find the L.C.M. for the following sets of numbers.

1. 8 and 10
2. 9 and 12
3. 10 and 16
4. 6, 8, 10
5. 6, 9, 15
6. 9, 12, 15
7. 3, 8, 12
8. 4, 5, 10
9. 3, 5, 12
10. 4, 10, 12
11. 6, 10, 12
12. 8, 10, 15

In all of these problems use the L.C.M.

13. Find the smallest number which will leave no remainder when divided by 8, 10 or 12.

14. Find the smallest number which leaves a remainder 9 when divided by 15 or 24. (Hint: you must first find the smallest number which will divide exactly by 15 or 24.)

15. What is the shortest length of string you must have to cut shorter lengths of 8 cm or 10 cm or 12 cm or 15 cm without any left over?

16. Three bells chime at different intervals: one every 3 minutes, another every 4 minutes and the third every 6 minutes; if they begin to chime together, after how many minutes will they next chime together again?

17. What is the smallest number of marbles you can put into sets of either 3 or 4 or 6?

18. Three toy cars move around a track. One takes 5 seconds, another takes 6 seconds, and the third takes 8 seconds. If they start off together how long will it be before they are all at the starting point again?

UNIT 4 Squares, square roots and factors

Highest common factor (H.C.F.)

Look at the factors of 12 and 18.

12 has factors 1, 2, 3, 4, 6 and 12	$12 = 2 \times 2 \times 3$ (using prime factors)
18 has factors 1, 2, 3, 6, 9 and 18	and $18 = 2 \times 3 \times 3$
The common factors are 1, 2, 3 and 6	One of the factors 2 is common to both 12 and 18
The **highest common factor** is 6	One of the factors 3 is also common
H.C.F. of 12 and 18 is 6	$2 \times 3 = 6$
	This is the H.C.F. of 12 and 18

If we write numbers as the product of their prime factors, the highest common factor (or H.C.F.) of the numbers is the product of the common factors of the numbers.

Example
Find the H.C.F. of 16 and 24
$16 = 2 \times 2 \times 2 \times 2 = 2^4$
$24 = 2 \times 2 \times 2 \times 3 = 2^3 \times 3$
H.C.F. $= 2 \times 2 \times 2 = 2^3 = 8$
[$2 \times 2 \times 2$ or 2^3 is common to both numbers: $2^4 = 2^3 \times 2$]

You can check that this is correct by writing out all the factors of 16 and 24.

Find the H.C.F. of the following pairs of numbers using prime factors.

1. 4, 8
2. 6, 9
3. 4, 12
4. 6, 12
5. 8, 12
6. 9, 12
7. 6, 18
8. 12, 18
9. 12, 20
10. 16, 24
11. 16, 20
12. 20, 32

Squares, square roots and factors UNIT 4

In questions 1 to 4 on page 48, check your answers by writing out all the factors of the pairs of numbers.

In all these problems use the H.C.F.

13. What is the largest number which will divide 24, 42 and 72 exactly?

14. What is the largest number which will divide 29 and 77 leaving a remainder of 5? (Hint: if you must have a remainder in each case, what numbers divide exactly?)

15. What is the largest number which will divide 115 and leave a remainder 7 and also divide 249 and leave a remainder 9?

16. What is the size of the largest square tile in cm which you can use to cover a walk 250 cm by 75 cm? (Hint: since the tile is square, the length of a side of the tile must divide the length and width of the walk exactly.)

17. Three bags contain 60 kg, 72 kg and 90 kg of potatoes. The potatoes have to be put into smaller bags of equal weight. What is the largest bag that can be made?

18. Three pieces of string measuring 48 cm, 64 cm and 80 cm must be cut up into smaller equal pieces. What is the longest piece that you can get?

5 Equivalent fractions

Every fraction has a **numerator** and **denominator**.

The numerator is the number above the fraction line.
The denominator is the number below the fraction line.

In the fraction $\frac{2}{3}$, the numerator is 2, the denominator is 3.
In the fraction $\frac{5}{12}$, the numerator is 5, the denominator is 12.

Remember that the denominator shows into **how many parts** the whole is divided; the numerator shows the **number of parts taken** to make the fraction.

From the shapes below we see that $\frac{1}{2} = \frac{2}{4}$, $\frac{1}{3} = \frac{2}{6}$, $\frac{1}{5} = \frac{2}{10}$.

Equivalent fractions

Complete the statements below.

1. $\frac{2}{3} = \frac{\Box}{6}$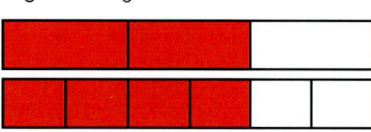

2. $\frac{3}{4} = \frac{\Box}{8}$

3. $\frac{5}{6} = \frac{\Box}{12}$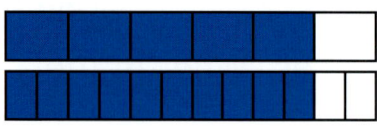

4. $\frac{3}{4} = \frac{\Box}{12}$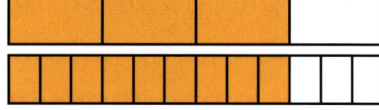

5. $\frac{1}{4} = \frac{\Box}{8} = \frac{\Box}{12}$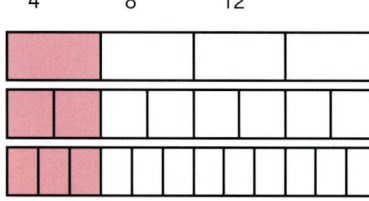

6. $\frac{1}{2} = \frac{\Box}{6} = \frac{\Box}{10}$

Equivalent fractions **UNIT 5**

Complete the statements.

7.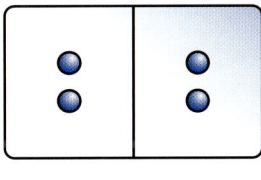
$\frac{1}{2} = \frac{\square}{4}$

8.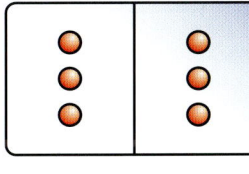
$\frac{1}{2} = \frac{\square}{6}$

9.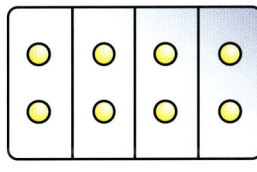
$\frac{1}{2} = \frac{\square}{8}$

10.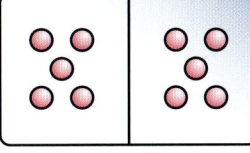
$\frac{1}{2} = \frac{\square}{10}$

11.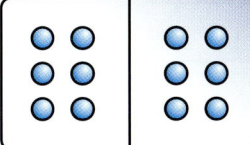
$\frac{1}{2} = \frac{\square}{12}$

12.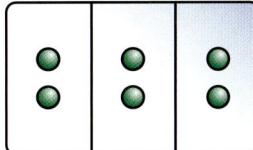
$\frac{1}{3} = \frac{\square}{6}$ $\frac{2}{3} = \frac{\square}{6}$

13.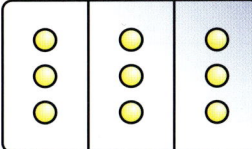
$\frac{1}{3} = \frac{\square}{9}$ $\frac{2}{3} = \frac{\square}{9}$

14.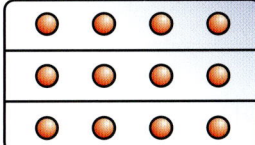
$\frac{1}{3} = \frac{\square}{12}$ $\frac{2}{3} = \frac{\square}{12}$

15.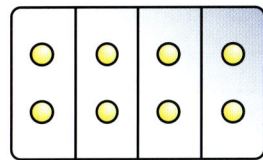
$\frac{1}{4} = \frac{\square}{8}$ $\frac{3}{4} = \frac{\square}{8}$

16.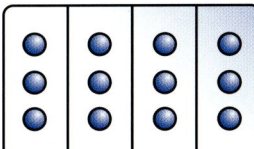
$\frac{1}{4} = \frac{\square}{12}$ $\frac{3}{4} = \frac{\square}{12}$

17.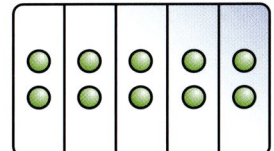
$\frac{1}{5} = \frac{\square}{10}$ $\frac{2}{5} = \frac{\square}{10}$

18.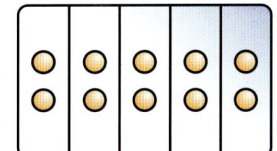
$\frac{3}{5} = \frac{\square}{10}$ $\frac{4}{5} = \frac{\square}{10}$

19.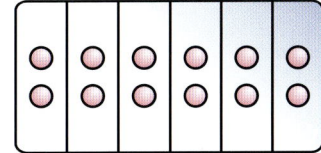
$\frac{1}{6} = \frac{\square}{12}$ $\frac{5}{6} = \frac{\square}{12}$

UNIT 5 Equivalent fractions

Ordering fractions

Look at these pictures.

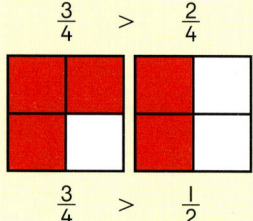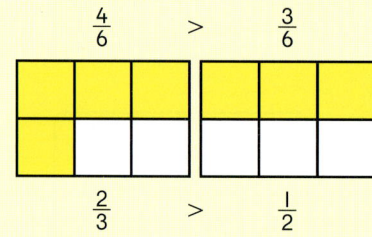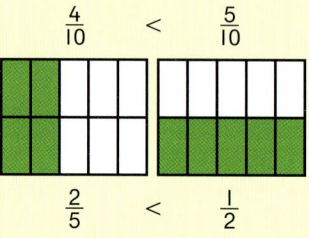

We are able to compare the fractions because the shapes are divided into the same number of parts.

Draw pictures to help you compare these fractions:

1. $\frac{3}{8}$ and $\frac{1}{4}$
2. $\frac{3}{4}$ and $\frac{5}{8}$
3. $\frac{1}{3}$ and $\frac{1}{2}$
4. $\frac{2}{3}$ and $\frac{5}{6}$
5. $\frac{7}{10}$ and $\frac{4}{5}$

Draw pictures to help you answer these questions.
Write the correct sign: >, < or =, between these pairs of fractions to make true statements.

6. $\frac{1}{3}$ ☐ $\frac{2}{9}$
7. $\frac{1}{5}$ ☐ $\frac{3}{10}$
8. $\frac{2}{3}$ ☐ $\frac{5}{9}$
9. $\frac{4}{10}$ ☐ $\frac{1}{2}$
10. $\frac{3}{4}$ ☐ $\frac{7}{8}$
11. $\frac{2}{3}$ ☐ $\frac{5}{6}$
12. $\frac{1}{2}$ ☐ $\frac{7}{12}$
13. $\frac{3}{4}$ ☐ $\frac{9}{12}$

Equivalent fractions UNIT 5

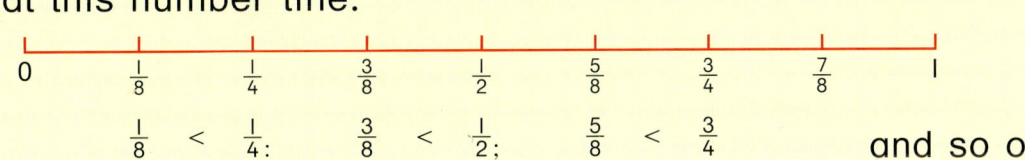

Look at this number line.

$\frac{1}{8} < \frac{1}{4}$; $\frac{3}{8} < \frac{1}{2}$; $\frac{5}{8} < \frac{3}{4}$ and so on.

Use number lines or shapes to help you arrange these fractions in order, starting with the smallest.

14. $\frac{1}{2}$ $\frac{1}{4}$ $\frac{3}{8}$ $\frac{3}{4}$ **15.** $\frac{3}{10}$ $\frac{1}{5}$ $\frac{1}{2}$ $\frac{7}{10}$ **16.** $\frac{2}{3}$ $\frac{5}{12}$ $\frac{1}{3}$ $\frac{5}{6}$

17. $\frac{1}{3}$ $\frac{3}{12}$ $\frac{3}{4}$ $\frac{1}{2}$

UNIT 5   Equivalent fractions

Use the chart on page 53 to help you answer the following.

You will need: a ruler or a straight-edge card.

Write the correct sign, > or <, between the pairs of fractions to make true statements.

18. $\frac{3}{8} \square \frac{1}{3}$ 19. $\frac{7}{8} \square \frac{5}{6}$ 20. $\frac{2}{3} \square \frac{5}{8}$

21. $\frac{5}{12} \square \frac{3}{8}$ 22. $\frac{3}{5} \square \frac{2}{3}$ 23. $\frac{5}{8} \square \frac{7}{9}$

24. $\frac{8}{9} \square \frac{5}{8}$ 25. $\frac{3}{8} \square \frac{4}{9}$ 26. $\frac{9}{10} \square \frac{11}{12}$

27. $\frac{5}{6} \square \frac{4}{5}$ 28. $\frac{3}{10} \square \frac{3}{8}$ 29. $\frac{3}{5} \square \frac{7}{12}$

Use the chart to help you arrange these fractions in order, smallest to largest.

30. $\frac{1}{3} \quad \frac{1}{4} \quad \frac{2}{9} \quad \frac{3}{10}$ 31. $\frac{1}{6} \quad \frac{1}{9} \quad \frac{1}{8} \quad \frac{1}{10}$

32. $\frac{3}{8} \quad \frac{1}{3} \quad \frac{4}{9} \quad \frac{2}{5}$ 33. $\frac{5}{12} \quad \frac{4}{9} \quad \frac{2}{5} \quad \frac{7}{8}$

34. $\frac{3}{4} \quad \frac{2}{3} \quad \frac{5}{6} \quad \frac{7}{9}$ 35. $\frac{5}{6} \quad \frac{4}{5} \quad \frac{8}{9} \quad \frac{7}{8}$

Use the chart to complete the following statements.

36. $\frac{1}{2} = \frac{\square}{4} = \frac{\square}{8}$ 37. $\frac{1}{2} = \frac{\square}{6} = \frac{\square}{12}$

38. $\frac{1}{2} = \frac{\square}{10}$ 39. $\frac{1}{3} = \frac{\square}{6} = \frac{\square}{12}$

40. $\frac{2}{3} = \frac{\square}{6} = \frac{\square}{12}$ 41. $\frac{2}{3} = \frac{\square}{9}$

42. $\frac{1}{4} = \frac{\square}{8}$ 43. $\frac{3}{4} = \frac{\square}{8}$

44. $\frac{1}{5} = \frac{\square}{10}$ 45. $\frac{2}{5} = \frac{\square}{10}$

46. $\frac{3}{5} = \frac{\square}{10}$ 47. $\frac{4}{5} = \frac{\square}{10}$

48. $\frac{1}{6} = \frac{\square}{12}$ 49. $\frac{5}{6} = \frac{\square}{12}$

Equivalent fractions UNIT 5

Creating equivalent fractions

> We have been able to rewrite our fractions by looking at our sets on page 51 and our chart on page 53.
>
> Look at these pairs of equivalent fractions:
>
> $\frac{1}{2} = \frac{2}{4}$ $\frac{1}{2} = \frac{4}{8}$ $\frac{1}{2} = \frac{6}{12}$
>
> What do you notice about the numerators and denominators in each pair of equivalent fractions?
> We see that:
>
> $\frac{1 \times 2}{2 \times 2} = \frac{2}{4}$ $\frac{1 \times 4}{2 \times 4} = \frac{4}{8}$ $\frac{1 \times 6}{2 \times 6} = \frac{6}{12}$
>
> We can find an equivalent fraction for every fraction by multiplying the numerator and denominator by the same number.

Multiply both the numerator and the denominator by 2 to get equivalent fractions for:

1. (a) $\frac{1}{2}$ (b) $\frac{2}{3}$ (c) $\frac{1}{4}$ (d) $\frac{2}{5}$ (e) $\frac{3}{5}$ (f) $\frac{1}{6}$ (g) $\frac{3}{8}$

Multiply both the numerator and the denominator by 3 to get equivalent fractions for:

2. (a) $\frac{1}{2}$ (b) $\frac{2}{3}$ (c) $\frac{1}{4}$ (d) $\frac{2}{5}$ (e) $\frac{3}{5}$ (f) $\frac{1}{6}$ (g) $\frac{3}{8}$

Multiply both the numerator and the denominator by 4 to get equivalent fractions for:

3. (a) $\frac{1}{4}$ (b) $\frac{3}{4}$ (c) $\frac{1}{3}$ (d) $\frac{2}{3}$ (e) $\frac{1}{5}$ (f) $\frac{2}{5}$ (g) $\frac{3}{5}$

Find the numbers for the boxes in these statements.

4. (a) $\frac{1}{3} = \frac{\square}{12}$ (b) $\frac{3}{5} = \frac{\square}{20}$ (c) $\frac{5}{6} = \frac{\square}{18}$

  (d) $\frac{2}{3} = \frac{\square}{9}$ (e) $\frac{3}{4} = \frac{\square}{16}$ (f) $\frac{3}{8} = \frac{\square}{16}$

UNIT 5 Equivalent fractions

Comparing fractions

We can use equivalent fractions to compare the **magnitude** or **size of fractions**.

We have to rewrite the fractions as equivalent fractions with the same denominator or, as we say, **a common denominator.**

We usually choose the smallest common denominator.

Example
To compare $\frac{1}{2}$ and $\frac{1}{3}$

We can rewrite $\frac{1}{2}$ as $\frac{2}{4}$ or $\frac{3}{6}$ or $\frac{4}{8}$ or $\frac{6}{12}$ and so on.

We can rewrite $\frac{2}{3}$ as $\frac{4}{6}$ or $\frac{6}{9}$ or $\frac{8}{12}$ and others.

Using the equivalent fractions with the smallest common denominator we have $\frac{1}{2} = \frac{3}{6}$ and $\frac{2}{3} = \frac{4}{6}$ [Note that the L.C.M. of 2 and 3 is 6]

Therefore $\frac{2}{3} > \frac{1}{2}$

Example
To compare $\frac{1}{3}$ and $\frac{3}{8}$

Multiples of 3 are 3, 6, 9, 12, 15, 18, 21, 24 ...

Multiples of 8 are 8, 16, 24, 27 ...

L.C.M. of 3 and 8 is 24

$$\frac{1}{3} = \frac{8}{24} \text{ and } \frac{3}{8} = \frac{9}{24}$$

Therefore $\frac{3}{8} > \frac{1}{3}$

Equivalent fractions   **UNIT 5**

Rewrite these pairs of fractions with the smallest common denominator.
Write the correct sign, > or <, to compare their size.

1. $\frac{1}{2}$ □ $\frac{2}{3}$ 2. $\frac{1}{3}$ □ $\frac{1}{4}$ 3. $\frac{2}{3}$ □ $\frac{3}{4}$

4. $\frac{1}{2}$ □ $\frac{2}{5}$ 5. $\frac{1}{2}$ □ $\frac{3}{5}$ 6. $\frac{4}{5}$ □ $\frac{3}{4}$

7. $\frac{4}{5}$ □ $\frac{5}{6}$ 8. $\frac{2}{3}$ □ $\frac{3}{5}$ 9. $\frac{3}{8}$ □ $\frac{2}{5}$

10. $\frac{7}{12}$ □ $\frac{3}{5}$ 11. $\frac{9}{10}$ □ $\frac{11}{12}$ 12. $\frac{5}{8}$ □ $\frac{2}{3}$

13. $\frac{2}{3}$ □ $\frac{5}{8}$ 14. $\frac{5}{6}$ □ $\frac{7}{8}$ 15. $\frac{3}{8}$ □ $\frac{4}{9}$

Rewrite each set of fractions with the smallest common denominator.

Arrange each set in order of size, starting with the smallest.

16. $\frac{1}{3}$ $\frac{1}{4}$ $\frac{1}{6}$ $\frac{1}{5}$ 17. $\frac{3}{4}$ $\frac{2}{3}$ $\frac{7}{10}$ $\frac{5}{12}$

18. $\frac{2}{3}$ $\frac{1}{2}$ $\frac{4}{9}$ $\frac{5}{6}$ 19. $\frac{2}{3}$ $\frac{5}{6}$ $\frac{1}{2}$ $\frac{3}{5}$

20. $\frac{3}{4}$ $\frac{2}{3}$ $\frac{5}{9}$ $\frac{1}{2}$ 21. $\frac{3}{8}$ $\frac{5}{6}$ $\frac{2}{3}$ $\frac{1}{2}$

22. $\frac{3}{5}$ $\frac{1}{2}$ $\frac{3}{4}$ $\frac{7}{10}$ 23. $\frac{5}{8}$ $\frac{4}{5}$ $\frac{7}{10}$ $\frac{1}{2}$

24. $\frac{2}{3}$ $\frac{5}{6}$ $\frac{3}{4}$ $\frac{7}{12}$ 25. $\frac{5}{6}$ $\frac{3}{4}$ $\frac{1}{2}$ $\frac{2}{5}$

UNIT 5 Equivalent fractions

Rewriting fractions with smaller denominators

> If I give away three of my twelve mangoes, what fraction of the mangoes have I given away?
> One answer is $\frac{3}{12}$.
>
> We always prefer to use an equivalent fraction with a smaller denominator if we can find one.
> Remember that in rewriting fractions with larger denominators we multiplied.
> In this case we can divide both numerator and denominator by 3.
> $$\frac{3 \div 3}{12 \div 3} = \frac{1}{4} \text{ so that } \frac{3}{12} \text{ is rewritten as } \frac{1}{4}.$$

Rewrite these fractions with smaller denominators.

1. $\frac{2}{16}$
2. $\frac{2}{10}$
3. $\frac{10}{12}$
4. $\frac{3}{21}$
5. $\frac{5}{20}$
6. $\frac{15}{50}$
7. $\frac{3}{30}$
8. $\frac{10}{24}$
9. $\frac{8}{18}$
10. $\frac{6}{15}$
11. $\frac{10}{25}$
12. $\frac{6}{16}$

> Look at the fraction $\frac{16}{20}$
>   16 has factors 2, 4 and 8
>   20 has factors 2, 4, 5 and 10
> so we can divide by either 2 or 4.
> 2 and 4 are common factors,
> $$\frac{16}{20} = \frac{16 \div 2}{20 \div 2} = \frac{8}{10} \text{ or } \frac{16}{20} = \frac{16 \div 4}{20 \div 4} = \frac{4}{5}$$
> To get the equivalent fraction with the smallest denominator we must divide by the highest common factor (H.C.F.).

Equivalent fractions UNIT 5

Find the highest common factors and write these fractions with the smallest denominators.

13. $\frac{8}{12}$
14. $\frac{12}{18}$
15. $\frac{16}{40}$
16. $\frac{12}{30}$
17. $\frac{16}{24}$
18. $\frac{4}{20}$
19. $\frac{18}{30}$
20. $\frac{10}{40}$
21. $\frac{16}{36}$
22. $\frac{24}{42}$
23. $\frac{24}{48}$
24. $\frac{36}{60}$

Write the answers to these questions as fractions with their smallest denominators.
What fraction of:

25. 24 is 16?
26. 36 is 20?
27. 48 is 16?
28. 60 is 36?
29. 72 is 48?
30. 75 is 15?
31. 96 is 42?
32. 84 is 36?
33. 100 is 40?

> **Example** What fraction of $1.00 is 40 cents?
> To answer this question we must first write $1.00 as 100 cents.
> The fraction is then $\frac{40}{100} = \frac{4}{10} = \frac{2}{5}$
> (dividing first by 10 and then by 2)
> 40 cents is $\frac{2}{5}$ of $1.00.

What fraction of $1.00 are the following:

34. 60 cents
35. 36 cents
36. 84 cents?

What fraction of:

37. $5.00 is $1.50
38. $10.00 is $7.50?

What fraction of:

39. 100 cm is 24 cm
40. 50 m is 36 m?

In these next two questions you must work in cm only.

41. 10 m is 200 cm
42. 6 m 40 cm is 1 m 20 cm?

UNIT 5 Equivalent fractions

Word problems

Work out the answers to these word problems. Show all your working.

1. John ate $\frac{3}{4}$ of his pie. Timmy ate $\frac{7}{8}$ of his. Which of the two boys ate most of his pie?

2. Devin had 20 plums. He gave Ravi $\frac{3}{10}$ and Kong $\frac{2}{5}$. Which boy got more? How many plums did he get?

3. How many cubes make up this block?
   How many cubes are in $\frac{1}{3}$ of the block?
   What fraction of the block is not red?
   How many blocks are not red?

4. Fifteen girls in a group of 45 are wearing red ribbons. What fraction of the group is this? What fraction is not wearing red ribbons?

5. A bottle of lemonade was poured into 15 glasses. The team drank 12 glasses. What fraction of the lemonade was left?

6. Three pies were cut into eighths. The class shared 20 pieces. What fraction of one pie was left?

7. Four cakes were cut up and shared equally among 12 girls. What fraction of one cake did each girl get?

8. Out of a class of 32 children, 20 are girls. What fraction is girls?

9. One fifth of my money is $240. How much money do I have altogether?

Assessment 3

Write these numbers as the product of their prime factors.

1. 30
2. 48

What is the L.C.M. of:

3. 6 and 10
4. 3, 5 and 10

What is the H.C.F. of:

5. 9 and 15
6. 12 and 16

Complete these statements:

7. $\frac{2}{3} = \frac{\square}{6} = \frac{\square}{18}$
8. $\frac{4}{5} = \frac{\square}{15} = \frac{\square}{30}$

Write the correct sign, > or <, between these pairs of fractions.

9. $\frac{1}{2} \square \frac{3}{5}$
10. $\frac{4}{5} \square \frac{3}{4}$

Arrange these fractions in ascending order of size.

11. $\frac{5}{6} \quad \frac{3}{4} \quad \frac{1}{2} \quad \frac{3}{5}$

Write these fractions with their smallest denominators.

12. $\frac{15}{25}$
13. $\frac{12}{16}$

14. What fraction of 60 is 45?

15. What fraction of 1 metre is 24 cm?

16. Randy sold 40 of his 60 marbles. What fraction of the marbles did he keep?

17. Thirty boys share five pies equally among themselves. What fraction of a pie did each boy get?

18. $5^2 + 7^2$
19. $12^2 - 5^2$
20. $\sqrt{144} + \sqrt{81}$

6 Mixed numbers and improper fractions

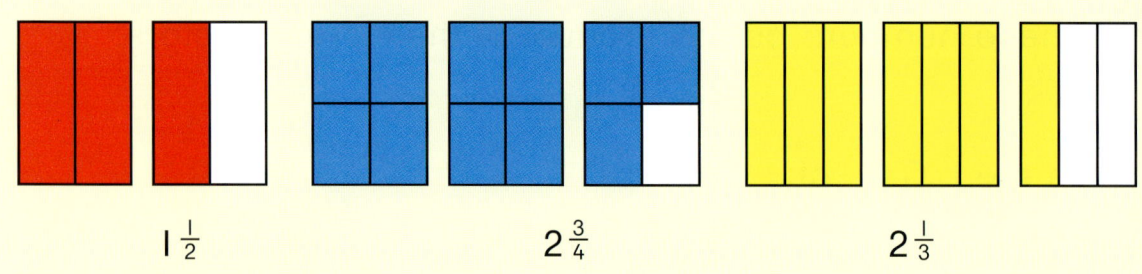

$1\frac{1}{2}$ $2\frac{3}{4}$ $2\frac{1}{3}$

Look at the drawings above.

$1\frac{1}{2} = 1 + \frac{1}{2} = 2$ halves $+ 1$ half $= (2 \times 1)$ halves $+ 1$ half
$= \frac{2}{2} + \frac{1}{2} = \frac{3}{2}$

$2\frac{3}{4} = 2 + \frac{3}{4} = (4 \times 2)$ quarters $+ 3$ quarters
$= 8$ quarters $+ 3$ quarters $= \frac{8}{4} + \frac{3}{4} = \frac{11}{4}$

$2\frac{1}{3} = 2 + \frac{1}{3} = (3 \times 2)$ thirds $+ 1$ third $= 6$ thirds $+ 1$ third
$= \frac{6}{3} + \frac{1}{3} = \frac{7}{3}$

Observe that the denominator of the improper fraction is the same as the denominator of the fraction in the mixed number. To get the numerator we multiply the whole number by the denominator and add the numerator of the fraction in the mixed number.

Examples $3\frac{1}{2} = \frac{7}{2}$ ($2 \times 3 + 1 = 7$)
and $5\frac{3}{4} = \frac{23}{4}$ ($4 \times 5 + 3 = 23$)

Write these mixed numbers as improper fractions.

1. $1\frac{1}{4}$
2. $1\frac{3}{4}$
3. $2\frac{1}{2}$
4. $3\frac{2}{3}$
5. $4\frac{2}{3}$
6. $4\frac{1}{4}$
7. $3\frac{3}{4}$
8. $2\frac{1}{5}$
9. $3\frac{3}{5}$
10. $5\frac{1}{2}$
11. $6\frac{2}{3}$
12. $4\frac{2}{5}$
13. $1\frac{4}{5}$
14. $2\frac{2}{5}$
15. $3\frac{1}{6}$
16. $2\frac{1}{8}$
17. $4\frac{3}{5}$
18. $5\frac{1}{4}$
19. $6\frac{1}{2}$
20. $1\frac{9}{10}$

Mixed numbers and improper fractions   **UNIT 6**

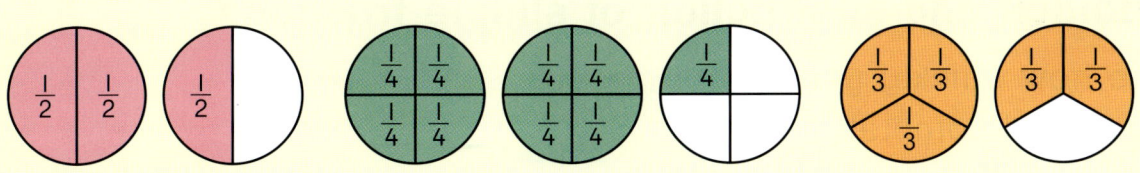

Look at the drawings above.

$\frac{3}{2}$ means 3 halves = 2 halves + 1 half = 1 + $\frac{1}{2}$ = $1\frac{1}{2}$

$\frac{9}{4}$ means 9 quarters = 8 quarters + 1 quarter = 2 + $\frac{1}{4}$ = $2\frac{1}{4}$

$\frac{5}{3}$ means 5 thirds = 3 thirds + 2 thirds = 1 + $\frac{2}{3}$ = $1\frac{2}{3}$

Notice how you obtain the mixed number.

You must divide the numerator of the improper fraction by the denominator.

The quotient gives the whole number part and the remainder gives the fraction part.

Note that the denominator of the fraction part of the mixed number is the same as the denominator of the improper fraction.

Examples $\frac{14}{3}$ = $4\frac{2}{3}$ (14 ÷ 3 = 4r2)

$\frac{7}{4}$ = $1\frac{3}{4}$ (7 ÷ 4 = 1r3)

Write these improper fractions as mixed numbers.

21. $\frac{5}{2}$ 22. $\frac{19}{3}$ 23. $\frac{17}{2}$ 24. $\frac{15}{8}$

25. $\frac{14}{4}$ 26. $\frac{16}{5}$ 27. $\frac{30}{4}$ 28. $\frac{17}{6}$

29. $\frac{13}{5}$ 30. $\frac{12}{8}$ 31. $\frac{21}{5}$ 32. $\frac{21}{4}$

33. $\frac{20}{3}$ 34. $\frac{14}{6}$ 35. $\frac{13}{4}$ 36. $\frac{17}{5}$

UNIT 6   Mixed numbers and improper fractions

Addition and subtraction of simple fractions

See how quickly you can do these.
Copy and complete.

1. $\frac{1}{8} + \frac{5}{8}$
2. $\frac{2}{5} + \frac{1}{5}$
3. $\frac{2}{9} + \frac{5}{9}$
4. $\frac{1}{12} + \frac{7}{12}$
5. $\frac{3}{10} + \frac{1}{10}$
6. $\frac{5}{12} + \frac{1}{12}$
7. $\frac{7}{10} + \frac{1}{10}$
8. $\frac{5}{12} + \frac{7}{12}$
9. $\frac{1}{8} + \frac{7}{8}$
10. $\frac{1}{6} + \frac{5}{6}$
11. $\frac{2}{5} + \frac{3}{5}$
12. $\frac{3}{8} + \frac{1}{8}$

Copy and complete.

13. $\frac{1}{3} + \frac{1}{12}$
14. $\frac{1}{5} + \frac{3}{10}$
15. $\frac{1}{4} + \frac{7}{12}$
16. $\frac{1}{2} + \frac{1}{8}$
17. $\frac{1}{6} + \frac{1}{3}$
18. $\frac{1}{6} + \frac{5}{12}$
19. $\frac{1}{3} + \frac{7}{12}$
20. $\frac{1}{5} + \frac{7}{10}$
21. $\frac{3}{10} + \frac{2}{5}$
22. $\frac{1}{6} + \frac{2}{3}$
23. $\frac{5}{8} + \frac{1}{4}$
24. $\frac{5}{12} + \frac{1}{3}$

Copy and complete.

25. $\frac{7}{8} - \frac{5}{8}$
26. $\frac{9}{10} - \frac{7}{10}$
27. $\frac{11}{12} - \frac{5}{12}$
28. $\frac{5}{8} - \frac{3}{8}$
29. $\frac{9}{10} - \frac{3}{10}$
30. $\frac{7}{10} - \frac{1}{10}$
31. $\frac{7}{8} - \frac{1}{8}$
32. $\frac{5}{6} - \frac{1}{6}$
33. $\frac{2}{3} - \frac{1}{12}$
34. $\frac{4}{5} - \frac{1}{10}$
35. $\frac{5}{6} - \frac{1}{3}$
36. $\frac{3}{4} - \frac{5}{12}$
37. $\frac{1}{2} - \frac{3}{10}$
38. $\frac{2}{3} - \frac{1}{6}$
39. $\frac{3}{5} - \frac{1}{10}$
40. $\frac{3}{4} - \frac{3}{8}$
41. $\frac{3}{4} - \frac{1}{6}$
42. $\frac{9}{10} - \frac{3}{5}$

Mixed numbers and improper fractions UNIT 6

> **Remember:** when we add fractions which have the same denominator, we simply add the numerators of the fractions to obtain the numerator of the resulting fraction.

Example $\frac{5}{8} + \frac{7}{8} = \frac{12}{8} = 1\frac{4}{8} = 1\frac{1}{2}$

> **Remember:** when we add fractions which have different denominators, we must change them to equivalent fractions which have a common denominator and then add.

Example $\frac{3}{4} + \frac{2}{3} = \frac{9}{12} + \frac{8}{12} = \frac{17}{12} = 1\frac{5}{12}$

In this example we used a common denominator 12 because the L.C.M. of 4 and 3 is 12.

These additions give an improper fraction as their answers. Change the improper fractions to mixed numbers as we have done in the examples above.
Also write the fraction part of the mixed number using the smallest denominator.

43. $\frac{5}{6} + \frac{5}{6}$ 44. $\frac{3}{5} + \frac{4}{5}$ 45. $\frac{7}{10} + \frac{9}{10}$

46. $\frac{5}{12} + \frac{11}{12}$ 47. $\frac{1}{2} + \frac{7}{12}$ 48. $\frac{3}{4} + \frac{5}{6}$

49. $\frac{2}{3} + \frac{3}{5}$ 50. $\frac{5}{8} + \frac{2}{3}$ 51. $\frac{5}{6} + \frac{5}{12}$

52. $\frac{3}{8} + \frac{5}{6}$ 53. $\frac{3}{4} + \frac{2}{5}$ 54. $\frac{4}{5} + \frac{1}{6}$

55. $\frac{2}{5} + \frac{5}{6}$ 56. $\frac{7}{10} + \frac{2}{3}$ 57. $\frac{9}{10} + \frac{3}{4}$

58. $\frac{2}{3} + \frac{7}{12}$ 59. $\frac{2}{3} + \frac{4}{5}$ 60. $\frac{3}{5} + \frac{7}{10}$

61. $\frac{5}{12} + \frac{5}{8}$ 62. $\frac{7}{8} + \frac{3}{4}$ 63. $\frac{1}{3} + \frac{1}{6}$

UNIT 6 Mixed numbers and improper fractions

Addition of mixed numbers

Remember: to add or subtract fractions we must rewrite the fractions with a common denominator if necessary.

The smallest common denominator is always the L.C.M. of the denominators of the fractions.

Example

$2\frac{1}{12} + 3\frac{7}{12}$ The fractions have a common denominator.
$= (2 + 3) + (\frac{1}{12} + \frac{7}{12})$ We add the fractions; we add the whole numbers.
$= 5 + \frac{8}{12}$ We can write $\frac{1}{12} + \frac{7}{12}$ as $\frac{1+7}{12} = \frac{8}{12}$
$= 5\frac{2}{3}$ $\frac{8}{12} = \frac{2}{3}$; we always write fractions with their smallest denominator.

When we rewrite a fraction with its smallest denominator, we say we have **reduced** the fraction to its **lowest terms**.

Copy and complete.

1. $1\frac{2}{5} + 2\frac{1}{5}$
2. $3\frac{1}{5} + 5\frac{3}{5}$
3. $2\frac{5}{12} + 1\frac{1}{12}$
4. $4\frac{1}{6} + 2\frac{5}{6}$
5. $4\frac{5}{12} + 3\frac{7}{12}$
6. $6\frac{3}{8} + 1\frac{1}{8}$
7. $1\frac{1}{8} + 3\frac{5}{8}$
8. $3\frac{7}{12} + 4\frac{5}{12}$
9. $2\frac{2}{9} + 3\frac{5}{9}$
10. $4\frac{3}{10} + 2\frac{1}{10}$
11. $4\frac{1}{6} + 3\frac{7}{6}$
12. $2\frac{7}{10} + 1\frac{1}{10}$

Example

$4\frac{1}{8} + 3\frac{3}{4}$ One denominator is a multiple of the other.
$= (4 + 3) + (\frac{1}{8} + \frac{3}{4})$ L.C.M. of 8 and 4 is 8, the larger denominator
$= 7 + \frac{1+6}{8}$ $\frac{3}{4} = \frac{6}{8}$
$= 7\frac{7}{8}$

Mixed numbers and improper fractions — UNIT 6

Copy and complete.

13. $2\frac{1}{4} + 1\frac{7}{12}$ 14. $3\frac{1}{6} + 2\frac{5}{12}$ 15. $4\frac{3}{10} + 1\frac{2}{5}$ 16. $3\frac{5}{12} + 2\frac{1}{3}$
17. $4\frac{1}{2} + 1\frac{1}{8}$ 18. $1\frac{1}{3} + 5\frac{7}{12}$ 19. $2\frac{1}{6} + 5\frac{2}{3}$ 20. $6\frac{1}{3} + 2\frac{1}{12}$
21. $6\frac{1}{5} + 2\frac{3}{10}$ 22. $7\frac{1}{6} + 3\frac{1}{3}$ 23. $4\frac{1}{5} + 9\frac{7}{10}$ 24. $3\frac{5}{8} + 5\frac{1}{4}$

Example

$12\frac{2}{3} + 9\frac{1}{2}$ We need to use the L.C.M. of 3 and 2.
$= (12 + 9) + (\frac{2}{3} + \frac{1}{2})$ L.C.M. of 3 and 2 is 6
$= 21 + \frac{4+3}{6}$ $\frac{2}{3} = \frac{4}{6}$ and $\frac{1}{2} = \frac{3}{6}$
$= 21 + \frac{7}{6}$
$= 22\frac{1}{6}$ $\frac{7}{6} = 1\frac{1}{6}$

Copy and complete.

25. $1\frac{1}{5} + 2\frac{1}{2}$ 26. $1\frac{3}{4} + 2\frac{1}{3}$ 27. $1\frac{2}{3} + 2\frac{1}{4}$
28. $3\frac{3}{4} + 2\frac{2}{3}$ 29. $3\frac{1}{2} + 2\frac{1}{3}$ 30. $3\frac{1}{5} + 2\frac{1}{2}$
31. $1\frac{3}{5} + 2\frac{1}{4}$ 32. $3\frac{3}{4} + 1\frac{2}{5}$ 33. $2\frac{2}{5} + 1\frac{1}{3}$
34. $3\frac{1}{2} + 2\frac{4}{5}$ 35. $3\frac{1}{3} + 1\frac{1}{5}$ 36. $4\frac{1}{4} + 2\frac{2}{5}$
37. $12\frac{2}{5} + 10\frac{1}{2}$ 38. $16\frac{3}{4} + 12\frac{1}{3}$ 39. $13\frac{2}{3} + 9\frac{1}{4}$
40. $15\frac{3}{4} + 6\frac{2}{3}$ 41. $9\frac{1}{2} + 18\frac{1}{3}$ 42. $14\frac{1}{5} + 9\frac{1}{2}$
43. $9\frac{3}{5} + 12\frac{1}{4}$ 44. $8\frac{3}{4} + 12\frac{2}{5}$ 45. $15\frac{2}{5} + 7\frac{1}{3}$
46. $18\frac{1}{2} + 10\frac{4}{5}$ 47. $6\frac{1}{3} + 18\frac{1}{5}$ 48. $5\frac{1}{4} + 16\frac{2}{5}$

UNIT 6 Mixed numbers and improper fractions

Subtraction of mixed numbers

Example

$5\frac{3}{4} - 1\frac{1}{4}$ — The fractions have a common denominator.

$= 5 + \frac{3}{4} - 1 - \frac{1}{4}$ — Remember you are subtracting 1 as well as $\frac{1}{4}$.

$= (5 - 1) + (\frac{3}{4} - \frac{1}{4})$ — Subtract fractions: subtract whole numbers.

$= 4 + \frac{2}{4}$ — Reduce $\frac{2}{4}$ to its lowest terms

$= 4\frac{1}{2}$ $\frac{2}{4} = \frac{1}{2}$

Copy and complete.

1. $5\frac{2}{3} - 1\frac{1}{3}$
2. $3\frac{5}{6} - 1\frac{1}{6}$
3. $6\frac{4}{5} - 2\frac{3}{5}$
4. $7\frac{5}{6} - 2\frac{1}{6}$
5. $4\frac{3}{5} - 2\frac{2}{5}$
6. $5\frac{8}{9} - 2\frac{4}{9}$
7. $2\frac{11}{12} - \frac{7}{12}$
8. $6\frac{9}{10} - 2\frac{1}{10}$
9. $8\frac{7}{12} - 2\frac{5}{12}$
10. $5\frac{4}{5} - 1\frac{2}{5}$
11. $4\frac{5}{9} - 1\frac{2}{9}$
12. $6\frac{3}{10} - 1\frac{1}{10}$
13. $6\frac{5}{12} - 2\frac{1}{12}$
14. $7\frac{7}{10} - 2\frac{3}{10}$
15. $6\frac{7}{9} - 2\frac{4}{9}$
16. $8\frac{5}{9} - 1\frac{1}{9}$

Copy and complete.

Example

$4\frac{1}{4} - 2\frac{3}{4}$ — The fraction part we are subtracting is larger than the fraction part we are subtracting from.

$= 4 + \frac{1}{4} - 2 - \frac{3}{4}$

$= (4 - 2) + (\frac{1}{4} - \frac{3}{4})$

$= 2 + (\frac{1}{4} - \frac{3}{4})$

$= 1 + (1\frac{1}{4} - \frac{3}{4})$ — Convert 1 whole to quarters and add to $\frac{1}{4}$.

$= 1 + (\frac{5}{4} - \frac{3}{4})$ $1\frac{1}{4} = \frac{5}{4}$

$= 1 + \frac{2}{4}$

$= 1\frac{1}{2}$ $\frac{2}{4} = \frac{1}{2}$

Mixed numbers and improper fractions   **UNIT 6**

17. $7\frac{1}{9} - 2\frac{5}{9}$ **18.** $6\frac{1}{10} - 2\frac{3}{10}$ **19.** $5\frac{1}{6} - 2\frac{5}{6}$

20. $4\frac{1}{10} - 1\frac{3}{10}$ **21.** $4\frac{1}{3} - 2\frac{2}{3}$ **22.** $4\frac{2}{5} - 1\frac{3}{5}$

23. $5\frac{4}{9} - 2\frac{8}{9}$ **24.** $8\frac{5}{12} - 2\frac{7}{12}$ **25.** $6\frac{4}{9} - 2\frac{7}{9}$

26. $3\frac{1}{6} - 1\frac{5}{6}$ **27.** $2\frac{7}{12} - \frac{11}{12}$ **28.** $6\frac{3}{5} - 2\frac{4}{5}$

29. $6\frac{1}{12} - 2\frac{5}{12}$ **30.** $5\frac{2}{5} - 1\frac{4}{5}$ **31.** $4\frac{2}{9} - 1\frac{5}{9}$

32. $7\frac{3}{10} - 2\frac{7}{10}$ **33.** $5\frac{1}{6} - 2\frac{3}{6}$ **34.** $4\frac{2}{10} - 2\frac{4}{10}$

Example

$4\frac{1}{3} - 1\frac{1}{9}$ One denominator is a multiple of the other.

$= (4 - 1) + (\frac{1}{3} - \frac{1}{9})$

$= 3 + \frac{3-1}{9}$ L.C.M. of 3 and 9 is 9.

$= 3\frac{2}{9}$

Copy and complete.

35. $5\frac{2}{3} - 1\frac{2}{9}$ **36.** $4\frac{5}{12} - 1\frac{1}{6}$ **37.** $5\frac{1}{3} - 1\frac{1}{6}$

38. $3\frac{7}{8} - 1\frac{1}{2}$ **39.** $4\frac{7}{12} - 2\frac{1}{6}$ **40.** $5\frac{5}{6} - 2\frac{2}{3}$

41. $3\frac{9}{10} - 1\frac{1}{5}$ **42.** $4\frac{2}{3} - 1\frac{1}{9}$ **43.** $5\frac{5}{8} - 1\frac{1}{4}$

44. $6\frac{2}{3} - 1\frac{5}{9}$ **45.** $4\frac{7}{10} - 1\frac{3}{5}$ **46.** $6\frac{2}{3} - 3\frac{1}{6}$

47. $5\frac{7}{8} - 1\frac{3}{4}$ **48.** $4\frac{9}{10} - 1\frac{2}{5}$ **49.** $3\frac{5}{8} - 2\frac{1}{2}$

50. $6\frac{2}{3} - 1\frac{4}{9}$ **51.** $3\frac{3}{8} - 2\frac{2}{9}$ **52.** $9\frac{1}{10} - 3\frac{1}{6}$

UNIT 6 Mixed numbers and improper fractions

Example

$4\frac{1}{9} - 1\frac{1}{3}$
$= (4-1) + (\frac{1}{9} - \frac{1}{3})$
$= 3 + (\frac{1}{9} - \frac{3}{9})$
$= 2 + (1\frac{1}{9} - \frac{3}{9})$ L.C.M. of 9 and 3 is 9.
$= 2 + \frac{10-3}{9}$ Convert 1 whole to $\frac{9}{9}$ and add to $\frac{1}{9}$.
$= 2\frac{7}{9}$

Copy and complete.

53. $5\frac{2}{9} - 1\frac{2}{3}$
54. $4\frac{1}{6} - 1\frac{5}{12}$
55. $5\frac{1}{6} - 1\frac{1}{3}$
56. $3\frac{1}{2} - 1\frac{7}{8}$
57. $4\frac{1}{6} - 2\frac{7}{12}$
58. $5\frac{2}{3} - 2\frac{5}{6}$
59. $3\frac{1}{5} - 1\frac{9}{10}$
60. $4\frac{1}{9} - 1\frac{2}{3}$
61. $5\frac{1}{4} - 1\frac{5}{8}$
62. $6\frac{5}{9} - 1\frac{2}{3}$
63. $4\frac{3}{5} - 1\frac{7}{10}$
64. $6\frac{1}{6} - 3\frac{2}{3}$
65. $5\frac{3}{4} - 1\frac{7}{8}$
66. $4\frac{2}{5} - 1\frac{9}{10}$
67. $3\frac{1}{2} - 2\frac{5}{8}$
68. $6\frac{4}{9} - 1\frac{2}{3}$

Example

$5\frac{1}{2} - 2\frac{1}{9}$
$= (5-2) + (\frac{1}{2} - \frac{1}{9})$ L.C.M. of 2 and 9 is 18.
$= 3 + (\frac{9}{18} - \frac{2}{18})$
$= 3 + \frac{9-2}{18}$
$= 3\frac{7}{18}$

Copy and complete.

69. $5\frac{2}{3} - 3\frac{1}{2}$
70. $3\frac{1}{3} - 1\frac{1}{4}$
71. $6\frac{2}{3} - 2\frac{1}{4}$
72. $5\frac{3}{4} - 1\frac{2}{3}$
73. $3\frac{5}{6} - 1\frac{3}{4}$
74. $4\frac{3}{4} - 2\frac{1}{6}$
75. $2\frac{5}{6} - 1\frac{1}{4}$
76. $5\frac{1}{2} - 2\frac{1}{5}$
77. $2\frac{3}{5} - 1\frac{1}{2}$
78. $4\frac{1}{2} - 1\frac{2}{5}$
79. $5\frac{4}{5} - 2\frac{1}{2}$
80. $4\frac{1}{3} - 1\frac{1}{5}$
81. $5\frac{1}{4} - 2\frac{1}{5}$
82. $4\frac{2}{3} - 1\frac{2}{5}$
83. $6\frac{2}{5} - 2\frac{1}{4}$
84. $3\frac{3}{4} - 1\frac{2}{5}$

Mixed numbers and improper fractions   UNIT 6

Example
$$5\tfrac{2}{5} - 1\tfrac{3}{4}$$
$$= (5 - 1) + (\tfrac{2}{5} - \tfrac{3}{4})$$
$$= 4 + (\tfrac{8}{20} - \tfrac{15}{20}) \quad \text{L.C.M. of 5 and 4 is 20.}$$
$$= 3 + (1\tfrac{8}{20} - \tfrac{15}{20})$$
$$= 3 + \tfrac{28 - 15}{20} \quad\quad 1\tfrac{8}{20} = \tfrac{28}{20}$$
$$= 3\tfrac{13}{20}$$

Copy and complete.

85. $5\tfrac{1}{2} - 3\tfrac{2}{3}$
86. $3\tfrac{1}{4} - 1\tfrac{1}{3}$
87. $6\tfrac{1}{4} - 2\tfrac{2}{3}$

88. $5\tfrac{2}{3} - 1\tfrac{3}{4}$
89. $3\tfrac{3}{4} - 1\tfrac{5}{6}$
90. $4\tfrac{1}{6} - 2\tfrac{3}{4}$

91. $2\tfrac{1}{4} - 1\tfrac{5}{6}$
92. $5\tfrac{1}{5} - 2\tfrac{1}{2}$
93. $2\tfrac{1}{2} - 1\tfrac{3}{5}$

94. $4\tfrac{2}{5} - 1\tfrac{1}{2}$
95. $5\tfrac{1}{2} - 2\tfrac{4}{5}$
96. $4\tfrac{1}{5} - 1\tfrac{1}{3}$

97. $5\tfrac{1}{5} - 2\tfrac{1}{4}$
98. $4\tfrac{2}{5} - 1\tfrac{2}{3}$
99. $6\tfrac{1}{4} - 2\tfrac{2}{5}$

100. $3\tfrac{2}{5} - 1\tfrac{3}{4}$
101. $5\tfrac{1}{5} - 3\tfrac{2}{3}$
102. $5\tfrac{1}{5} - 2\tfrac{3}{4}$

103. $4\tfrac{2}{9} - 1\tfrac{1}{2}$
104. $3\tfrac{1}{9} - 1\tfrac{5}{6}$
105. $6\tfrac{1}{2} - 5\tfrac{1}{3}$

7 Multiplication and division of fractions

Multiplying a fraction by a whole number

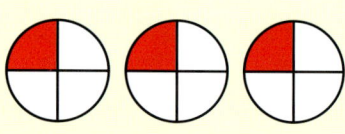 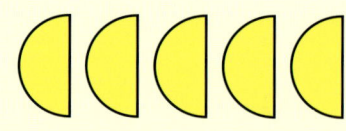 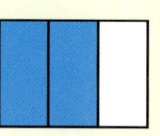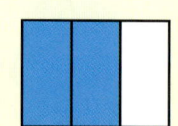

$\frac{1}{4}$ put out 3 times $\qquad$ $\frac{1}{2}$ put out 5 times $\qquad$ $\frac{2}{3}$ put out 2 times

$\frac{1}{4} + \frac{1}{4} + \frac{1}{4}$ $\qquad$ $\frac{1}{2} + \frac{1}{2} + \frac{1}{2} + \frac{1}{2} + \frac{1}{2}$ $\qquad$ $\frac{2}{3} + \frac{2}{3}$

$\frac{1}{4} \times 3$ $\qquad$ $\frac{1}{2} \times 5$ $\qquad$ $\frac{2}{3} \times 2$

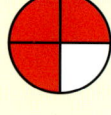 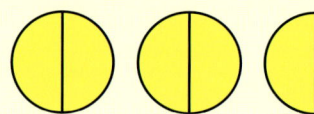 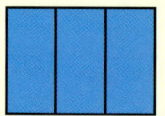

3 quarters = $\frac{3}{4}$ $\qquad$ 5 halves = $\frac{5}{2}$ $\qquad$ 4 thirds = $\frac{4}{3}$

$\frac{1}{4} \times 3 = \frac{3}{4}$ $\qquad$ $\frac{1}{2} \times 5 = \frac{5}{2} = 2\frac{1}{2}$ $\qquad$ $\frac{2}{3} \times 2 = \frac{4}{3} = 1\frac{1}{3}$

Look at the numerator of each of the fractions which we are multiplying in the examples above. Look also at the multiplier (the number we are multiplying by). Now look at the numerator of the product in each case. What do you notice? We must multiply the numerator in the fraction by the multiplier to get the numerator in the product fraction.

Example $\frac{3}{4} \times 5 = \frac{3 \times 5}{4} = \frac{15}{4} = 3\frac{3}{4}$

Draw pictures to show these products. Use circles or square shapes.

1. $\frac{1}{2} \times 3$ 2. $\frac{1}{4} \times 2$ 3. $\frac{1}{3} \times 4$ 4. $\frac{1}{8} \times 5$

Write answers to:

5. $\frac{1}{2} \times 7$ 6. $\frac{1}{3} \times 5$ 7. $\frac{1}{4} \times 4$ 8. $\frac{1}{5} \times 6$
9. $\frac{2}{3} \times 4$ 10. $\frac{3}{4} \times 3$ 11. $\frac{2}{5} \times 4$ 12. $\frac{3}{8} \times 3$
13. $\frac{2}{9} \times 4$ 14. $\frac{5}{6} \times 3$ 15. $\frac{3}{4} \times 3$ 16. $\frac{5}{8} \times 2$

Multiplication and division of fractions UNIT 7

Multiplying a whole number by a fraction

4 × 2 means 2 groups of 4
4 × 3 means 3 groups of 4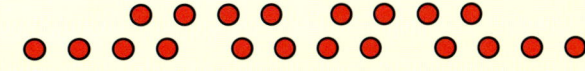

The **multipliers** 2 and 3 (the numbers you multiply by) show the number of groups or sets.

So $3 \times \frac{1}{2}$ would mean $\frac{1}{2}$ of a set of 3 or $\frac{1}{2}$ of 3
and $4 \times \frac{2}{3}$ would mean $\frac{2}{3}$ of a set of 4 or $\frac{2}{3}$ of 4.

 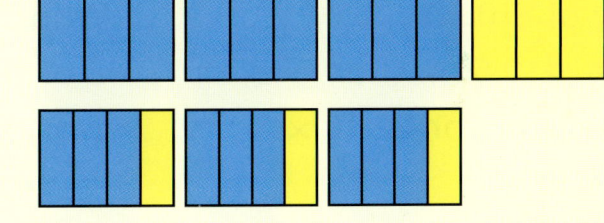

Put 3 into 2 equal groups.
$\frac{1}{2}$ of $3 = 1\frac{1}{2} = \frac{3}{2}$
$3 \times \frac{1}{2} = \frac{1}{2}$ of $3 = \frac{3}{2}$

Put 4 into 3 equal groups.
$\frac{1}{3}$ of $4 = 1\frac{1}{3} = \frac{4}{3}$
$4 \times \frac{2}{3} = \frac{2}{3}$ of $4 = \frac{8}{3}$

Remember: $\frac{1}{2} \times 3 = \frac{3}{2}$, 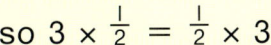 **Remember:** $\frac{2}{3} \times 4 = \frac{8}{3}$,

so $3 \times \frac{1}{2} = \frac{1}{2} \times 3$ so $4 \times \frac{2}{3} = \frac{2}{3} \times 4$

To multiply a whole number by a fraction is just like multiplying the fraction by the number.

Example $3 \times \frac{2}{5} = \frac{3 \times 2}{5} = \frac{6}{5} = 1\frac{1}{5}$

Find these products.

1. $5 \times \frac{1}{3}$
2. $7 \times \frac{1}{3}$
3. $9 \times \frac{1}{4}$
4. $4 \times \frac{3}{5}$
5. $7 \times \frac{2}{3}$
6. $6 \times \frac{3}{5}$
7. $8 \times \frac{2}{5}$
8. $7 \times \frac{3}{10}$
9. $3 \times \frac{5}{6}$
10. $2 \times \frac{3}{10}$
11. $5 \times \frac{3}{4}$
12. $4 \times \frac{1}{6}$
13. $6 \times \frac{7}{8}$
14. $9 \times \frac{3}{5}$
15. $8 \times \frac{1}{4}$
16. $6 \times \frac{2}{3}$

UNIT 7 Multiplication and division of fractions

Fractional parts of concrete quantities

Remember: $30 \times \frac{1}{3}$ means $\frac{1}{3}$ of 30 and $90 \times \frac{2}{5}$ means $\frac{2}{5}$ of 90, and so on.

We can use this to help us find fractional parts of money, length, volume, weight and all other measurements.

Examples

Find $\frac{3}{5}$ of $10.50

$\frac{3}{5}$ of $10.50
$= \$10.50 \times \frac{3}{5}$ or $\frac{\$10.50 \times 3}{5}$
$= \frac{\$31.50}{5}$ or $\$2.10 \times 3$
$= \$6.30$

$\frac{3}{4}$ of a length of rope is 42 m.
What is the total length?

$\frac{3}{4}$ of the length $= 42$ m
$\frac{1}{4}$ of the length $= 42$ m $\div 3$
$= 14$ m
total length $(\frac{4}{4}) = 14$ m $\times 4$
$= 56$ m

Copy and complete.

1. $\frac{3}{4}$ of 24
2. $\frac{2}{3}$ of 30
3. $\frac{2}{5}$ of 75
4. $\frac{5}{6}$ of 30
5. $\frac{3}{4}$ of 60
6. $\frac{5}{12}$ of 48
7. $\frac{4}{5}$ of $7.50
8. $\frac{3}{4}$ of 100 cm
9. $\frac{3}{5}$ of 1 metre
10. $\frac{2}{3}$ of 9 litres
11. $\frac{1}{4}$ of 2 kilograms
12. $\frac{3}{4}$ of $15.00

Work out the answers to these word problems. Show all your working.

13. Three fifths of a sum of money is $15.00. What is the sum?
14. Five sixths of a length of rope is 75 m. What is the length of the rope?
15. Two thirds of a tank is 1200 litres. How much will it hold when full?

Multiplication and division of fractions — UNIT 7

Word problems

Work out the answers to these word problems. Show all your working.

1. (a) A man spent $\frac{1}{3}$ of his wages on food and $\frac{1}{5}$ on rent. What fraction does he spend on food and rent together?
   (b) From (a), say what fraction of his wages is left to spend on other things.
   (c) If in a month the same man spends $450 on food, what is his monthly wage?
   (d) How much money does this man spend on rent?

2. Two thirds of a class of 36 girls and three quarters of another class of 40 girls went on a school outing. How many girls altogether went on the outing?

3. Four fifths of a tank of water is 1200 litres. How much water does the tank hold?

4. A cake weighing $1\frac{1}{2}$ kg was divided into 10 equal pieces. How much did each piece weigh?

5. From a tank holding $16\frac{1}{2}$ litres of petrol, a motorist used $5\frac{1}{3}$ litres. How much petrol remained in the tank?

6. Bal received $10 as pocket money. He spent $\frac{1}{2}$ on snacks, $\frac{1}{5}$ on sweets and kept the rest in his savings box. How much did he keep?

7. The vendor sold $\frac{1}{4}$ of her mangoes on Monday, $\frac{1}{6}$ on Tuesday and $\frac{1}{5}$ on Wednesday. What fraction of the total did she have left?

8. Three tenths of Ashley's salary is $600. What is his total salary?

UNIT 7 Multiplication and division of fractions

Division by a fraction

Remember: 20 ÷ 4 sometimes means how many fours there are in 20. 18 ÷ 3 and 15 ÷ 3 mean how many threes there are in 18 and 15.

$1 \div \frac{1}{2}$, $2 \div \frac{1}{2}$ and $3 \div \frac{1}{2}$ will mean how many halves there are in 1 and 2 and 3. Look at the pictures below:

 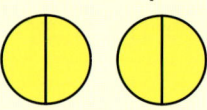 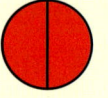

$1 \div \frac{1}{2} = 2$ $\qquad$ $2 \div \frac{1}{2} = 4$ $\qquad$ $3 \div \frac{1}{2} = 6$

We know
$1 \times \frac{2}{1} = 2$ and $2 \times \frac{2}{1} = 4$ and $3 \times \frac{2}{1} = 6$

Therefore
$1 \div \frac{1}{2} = 1 \times \frac{2}{1}$ and $2 \div \frac{1}{2} = 2 \times \frac{2}{1}$ and $3 \div \frac{1}{2} = 3 \times \frac{2}{1}$

Now look at these pictures: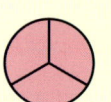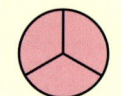

$2 \div \frac{2}{3} = 3$ $\qquad$ $3 \div \frac{3}{4} = 4$

We know $2 \times \frac{3}{2} = 3$ and $3 \times \frac{4}{3} = 4$

So that $2 \div \frac{2}{3} = 2 \times \frac{3}{2}$ and $3 \div \frac{3}{4} = 3 \times \frac{4}{3}$

Can you spot the rule for division by a fraction? Here are two worked examples which should help you with the rule.

$5 \div \frac{2}{3} = 5 \times \frac{3}{2} = \frac{15}{2} = 7\frac{1}{2}$ $\qquad$ $6 \div \frac{3}{4} = 6 \times \frac{4}{3} = \frac{24}{3} = 8$

Copy and complete.

1. $4 \div \frac{1}{2}$
2. $5 \div \frac{1}{4}$
3. $6 \div \frac{1}{3}$
4. $8 \div \frac{3}{4}$
5. $16 \div \frac{4}{5}$
6. $10 \div \frac{5}{8}$
7. $12 \div \frac{2}{3}$
8. $15 \div \frac{3}{5}$
9. $18 \div \frac{9}{10}$
10. $24 \div \frac{2}{9}$
11. $20 \div \frac{5}{12}$
12. $12 \div \frac{3}{5}$
13. $15 \div \frac{5}{6}$
14. $15 \div \frac{3}{8}$
15. $16 \div \frac{8}{9}$
16. $14 \div \frac{7}{10}$

8 Angles

Clockwise and anti-clockwise turns

If we are walking along in one direction and we need to go in another direction we must make a turn.
If we are facing North and we want to face East we must turn.

The direction in which the hands of a clock turn is called **clockwise**. The opposite direction is **anti-clockwise**.

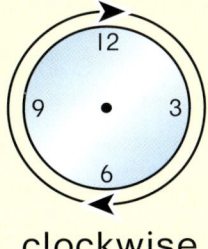
clockwise

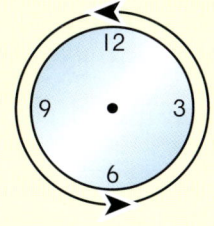
anti-clockwise

Say whether these turns are clockwise or anti-clockwise.

1.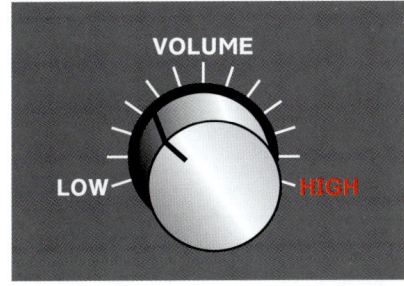
Turning up the volume.

2.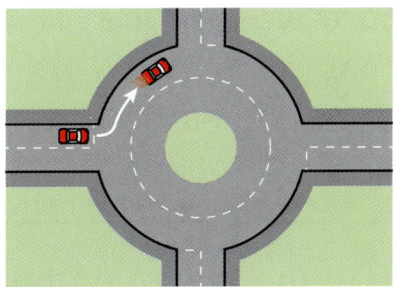
Driving around a roundabout.

3.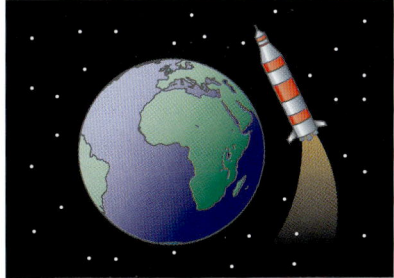
Rocket orbiting the Earth.

UNIT 8   Angles

Comparing angles

> **You will need: cardboard, pencil, ruler, scissors, paper fastener.**
>
> - Cut the cardboard into two strips, each 2 cm wide and 10 cm long.
> - Fasten the strips together with the paper fastener to make an **angle measurer**.
> - We can move one arm of the angle measurer by itself, or we can move both arms.
> - We can **rotate** or **turn** them in either a clockwise or anti-clockwise direction.
>
>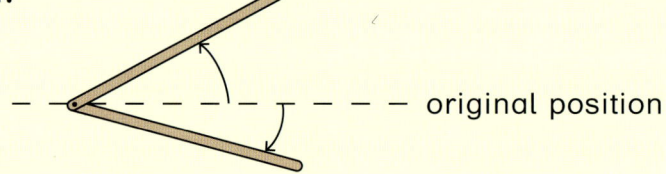
>
> When we **rotate** our strips they turn **through an angle**. The more we turn the larger the angle.
> Would the angles be larger if the strips were longer?
>
>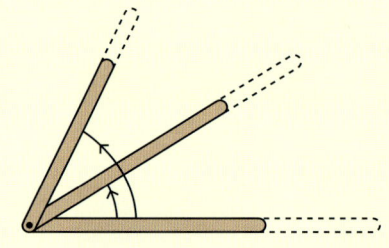

1. Look at the diagrams below. Draw them in order according to the size of the angle, starting with the smallest.

(a)    (b)    (c)

(d)    (e)

Angles UNIT 8

Lines and angles

> We can replace our cardboard strips by straight lines. The straight lines meet at a point and an angle is formed. The point represents the position of the fastener and the lines can be said to rotate about that point.
>
> The straight lines forming the angle are called the **arms** of the angle.
> The point where they meet is called the **vertex**.

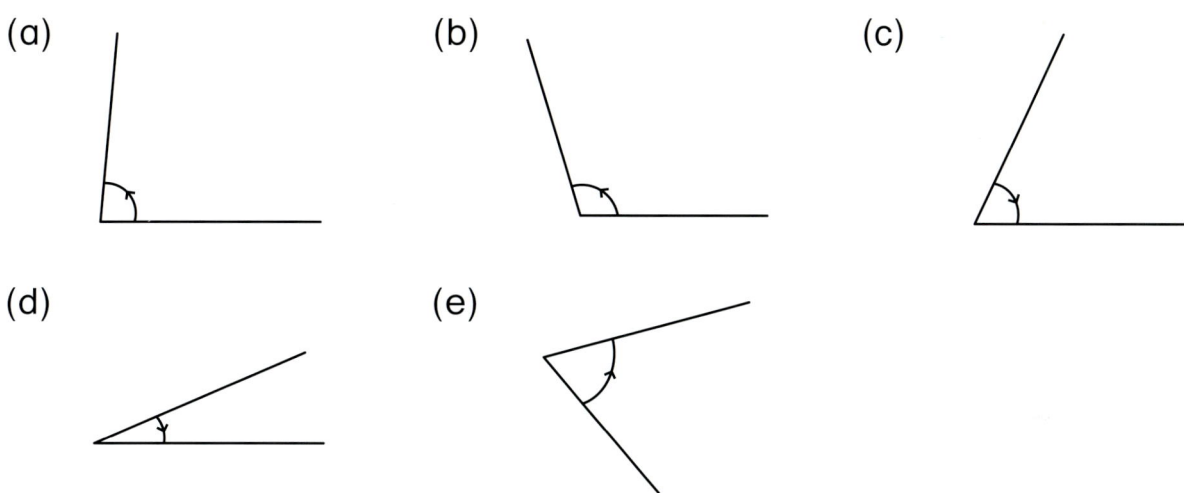

1. Draw the angles above in order of magnitude (size) starting with the smallest.
2. Which two angles appear to be equal in size?
3. How much larger than angle (d) would you say angle (b) is?
4. How much larger than angle (d) would you say angle (a) is?

In our next exercise you will measure these angles and find out whether you were right.

UNIT 8   Angles

Measuring angles

You will need: cardboard and scissors.

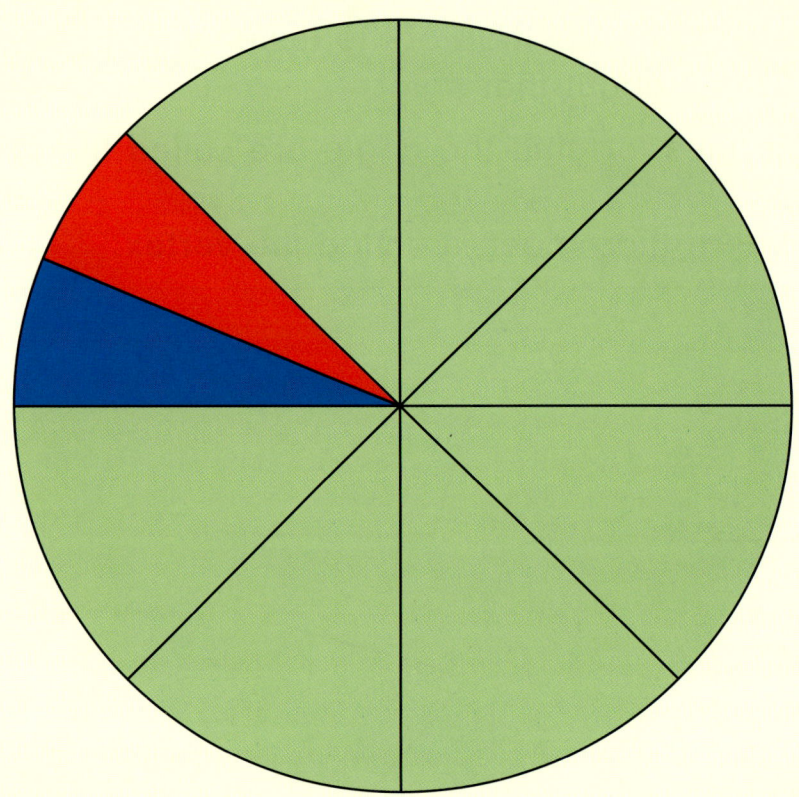

Trace the coloured shapes on cardboard and cut them out.
Each of these shapes is called a **sector** of the circle.
In each sector there is an angle formed where the straight lines meet.
The angle in the green sector measures 1 unit.
What will the angles in the red and blue sectors measure?

Angles   UNIT 8

Say how many units each of the following angles measure.

1.

2.
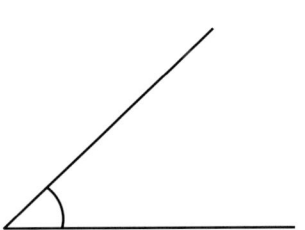

3.
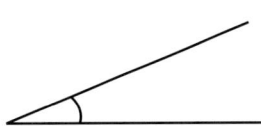

4.
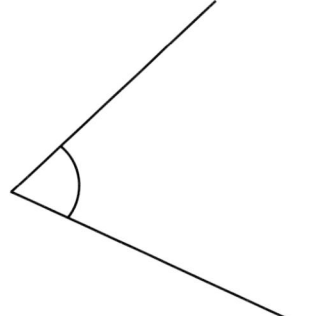

5.
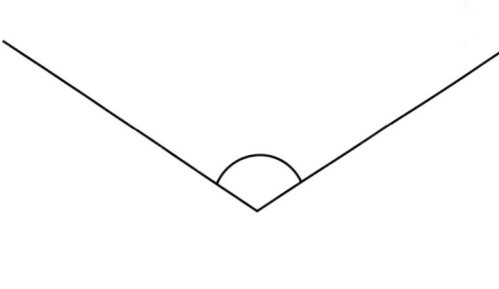

6.
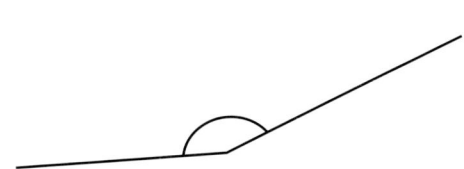

7.
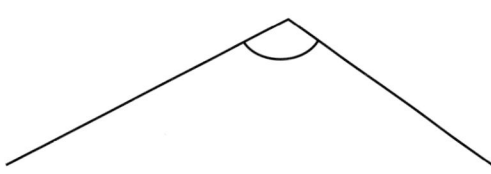

8. Go back to the angles on page 79 and measure these angles to the nearest unit.
Were the answers you gave for questions 1 to 4 on page 79 correct?

UNIT 8   Angles

Right angles

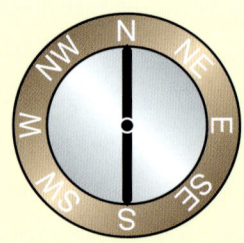

Here is a picture of a compass.

A compass helps you to find directions.

If you are facing North (N) what kind of turn must you make to face East (E) in the shortest time? What kind of turn must you make to face West (W)? To face South (S)?

Stand facing the North.

Make a complete clockwise turn. Where are you now facing?
Make a half turn clockwise. Where are you now facing?
Make a quarter turn clockwise. Where are you facing?
Repeat these turns in an anti-clockwise motion.
State the direction you face on the full turn, half turn and quarter turn.

If you are facing North and you make a quarter turn to face East you have turned through one right angle. This is a clockwise turn.

If you are facing North and you make a quarter turn to face West you have also turned through one right angle. This is an anti-clockwise turn.

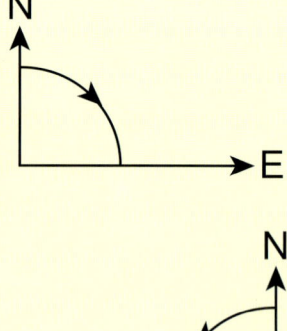

Every time you make a quarter turn, clockwise or anti-clockwise, you have turned one **right angle**.

82

Angles UNIT 8

Answer these questions. Draw diagrams to show the turns.

1. You are facing N and you turn clockwise to face S.

   How many right angles do you turn?

2. You are facing E and you turn anti-clockwise to face N.

   How many right angles do you turn?

3. You are facing E and you turn two right angles clockwise.

   Which direction are you facing now?

4. You are facing N and you turn three right angles clockwise.

   Which direction are you now facing?

5. If you turn clockwise through four right angles, where would you face if you started facing North?

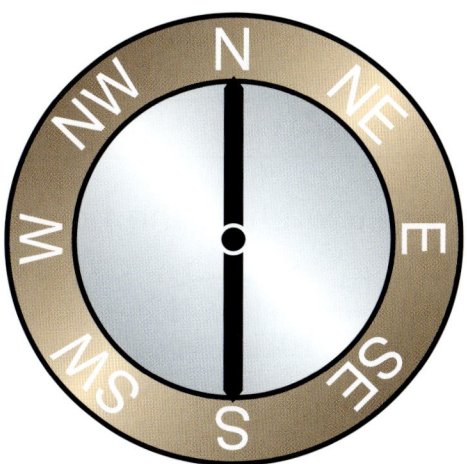

UNIT 8   Angles

Identifying right angles

Right angles are often called square corners.

Here are some objects with right angles or square corners.

Find other examples in the classroom or at home.

Make a right-angle tester by folding a circle into quarters.

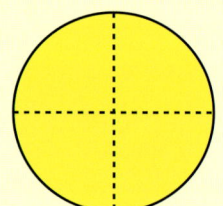 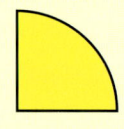

You will need: a paper circle.

You can also use a set square to find right angles.

This is what a set square looks like.

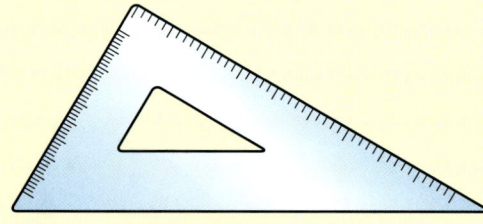

1. Which of the clocks below show the hands at right angles?

(a) 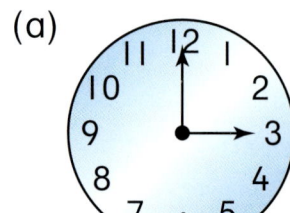   (b) 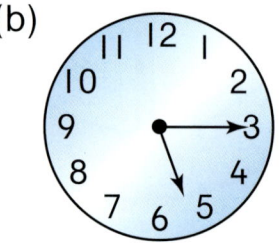   (c)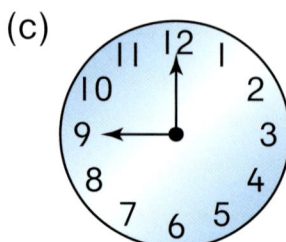

84

Angles   UNIT 8

Look at the shapes below. Copy and mark the right angles with dots.

2. 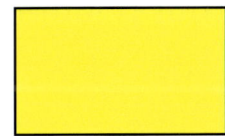 3. 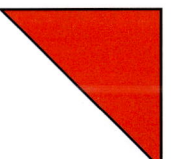 4.  5.

6. If you are facing NE and you turn clockwise through one right angle, in which direction would you be facing?

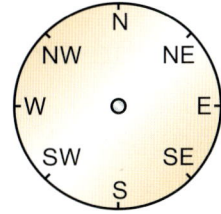

Use your set square or your angle tester to find out which of these angles are smaller and which are larger than one right angle.

7. 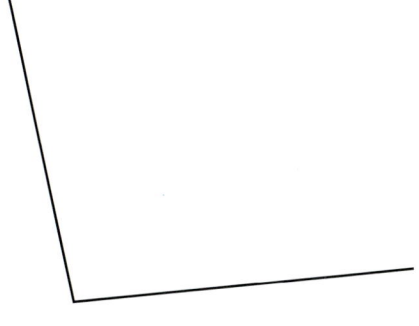   8.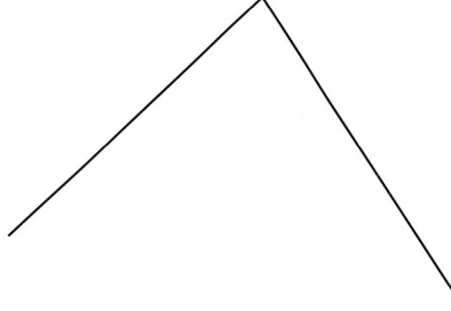

9. 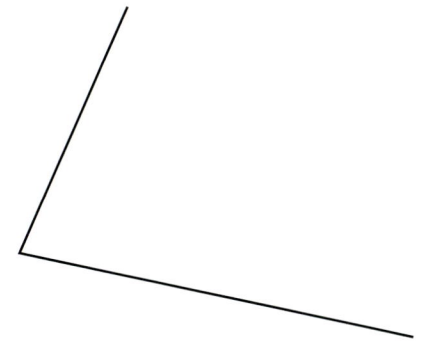   10.

85

UNIT 8 Angles

Measurement of angles

Use the angle tester you made on page 84 or cut out another circle and fold it in quarters.

- Open out and draw the folding lines.

How many angles have you made at the centre of the circle?

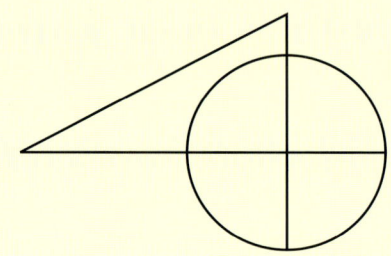

- Match the angles at the centre with the right angle of your set square.

How many right angles do you have at the centre of the circle?

The long hand of a clock turns a full circle when it goes around every hour. If you make a complete turn you have turned a full circle.

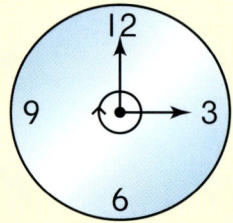

When you make a complete turn you have turned through four right angles. If you have made a $\frac{1}{4}$ turn, how many right angles is this? If you have made a $\frac{1}{2}$ turn, how many right angles is this? When you have turned a full circle we say you have turned through 360 degrees, which is written as 360°. How many degrees is a $\frac{1}{4}$ turn?

How many degrees is a $\frac{1}{2}$ turn? How many degrees is one right angle? How many degrees are two right angles?

Angles   UNIT 8

Copy and complete this table.

Turn	Fraction of turn	Number of degrees
N to E clockwise		
N to S clockwise		
N to W clockwise		
S to N clockwise		
N to S anti-clockwise		
NE to SW clockwise		
W to S anti-clockwise		

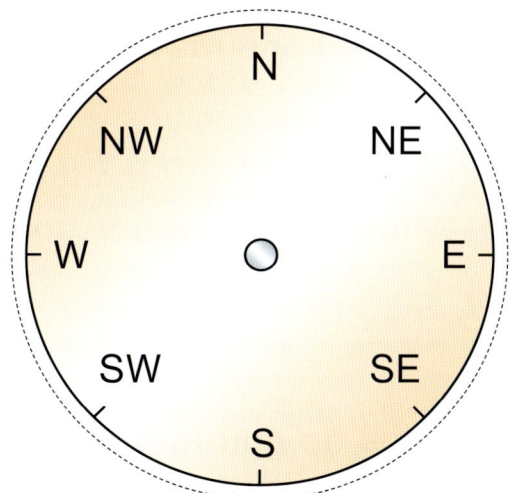

Assessment

Assessment 4

Write these mixed numbers as improper fractions:

1. $4\frac{1}{5}$
2. $5\frac{1}{3}$

Write these improper fractions as mixed numbers:

3. $\frac{24}{5}$
4. $\frac{31}{6}$

Work out the following calculations.

5. $13\frac{1}{3} + 2\frac{3}{5}$
6. $4\frac{1}{4} + 12\frac{2}{5}$
7. $12\frac{5}{6} - 2\frac{1}{4}$
8. $15\frac{1}{5} - 12\frac{3}{4}$
9. $2 \times \frac{4}{5}$
10. $\frac{3}{4} \times 12$

11. What is $\frac{3}{8}$ km in metres?

12. Three fifths of a sum of money is $30. What is the total sum of money?

13. A vendor sold $\frac{1}{4}$ of her goods on Monday, $\frac{1}{5}$ on Tuesday and $\frac{1}{3}$ on Wednesday. What fraction of her goods did she have left?

14. $12 \div \frac{2}{3}$
15. $24 \div \frac{3}{4}$

16. How many right angles do you turn through in moving from West to East in (a) a clockwise direction, (b) an anti-clockwise direction?

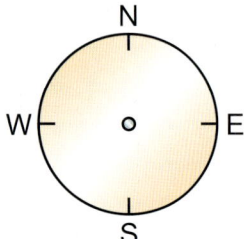

9 Decimals

Revision of tenths

For each of the shapes below write the fraction and decimal number to show how much of the shape is shaded.

1.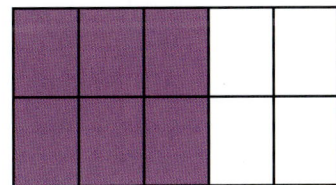
2.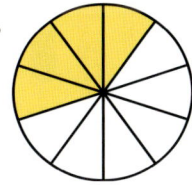
3.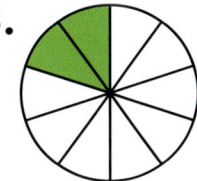

4. Copy the number line below.
   Write in the decimal numbers for each point on the line marked by an arrow.

   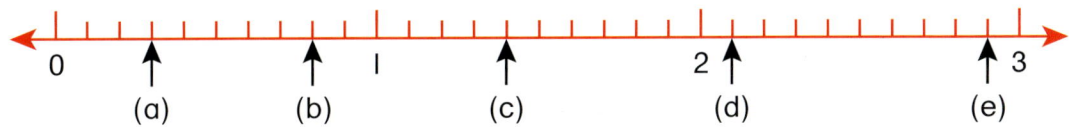

Write decimal numbers for the following:

5. $\frac{3}{10}$
6. $\frac{2}{5}$
7. $2\frac{1}{2}$
8. $3\frac{3}{5}$

Write as fractions or mixed numbers:

9. 0·2
10. 1·3
11. 2·4
12. 3·5

13. Arrange these numbers in ascending order (smallest to largest).

    12·8   11·7   12·2   11·3

Write the decimal numbers shown with the blocks and on the abacuses.

14.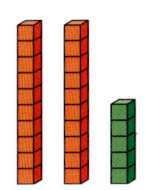
15.
16.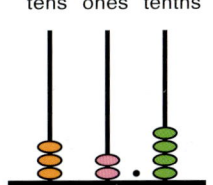
17.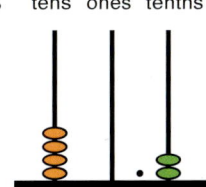

UNIT 9 Decimals

Addition of decimals

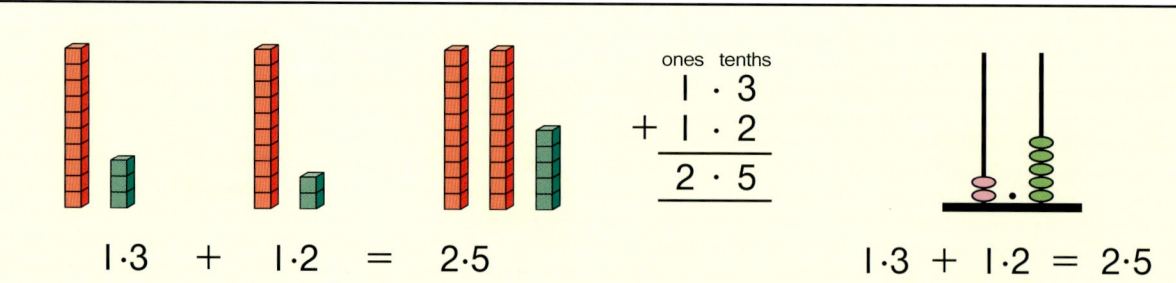

1·3 + 1·2 = 2·5   1·3 + 1·2 = 2·5

Add the tenths, then add the ones.

Copy and complete these calculations.
Draw abacus pictures if you need to.

1. 3·2 + 4·6   2. 5·1 + 4·3   3. 1·4 + 6·5   4. 2·3 + 5·2
5. 1·1 + 2·7   6. 0·4 + 5·3   7. 2·6 + 4·3   8. 4·1 + 3·8
9. 2·2 + 3·2   10. 4·1 + 2·7   11. 1·6 + 2·1   12. 3·3 + 2·5

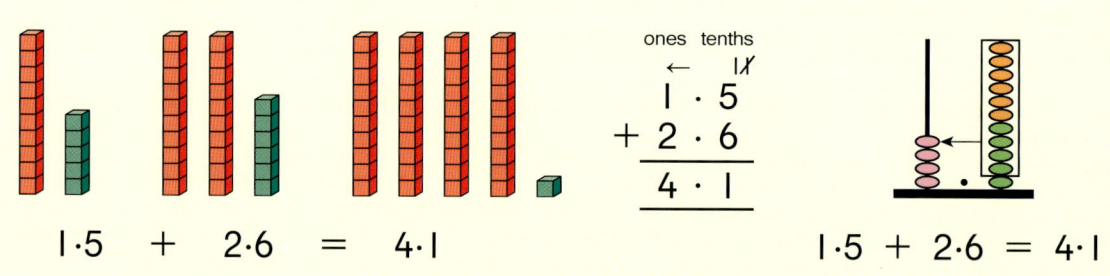

Carrying tenths in addition

1·5 + 2·6 = 4·1   1·5 + 2·6 = 4·1

Add the tenths: 6 + 5 = 11 tenths = 1 whole and 1 tenth.
Carry 1 whole one and add the ones.

Use your rods and blocks, or abacus, to help you if you need to.

13. 1·5 + 3·7   14. 2·4 + 2·6   15. 3·4 + 2·7   16. 4·3 + 2·9
17. 2·8 + 2·5   18. 1·7 + 2·4   19. 3·2 + 1·8   20. 5·6 + 2·8
21. 2·3 + 3·8   22. 3·3 + 4·9   23. 1·3 + 5·7   24. 6·4 + 4·9

Decimals UNIT 9

Subtraction of decimals

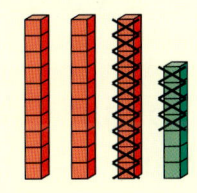

ones tenths
3 . 7
− 1 . 4
———
2 . 3

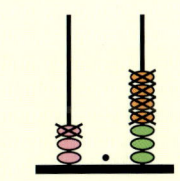

3·7 − 1·4 = 2·3

3·7 − 1·4 = 2·3

Subtract the tenths, then subtract the ones.

Draw pictures to show these subtractions if you need to.

1. 6·6 − 2·1
2. 5·5 − 1·4
3. 8·8 − 6·1
4. 5·9 − 1·7
5. 6·3 − 2·0
6. 6·9 − 1·3
7. 4·4 − 1·1
8. 8·6 − 2·4
9. 5·7 − 3·2
10. 7·5 − 3·0
11. 6·7 − 4·3
12. 3·5 − 2·5

Changing to tenths

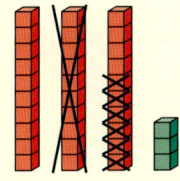

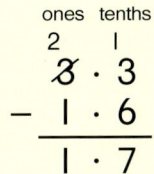

ones tenths
  2   13
  3̶ . 3̶
− 1 . 6
———
  1 . 7

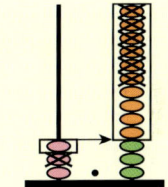

3·3 − 1·6 = 1·7

3·3 − 1·6 = 1·7

Change 1 whole to tenths: 3 wholes 3 tenths → 2 wholes 13 tenths.

  Subtract tenths   13 − 6 = 7 tenths
  Subtract ones   2 − 1 = 1

Use your abacus or rods to help you if you need to.

13. 3·3 − 1·8
14. 6·2 − 1·8
15. 6·1 − 3·8
16. 7·5 − 2·9
17. 4·1 − 2·9
18. 5·4 − 1·9
19. 7·2 − 4·3
20. 9·4 − 6·6
21. 5·0 − 1·8
22. 6·0 − 2·4
21. 3·2 − 2·9
24. 10·3 − 2·9

UNIT 9 Decimals

Word problems

Work out the answers to these word problems. Show all your working.

1. (a) Maisie bought $2\frac{1}{2}$ metres of ribbon. Tisha bought $1\frac{1}{2}$ metres. How much did they have together?
   (b) From (a) above write $2\frac{1}{2}$ and $1\frac{1}{2}$ as decimal numbers. How much ribbon did they now have?

2. Millie ran a 100 m sprint race in 12·6 seconds. Anil was second in 13·1 seconds. How many seconds more did Anil take?

3. Dave mixed 1·2 litres of lime juice with 1·5 litres of orange juice. How much punch did he make?

4. Susan bought 2·5 m of ribbon. She used 1·5 m for decorations. How much did she have left?

5. In a wheel of fortune game, Rory scored 3·2 and Vindra scored 2·5.
   What was the total score? How much more did Rory score?

6. The perimeter of a triangle is 10 cm. One side is 2·4 cm; another is 4·3 cm. What is the length of the third side?

7. (a) A fruit punch is made using 0·5 litres of syrup, 1·2 litres of pineapple juice and 1·5 litres of orange juice. How many litres of punch are made?
   (b) If 2·5 litres of the punch made in (a) were given away, how many litres remained?

8. A rectangle measures 4·5 cm by 2·3 cm. What is its perimeter?

Decimals UNIT 9

Decimal numbers – hundredths

Look at the square below. It is divided into smaller squares.

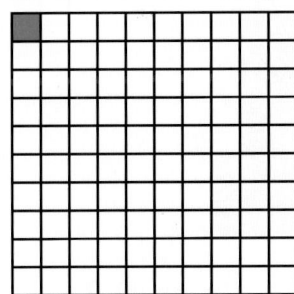

How many small squares make up the larger square?
What fraction of the large square is each of the smaller squares?

You will see that there are 100 small squares in the large square. Each small square is $\frac{1}{100}$ of the large square.
$\frac{1}{100}$ is read as one hundredth.
Another way of writing $\frac{1}{100}$ is ·01 or 0·01. We say these as point zero one, or zero point zero one.

2 squares = $\frac{2}{100}$. This is written as ·02 or 0·02.
Make a list like the one below up to
9 squares = $\frac{9}{100}$ = 9 hundredths = ·09 or 0·09

1 square = $\frac{1}{100}$ = 1 hundredth = ·01 or 0·01
2 squares = _____ = _____ = _____

Look at the square below. Count the number of hundredths in one tenth.

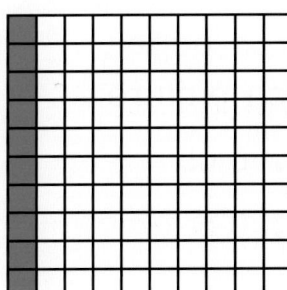

What fraction is shaded?
How many hundredths are shaded?
1 tenth = _____ hundredths
$\frac{1}{10} = \frac{\square}{100}$
Write the decimal numbers for both fractions.
_____ = _____

UNIT 9   Decimals

The pictures below show three decimal numbers.

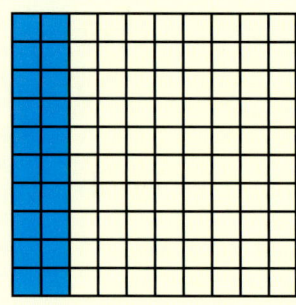
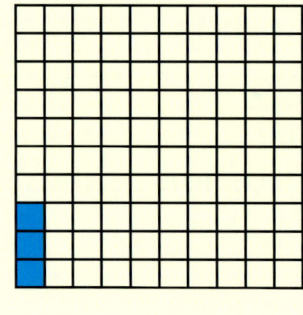
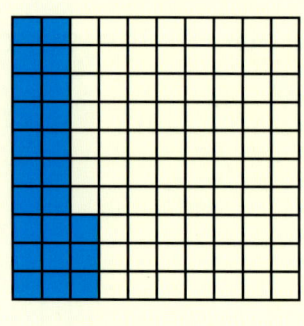

$\frac{2}{10} = \frac{20}{100} = 0.20$ $\frac{3}{100} = 0.03$ $\frac{23}{100} = 0.23$

What are 0·3, 0·4, 0·5, 0·6, 0·7, 0·8 and 0·9 as a decimal number in hundredths?

Write the decimal numbers shown by these pictures.

1.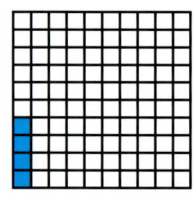
2.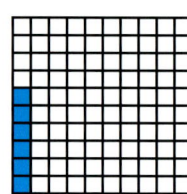
3.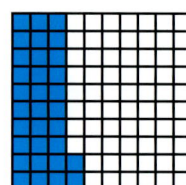

4.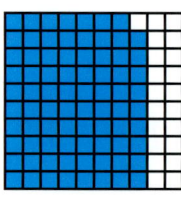
5.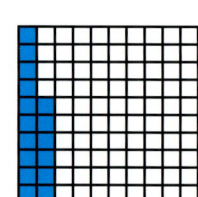
6.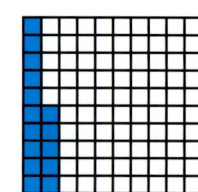

Draw pictures to show these decimals. Use squared paper. Write the decimal number and the fraction for each picture.

7. 0·42   8. 0·24   9. 0·05

10. 0·50   11. 0·06   12. 0·6

Decimals   UNIT 9

Look at the squares below; they show decimal numbers greater than 1. Each block of 100 squares is 1 whole, each strip of 10 squares is $\frac{1}{10}$ or 0·1 and each small square is $\frac{1}{100}$ or 0·01.

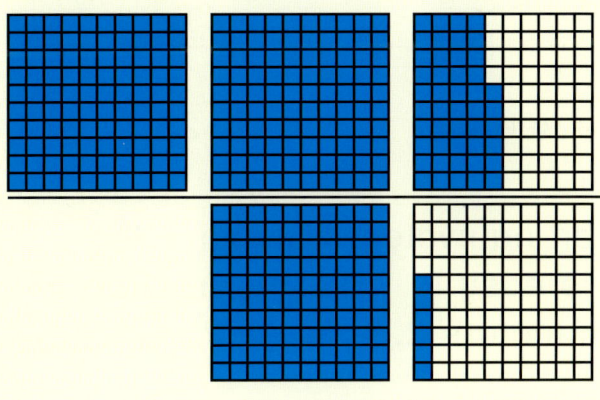

ones	tenths	hundredths
2	4	6
1	0	6

We can also use an abacus to show decimal numbers.

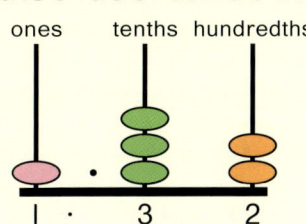   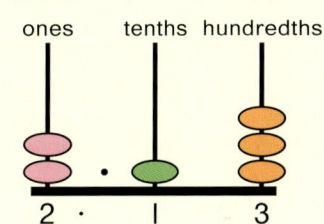

Write the decimal numbers shown.

13. 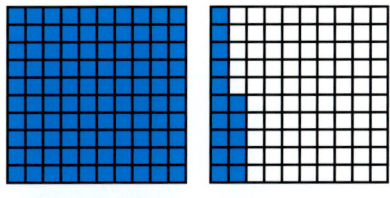   14.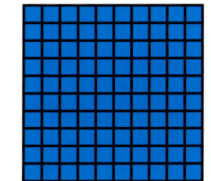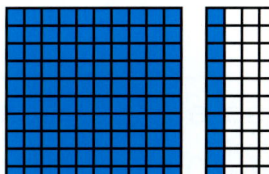

15. 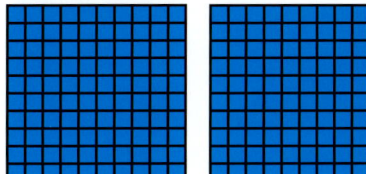   16.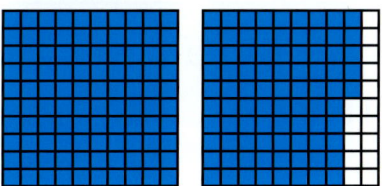

17. 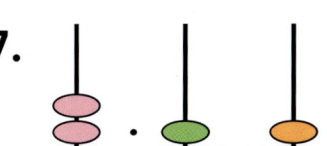   18.    19.

95

UNIT 9 Decimals

Converting fractions to decimals

We can show equivalent fractions on a number line.

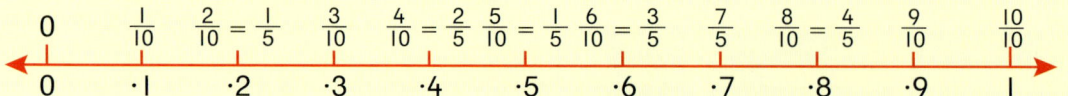

From the number line above we see that $\frac{1}{5} = \frac{2}{10} = \cdot 2$, $\frac{1}{2} = \frac{5}{10} = \cdot 5$, and so on.

If we can rewrite a fraction as an equivalent fraction with denominator 10, or 100, then it is easy to write the fraction as a decimal. Fractions with denominators 2, 4, 5, 20, 25 and 50 are easy to convert to decimals.

Examples $\frac{1}{25} = \frac{4}{100} = 0.04$ $\frac{11}{50} = \frac{22}{100} = 0.22$

Write the following fractions as decimal numbers:

1. $\frac{3}{4}$
2. $\frac{2}{5}$
3. $\frac{13}{25}$
4. $\frac{4}{5}$
5. $\frac{1}{20}$
6. $\frac{3}{20}$
7. $\frac{2}{25}$
8. $\frac{3}{50}$
9. $\frac{7}{20}$
10. $\frac{9}{50}$
11. $\frac{3}{5}$
12. $\frac{3}{10}$
13. $\frac{7}{10}$
14. $\frac{9}{10}$
15. $\frac{7}{20}$
16. $\frac{11}{20}$
17. $\frac{9}{50}$
18. $\frac{17}{20}$
19. $\frac{13}{50}$
20. $\frac{4}{25}$

It is also easy to convert decimals to fractions.
Example $0.55 = \frac{55}{100} = \frac{11}{20}$

Now rewrite these decimals as fractions.

21. 0·85
22. 0·10
23. 0·35
24. 0·64
25. 0·65
26. 0·32
27. 0·45
28. 0·16
29. 0·95
30. 0·72
31. 0·24
32. 0·15
33. 0·88
34. 0·44
35. 0·38
36. 0·90
37. 0·09
38. 0·40
39. 0·50
40. 0·05

Decimals UNIT 9

Thousands to hundredths – the place value chart

Remember: 0·1 is $\frac{1}{10}$ (one tenth) and 0·01 is $\frac{1}{100}$ (one hundredth)

Example 2·1 is $2\frac{1}{10}$ (two and one tenth)

and 3·01 is $3\frac{1}{100}$ (three and one hundredth)

We can now show decimal numbers in an extended place value chart which includes tenths and hundredths.

Number	whole number part				decimal part		number in words
	Th	H	T	U	tenths	hundredths	
2·1				2	1		two and one tenth
2·01				2	0	1	two and one hundredth
35·48			3	5	4	8	thirty-five and forty-eight hundredths
216·05		2	1	6	0	5	two hundred and sixteen and five hundredths
4109·7	4	1	0	9	7		four thousand, one hundred and nine and seven tenths

Write these numbers in words.

1. 5·3
2. 2·41
3. 4·07
4. 9·25
5. 1·11
6. 1·10
7. 6·2
8. 6·20
9. 28·7
10. 35·21
11. 145·9
12. 515·37
13. 1512·3
14. 2130·17
15. 1009·2
16. 2301·01

Write decimal numbers for the following.

17. two and seven tenths
18. two and seven hundredths
19. four and seventeen hundredths

UNIT 9 Decimals

20. five and thirty-five hundredths
21. three and three tenths
22. three and thirty hundredths
23. thirty-six and three tenths
24. fifty-three and nineteen hundredths
25. two hundred and twenty and seven tenths
26. four thousand, two hundred and six and forty-one hundredths
27. five thousand and fifty and five tenths
28. one thousand and one and one hundredth

Decimal numbers in expanded form – thousands to hundredths

We can now write decimal numbers in expanded form.

	Th	H	T	U	tenths	hundredths
524·3		5 500 5 × 100	2 + 20 + 2 × 10	4 + 4 + 4 × 1	3 + $\frac{3}{10}$ + 3 × $\frac{1}{10}$	
6205·76	6 6000 6 × 1000	2 200 + 2 × 100	0	5 5 + 5 × 1	7 $\frac{7}{10}$ + 7 × $\frac{1}{10}$	6 $\frac{6}{100}$ + 6 × $\frac{1}{100}$

Write these numbers in expanded form.

1. 15·6   **2.** 29·35   **3.** 342·8   **4.** 592·24
5. 2164·2   **6.** 3062·42   **7.** 5150·5   **8.** 1001·11

Write the value of the red digits in these numbers.

9. 112·2   **10.** 220·2   **11.** 5050·15   **12.** 3118·2
13. 2412·22   **14.** 1555·15   **15.** 2331·31   **16.** 1516·16

Decimals UNIT 9

Ordering decimal numbers

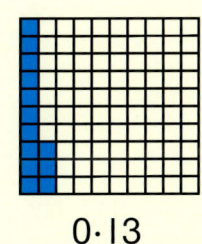

0·13

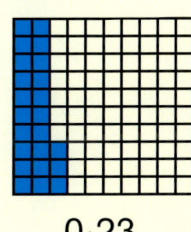

0·23

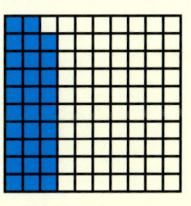

0·29

0·13 < 0·23
The tenths digit in 0·13 is smaller than the tenths digit in 0·23.

0·29 > 0·23
the tenths digit is the same, but the hundredths digit is larger in 0·29.

We can also use a number line to compare decimals.

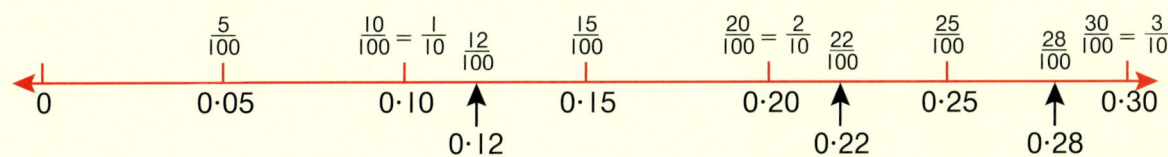

0·12 < 0·22
the tenths digit is smaller.

0·28 > 0·22
The tenths digit is the same, but the hundredths digit is larger.

Write the next five decimal numbers in these sets.

1. 0·06, 0·07, _____, _____, _____, _____, _____

2. 1·23, 1·26, _____, _____, _____, _____, _____

Write the correct sign <, > or = between these pairs of numbers.

3. 1·05 ☐ 1·50   4. 2·01 ☐ 1·01   5. 0·6 ☐ 0·06

Arrange each set of numbers in order starting with the smallest.

6. 14·2   18·1   16·3   12·9   7. 5·81   3·18   7·21   5·18
8. 0·05   0·10   0·04   0·01   9. 1·11   1·01   1·10   1·01

UNIT 9   Decimals

Place value – millions to hundredths

number	hundred millions	ten millions	millions	hundred thousands	ten thousands	thousands	hundreds	tens	units	tenths	hundredths	
4 123·52						4	1	2	3	5	2	four thousand, one hundred and twenty-three and fifty-two hundredths
21 346·1					2	1	3	4	6	1		twenty-one thousand, three hundred and forty-six and one tenth
15 021·36					1	5	0	2	1	3	6	fifteen thousand and twenty-one and thirty-six hundredths
105 201·36				1	0	5	2	0	1	3	6	one hundred and five thousand, two hundred and one and thirty-six hundredths
1 054 326·15			1	0	5	4	3	2	6	1	5	one million, fifty-four thousand, three hundred and twenty-six and fifteen hundredths

Note carefully where zeros have been used in the last three numbers.

Write these numbers in words.

1. 7125·2   2. 6242·35   3. 1421·01   4. 2005·27
5. 30 192·16   6. 20 191·05   7. 310 218·1   8. 152 410·01

Write these numbers in figures.

9. twenty-three thousand, four hundred and twenty-seven and nine tenths

100

Decimals   UNIT 9

10. forty-two thousand, one hundred and sixty-five and eleven hundredths
11. eighty-seven thousand and seventy-four and fifteen hundredths
12. one hundred and thirty-four thousand, two hundred and nineteen and one tenth

Decimal numbers in expanded form – hundred thousands to hundredths

	hundred thousands 100 000	ten thousands 10 000	thousands 1000	hundreds 100	tens 10	units 1	tenths $\frac{1}{10}$	hundredths $\frac{1}{100}$
1346·27			1 1 × 1000	3 3 × 100	4 4 × 10	6 6 × 1	2 2 × $\frac{1}{10}$	7 7 × $\frac{1}{100}$
39 028·15		3 3 × 10 000	9 9 × 1000	0	2 2 × 10	8 8 × 1	1 1 × $\frac{1}{10}$	5 5 × $\frac{1}{100}$
312 147·09	3 3 × 100 000	1 1 × 10 000	2 2 × 1000	1 1 × 100	4 4 × 10	7 7 × 1	0	9 9 × $\frac{1}{100}$

Use the examples above to write these numbers in expanded form.

1. 123·1
2. 413·21
3. 5162·3
4. 3592·01
5. 15 001·25
6. 1781·02
7. 150 215·1
8. 275 391·24
9. 21 001·11

Write the value of the red digits in these numbers.

10. 156·35
11. 2578·02
12. 51 212·13
13. 135 206·1
14. 212 415·15
15. 39 003·03

UNIT 9   Decimals

Approximation to the nearest tenth

Remember: when we round numbers we are giving approximate values to those numbers.

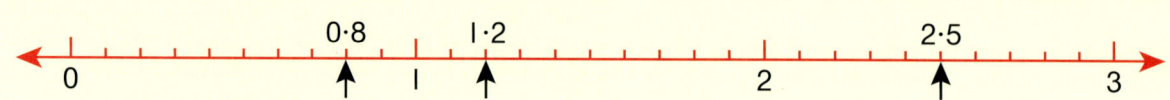

The nearest whole number to 0·8 is 1.
We round 0·8 to 1 and say 0·8 is approximately equal to 1.
The nearest whole number to 1·2 is 1; now we round down.
1·2 to the nearest whole number is 1.
2·5 is midway between 2 and 3; in such cases we always round up.
So 2·5 to the nearest whole number is 3.

In the number line here, tenths are shown above the line and hundredths below.

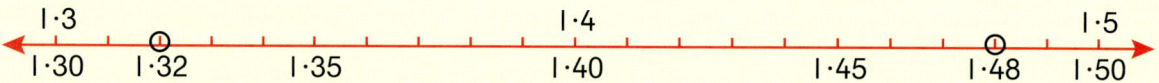

1·32 is nearer to 1·3 than to 1·4; so 1·32 is 1·3 to the nearest tenth.
1·48 is nearer to 1·5 than to 1·4; so 1·48 is 1·5 to the nearest tenth.
1·35 is midway between 1·3 and 1·4 and 1·45 is midway between 1·4 and 1·5.
So 1·35 is 1·4 to the nearest tenth, and 1·45 is 1·5 to the nearest tenth.
We can write 1·32 ≈ 1·3; 1·48 ≈ 1·5; and 1·35 ≈ 1·4
≈ means is approximately equal to

Write these numbers as approximations to the nearest tenth and to the nearest whole number.

1. 0·12	2. 0·81	3. 0·65	4. 0·55
5. 1·71	6. 2·28	7. 6·25	8. 4·01
9. 25·19	10. 140·36	11. 20·09	12. 20·99
13. 212·85	14. 69·31	15. 104·92	16. 50·51

Assessment 5

1. 13·2 + 5·7
2. 4·8 + 15·7
3. 14·8 − 6·3
4. 15·2 − 10·9
5. The perimeter of a triangle is 15 cm. Two of its sides are 4·4 cm and 5·8 cm. What is the length of the third side?

Write as decimal numbers:

6. $\frac{7}{100}$
7. $\frac{3}{50}$

Write as fractions in their lowest terms:

8. 0·35
9. 0·08

Write in words:

10. 15·4
11. 245·12
12. 3005·01

Write numerals for:

13. one hundred and twelve and seven hundredths
14. two thousand and seven and nine tenths

Write in expanded form:

15. 24·35
16. 510·07

What is the value of the red digits?

17. 274·2**1**
18. 1462·0**5**

Round to the nearest whole number and to the nearest tenth:

19. 510·62
20. 4134·08

10 Addition and subtraction of decimals

Adding decimal numbers in hundredths

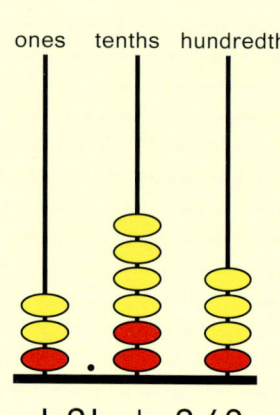

1·21 + 2·43

Add hundredths 1 + 3 = 4
Add tenths 4 + 2 = 6
Add ones 2 + 1 = 3

```
  1·21
+ 2·43
------
     4
   ·64
  3·64
```

What number do the red beads represent?
What number do the yellow beads represent?
The steps for doing the addition are shown on the right.

Copy and complete these calculations.

1. 2·13
  + 1·42

2. 3·25
  + 2·01

3. 1·61
  + 4·26

4. 3·20
  + 1·49

5. 3·14
  + 2·53

6. 6·26
  + 3·43

7. 5·38
  + 2·41

8. 7·27
  + 3·32

9. 3·23
    1·41
  + 5·14

10. 2·04
     1·50
   + 2·45

11. 4·11
     3·48
   + 2·30

12. 1·12
     3·53
   + 2·24

13. 4·13 + 2·05 + 1·20

14. 1·41 + 2·24 + 5·02

Addition and subtraction of decimals UNIT 10

Regrouping hundredths in adding

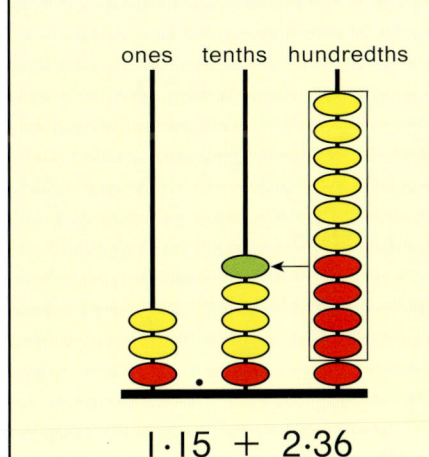

1·15 + 2·36

Add hundredths
6 + 5 = 11

Add tenths
1 + 3 + 1 = 5

Add ones
2 + 1 = 3

10 hundredths = 1 tenth

```
   ←1
  1·1 5
+ 2·3 6
───────
       1
   ·5 1
───────
  3·5 1
```

Copy and complete.

1. 2·2 8
   + 1·1 4
   ───────

2. 4·0 7
   + 2·1 7
   ───────

3. 3·2 9
   + 1·0 4
   ───────

4. 3·0 2
   + 2·8 9
   ───────

5. 4·1 5
   + 2·2 7
   ───────

6. 3·4 8
   + 1·3 4
   ───────

7. 5·4 6
   + 2·4 4
   ───────

8. 3·2 7
   + 2·1 8
   ───────

9. 1·1 8
    2·1 3
   + 4·2 4
   ───────

10. 2·4 8
     2·3 2
    + 1·1 7
    ───────

11. 5·3 4
     2·0 6
    + 1·4 8
    ───────

12. 4·4 7
     2·3 4
    + 1·1 6
    ───────

13. 2·56 + 3·28

14. 1·42 + 3·39

15. 1·05 + 1·36 + 2·17

16. 2·12 + 3·23 + 4·29

105

UNIT 10 Addition and subtraction of decimals

Regrouping tenths in adding

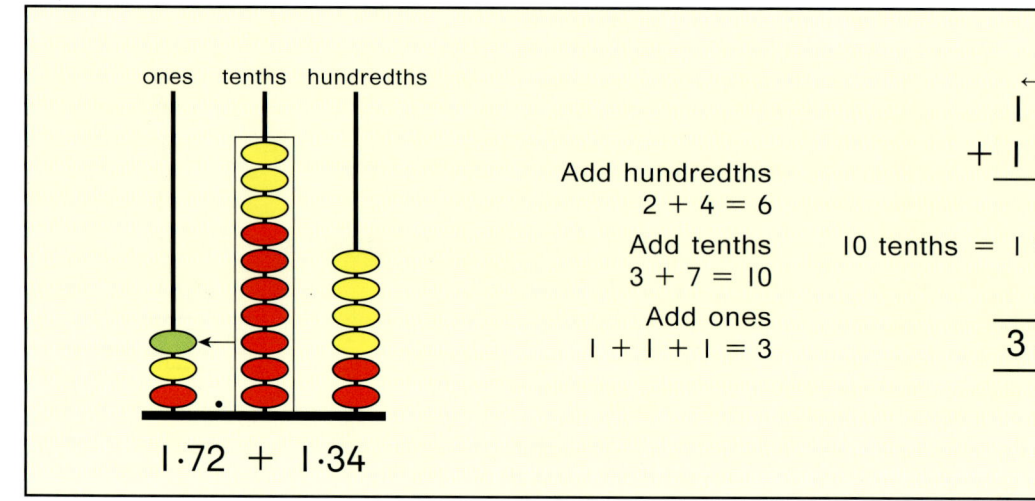

Copy and complete these calculations.

1.	3·42 +2·71	2.	4·62 +3·84	3.	5·70 +2·62	4.	3·81 +1·95
5.	2·91 +4·74	6.	5·85 +2·43	7.	7·27 +2·82	8.	2·62 +1·93
9.	2·88 +3·71	10.	2·75 +3·92	11.	2·90 +2·74	12.	5·51 +3·94
13.	1·82 2·45 +3·31	14.	4·95 2·81 +1·13	15.	5·54 4·91 +3·32	16.	5·02 2·94 +1·83

Now check your answers using a calculator.

Addition and subtraction of decimals UNIT 10

Subtraction of hundredths

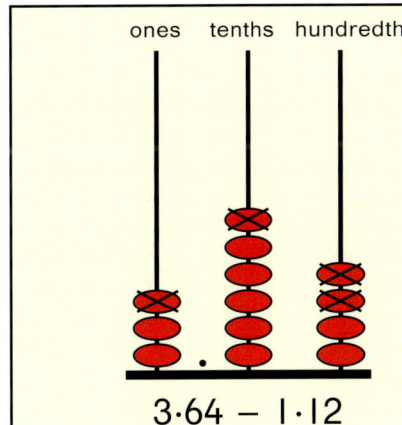

3·64 − 1·12

Subtract hundredths 4 − 2 = 2
Subtract tenths 6 − 1 = 5
Subtract ones 3 − 1 = 2

```
  3·6 4
− 1·1 2
───────
      2
    ·5 2
  2·5 2
```

Copy and complete these calculations.

1. 4·68 − 2·35
2. 7·54 − 3·42
3. 6·85 − 1·72
4. 5·39 − 2·07

5. 5·93 − 2·71
6. 4·72 − 3·10
7. 3·68 − 1·22
8. 4·36 − 2·02

9. 4·66 − 2·02
10. 6·28 − 4·15
11. 5·76 − 4·24
12. 3·42 − 3·11

13. 5·99 − 3·67
14. 6·86 − 4·23
15. 7·54 − 1·32
16. 8·56 − 3·22

Now check your answers using a calculator.

UNIT 10 Addition and subtraction of decimals

Regrouping hundredths in subtraction

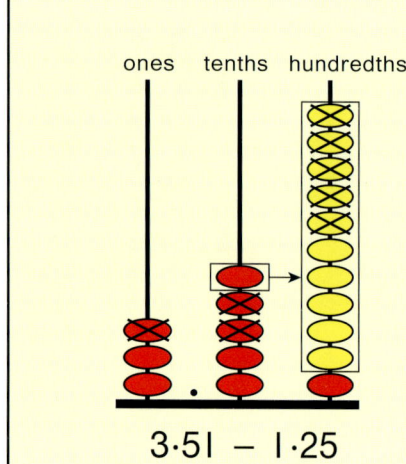

Change 1 tenth to 10 hundredths
Subtract hundredths 11 − 5 = 6
Subtract tenths 4 − 2 = 2
Subtract ones 3 − 1 = 2

$$\begin{array}{r} \overset{4}{}\overset{1}{} \\ 3\cdot\!\not{5}\,1 \\ -\,1\cdot 2\,5 \\ \hline 6 \\ \cdot 2\,6 \\ \hline 2\cdot 2\,6 \end{array}$$

3·51 − 1·25

Copy and complete these calculations.

1. 6·73   2. 5·50   3. 3·84   4. 2·42
   −4·26   −2·36   −1·26   −1·08

5. 7·64   6. 4·40   7. 3·92   8. 2·85
   −2·36   −1·06   −1·47   −1·58

9. 3·61   10. 2·20   11. 3·45   12. 3·33
   −2·44   −1·08   −1·28   −1·24

13. 3·75   14. 2·15   15. 5·64   16. 3·76
   −0·18   −1·08   −2·28   −1·28

Now check your answers using a calculator.

108

Addition and subtraction of decimals UNIT 10

Regrouping tenths in subtraction

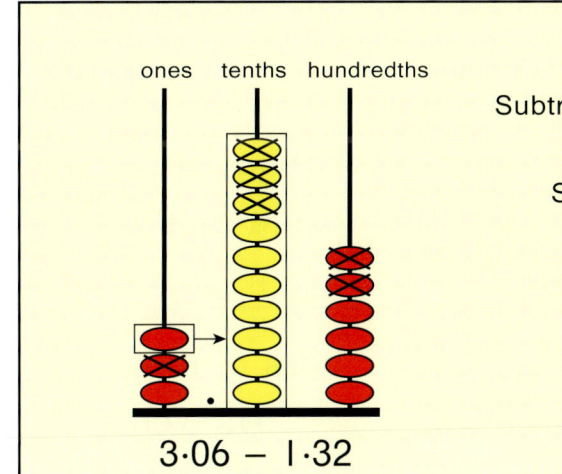

Subtract hundredths 6 − 2 = 4
Change 1 to tenths
Subtract tenths 10 − 3 = 7
Subtract ones 2 − 1 = 1

```
   2 1
   3̶·0 6
 − 1·3 2
   ─────
       4
     ·7 4
   ─────
   1·7 4
```

3·06 − 1·32

Copy and complete these calculations.

1. 3·06   2. 4·28   3. 5·36   4. 3·64
   −1·22   −2·84   −1·42   −2·92

5. 4·48   6. 3·35   7. 5·58   8. 6·48
   −1·63   −1·72   −1·85   −2·54

9. 4·08   10. 3·29   11. 4·67   12. 6·08
   −1·72   −1·75   −2·93   −1·97

13. 2·26   14. 5·18   15. 3·25   16. 6·25
   −0·62   −2·90   −1·73   −1·95

Now check your answers using a calculator.

109

UNIT 10 Addition and subtraction of decimals

Decimal numbers in linear measurement

Remember: 1 m = 100 cm.

So $\frac{1}{10}$ m = 10 cm and $\frac{1}{100}$ m = 1 cm.

We can write 10 cm as 0·1 m; 20 cm as 0·2 m; and 30 cm as 0·3 m; and so on. We can write 1 cm as 0·01 m; 2 cm as 0·02 m; and 3 cm as 0·03 m; and so on.

Now write these measurements as decimal numbers of metres.

1. 50 cm **2.** 90 cm **3.** 6 cm **4.** 8 cm
5. 15 cm **6.** 36 cm **7.** 99 cm **8.** 42 cm

Do you remember Salick whom we met in Book 3? He was about 115 cm tall or 1 m 15 cm. We learnt that we could write 1 m 15 cm as 1·15 m in the same way that we could write 1 dollar and 15 cents as $1.15.

We can write 125 cm as 100 cm + 20 cm + 5 cm

or as

m	$\frac{1}{10}$ m	$\frac{1}{100}$ m
1	2	5

or as 1 . 2 5 m.

Look at the examples below and note carefully the use of the zeros.

	m	$\frac{1}{10}$ m	$\frac{1}{100}$ m	
250 cm = 2 m 50 cm =	2	5	0	= 2·50 m
205 cm = 2 m 5 cm =	2	0	5	= 2·05 m
25 cm = 0 m 25 cm =	0	2	5	= 0·25 m

Addition and subtraction of decimals — UNIT 10

Write these lengths as decimal numbers in metres.

9. 1 m 15 cm **10.** 12 m 25 cm **11.** 3 m 15 cm
12. 14 m 24 cm **13.** 20 m 10 cm **14.** 15 m 50 cm
15. 125 cm **16.** 240 cm **17.** 305 cm

Write the correct signs <, > or = between these lengths.

18. 1·15 m ☐ 1·18 m **19.** 2·16 m ☐ 2·06 m
20. 1·92 m ☐ 2·92 m **21.** 3·05 m ☐ 3·50 m

Round off these to the nearest metre.

22. 4·23 m **23.** 2·56 m **24.** 3·08 m **25.** 10·10 m

Arrange each set of lengths in order from longest to shortest.

26. 2·25 m 2·95 m 2·15 m **27.** 5·18 m 5·81 m 5·01 m
28. 3·96 m 3·69 m 3·06 m **29.** 7·20 m 7·50 m 7·30 m

Copy and complete these calculations.

30.   m   **31.**   m   **32.**   m   **33.**   m
　　1·64　　　　　　　　6·10　　　　　　　　5·21　　　　　　　　8·01
　　2·32　　　　　　　　2·03　　　　　　　− 2·84　　　　　　　− 2·92
　+ 1·86　　　　　　　+ 0·18

34. Find the sum of 5·96 m, 0·24 m and 1·30 m.

35. Subtract 5·65 m from 8·92 m.

36. Find the difference between 3·01 m and 6·10 m.

UNIT 10 Addition and subtraction of decimals

Problem solving

1. Look at this table.
   It shows the distance which five toy cars travelled before stopping.

car A	car B	car C	car D	car E
11·60 m	16·40 m	8·20 m	20·40 m	12·60 m

   (a) Copy and rearrange the table. Put the car that travelled the furthest distance first, the one that travelled next furthest second and so on.

1st	2nd	3rd	4th	5th
car ____	car ____	car ____	car ____	car ____
____ m	____ m	____ m	____ m	____ m

   Using the completed table from (a), work out the distances between the cars when they stopped. Show all your working.

   (b) 1st and 2nd   (c) 2nd and 3rd   (d) 3rd and 4th
   (e) 4th and 5th   (f) 1st and 5th

   (g) Which two cars were nearest each other when they stopped?
   (h) How much further did the first car travel than the last?
   (i) How much further did the third car have to go to travel the same distance as the first car?
   (j) Which car travelled exactly twice as far as another car?
   (k) Which two distances when added together would be less than the furthest distance travelled?

Addition and subtraction of decimals UNIT 10

2. In a magic square the numbers in each row, each column and along each diagonal add up to the same total.
Complete these magic squares:

(a)
4·24		2·20
	2·05	1·33

(b)
		0·88
0·61	2·72	4·20

(c)
	4·10	
		0·82
	2·06	1·26

Work out the answers to these word problems. Show all your working.

3. Mala was 1·62 m tall; Cindy was 1·51 m. How much taller was Mala? Give your answer in metres and also in centimetres.

4. Paul weighed 42·5 kg and Ronnie weighed 40·25 kg. What was the total weight?

5. From a piece of carpet 5·5 m long, a piece 3·25 m was cut off. How much was left?

6. Three pieces of string 6 m 25 cm, 4 m 20 cm and 5 m 80 cm were placed end to end on the floor. What was the total length of string in metres?

7. What is the perimeter of a rectangle which is 2·5 m long and 2·25 m wide?

8. Tony weighs 50·2 kg and Mikey weighs 51·5 kg. What is their combined weight?

9. Mavis cut off 2·75 m from a piece of ribbon 5·50 m long. What length of ribbon was left?

11 Percentages

Fractions as percentages

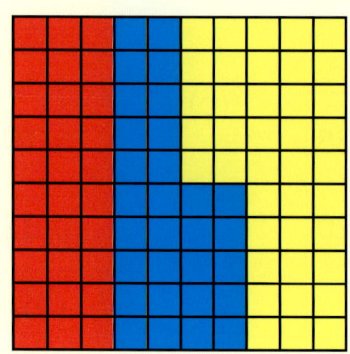

The shape on the left is divided into 100 squares.
How many squares are shaded red? How many are blue? How many are yellow? What fraction is shaded red? What fraction is blue? What fraction is yellow?

The fraction $\frac{1}{100}$ can be written as a decimal, 0·01.

The fraction $\frac{2}{100}$ can be written as 0·02.

The fraction $\frac{1}{100}$ can also be written as 1% which we read as 1 per cent.

The fraction $\frac{2}{100}$ can be written as 2% (2 per cent), and so on.

Per cent or **percentage** means **out of each hundred**; % is really 100 written in a special way.

$\frac{30}{100}$ of the shape is red; the percentage shaded red is 30%. What per cent is blue? What per cent is yellow?

What fraction and percentage of these shapes is shaded?

 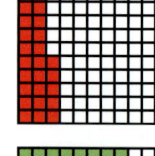   2. 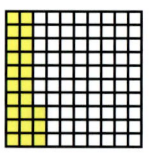   3. 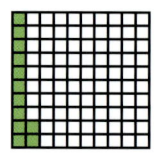   4.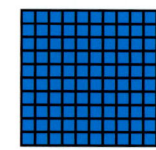

5. 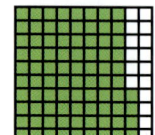   6. 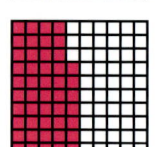   7. 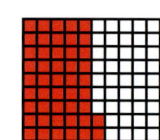   8.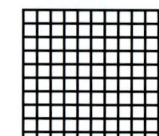

Percentages UNIT 11

The whole – 100%

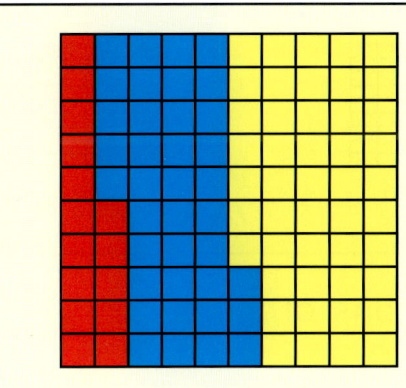

Look at the shape on the left. What percentage is red?
What percentage is blue?
What percentage is yellow?
What is the total percentage shaded?

Red + Blue + Yellow = ☐ %

The whole is always 100%

1. What percentages of these shapes are shaded red, blue, yellow?
   Copy and complete the table below: the letters R, B, Y represent the colours.

A 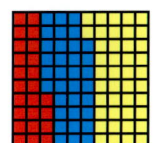   B 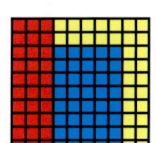   C 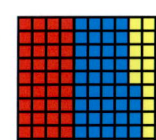   D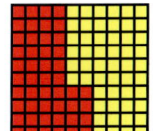

	percentage shaded			
shape	R	B	Y	R + B + Y
A				
B				
C				
D				

Use the table above to answer these questions. Use the pictures to check your answers. What percentage is shaded:

2. Red and blue in shape A?
3. Red and yellow in shape B?
4. Blue and yellow in shape C?
5. Red and yellow in shape D?

UNIT 11 Percentages

Percentages and fractions

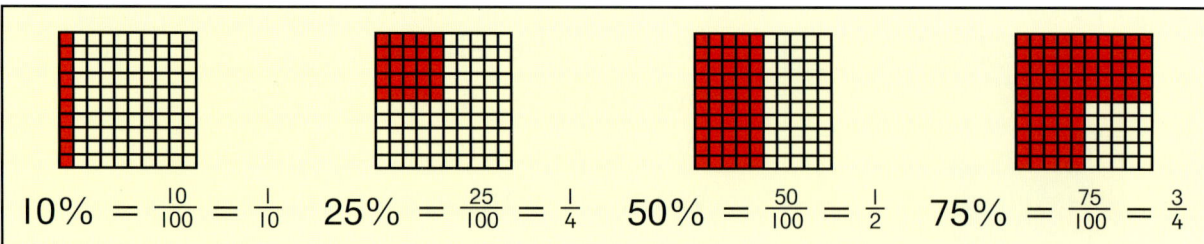

$10\% = \frac{10}{100} = \frac{1}{10}$ $25\% = \frac{25}{100} = \frac{1}{4}$ $50\% = \frac{50}{100} = \frac{1}{2}$ $75\% = \frac{75}{100} = \frac{3}{4}$

Draw pictures to show the equivalent fractions of these percentages.

1. 20%   **2.** 30%   **3.** 40%   **4.** 60%

Write the equivalent fractions for these percentages.

5. 70%   **6.** 80%   **7.** 90%

Remember: a percentage is a fraction with a denominator of 100. We can write any percentage as a fraction.

What fraction is equivalent to 12%? 35%?
$12\% = \frac{12}{100} = \frac{3}{25}$
(divide both numerator and denominator by H.C.F. 4)
$35\% = \frac{35}{100} = \frac{7}{20}$
(divide both numerator and denominator by H.C.F. 5)

Work out the fractions that are equivalent to these percentages.

8. 45%   **9.** 24%   **10.** 65%   **11.** 64%
12. 18%   **13.** 55%   **14.** 66%   **15.** 33%
16. 28%   **17.** 32%   **18.** 36%   **19.** 42%
20. 56%   **21.** 85%   **22.** 72%   **23.** 95%

Percentages UNIT 11

24. In a survey, people were asked what type of TV show they preferred to watch. The answers are shown as percentages in the chart below.

Programme	People's preference
Sports	20
Nature	10
Films	15
Comedies	30
News	25

Percentage: 0, 5, 10, 15, 20, 25, 30, 35, 40

Use the chart above to answer the following.

(a) What percentage of the people surveyed preferred the news?
(b) What fraction gave nature programmes as their first choice?
(c) Express as a decimal the number who preferred sports.
(d) What fraction preferred comedies?
(e) Write as a decimal the number who liked films the most.

The report did not say how many people were questioned. If 200 people were in the survey:
(f) How many would prefer news programmes?
(g) How many would prefer sports programmes?

If 400 people were questioned:
(h) How many would prefer films?
(i) How many would have said nature programmes?

If 1000 people were in the survey:
(j) How many would have said comedies?

UNIT 11 Percentages

Finding percentages

> **Remember:** per cent or percentage means **out of each hundred**. If we have a fraction with 100 as the denominator it is easy to write the equivalent percentage.
>
> **Examples** $\frac{10}{100} = 10\%$ $\frac{25}{100} = 25\%$ $\frac{33}{100} = 33\%$
>
> **Problem 1**
> In a bag of 200 marbles, 80 are red and the rest green. What per cent are red? What per cent are green?
> Fraction red = $\frac{80}{200} = \frac{40}{100}$ Percentage red = 40%
> Percentage green = 100 − 40 = 60%
>
> **Problem 2**
> In a class of 50 pupils, 28 are boys. What per cent are boys?
> Boys = $\frac{28}{50} = \frac{56}{100}$ Percentage of boys = 56%
>
> In both problems above we had to find the equivalent fractions with denominator 100.

Answer these questions.

1. What per cent of 200 is 60?
2. What per cent of 50 is 18?
3. What per cent of 300 is 45?
4. What per cent of $1.00 is 42 cents?
5. What per cent of $2.00 is 42 cents?
6. In a mathematics test Ram made 85 out of 100. What per cent did he score?
7. In a basket of mangoes 12 out of the 200 were spoilt. What per cent were good?
8. In a class of 50 pupils 26 were girls. What per cent were boys?

Percentages UNIT 11

Finding percentages of quantities

Some common percentages and fractions.

10% = $\frac{1}{10}$ 30% = $\frac{3}{10}$ 50% = $\frac{1}{2}$ 70% = $\frac{7}{10}$ 80% = $\frac{4}{5}$
20% = $\frac{1}{5}$ 40% = $\frac{2}{5}$ 60% = $\frac{3}{5}$ 75% = $\frac{3}{4}$ 90% = $\frac{9}{10}$

Problem 1   What is 25% of 60?
[25% = $\frac{1}{4}$ and 25% of 60 means $\frac{1}{4}$ of 60]
25% of 60 = 60 × $\frac{1}{4}$ = $\frac{60}{4}$ = 15

Remember: in work on fractions, 'of' means ×.

Problem 2   What is 75% of 80?
[75% = $\frac{3}{4}$ and 75% of 80 means $\frac{3}{4}$ of 80]
75% of 80 = $\frac{3}{4}$ × 80 = $\frac{240}{4}$ = 60

Answer these questions.

1. What is 20% of 30?
2. What is 30% of 40?
3. What is 25% of 50?
4. What is 75% of 120?
5. Javed had 150 newspapers and sold 80%. How many did he sell?
6. In a class of 40 children 25% wore white sneakers and 20% wore black sneakers. How many children wore white sneakers and how many wore black?
7. In a class of 32 children 75% went on an outing. How many was this?
8. In a bag of 150 mangoes 10% were spoilt. How many were unspoilt?
9. In a hall that could seat 300 persons only 60% of the seats were taken. How many chairs remained empty?

UNIT 11 Percentages

> We will not always have easy percentages like 10%, 20%, 25% and so on to work with. Working with other percentages would be easier if we are able to multiply and divide by 100 and its multiples.

Copy and complete these calculations.

10. 24 × 2 =   **11.** 45 × 3 =   **12.** 24 × 100 =

13. 45 × 100 =   **14.** 24 × 200 =   **15.** 45 × 300 =

16. 22 × 400 =   **17.** 2400 ÷ 100 =   **18.** 4500 ÷ 100 =

19. 4800 ÷ 200 =   **20.** 13 500 ÷ 300 =   **21.** 8800 ÷ 400 =

Now check your answers using a calculator.

> **Examples**
> 12% of 200 = $\frac{12}{100}$ of 200   8% of 125 = $\frac{8}{100}$ of 125
> $\phantom{12\% \text{ of } 200}$ = 200 × $\frac{12}{100}$ = $\frac{2400}{100}$ $\phantom{8\% \text{ of } 125}$ = 125 × $\frac{8}{100}$ = $\frac{1000}{100}$
> $\phantom{12\% \text{ of } 200}$ = 24 $\phantom{8\% \text{ of } 125}$ = 10

Copy and complete.

22. 15% of 60   **23.** 24% of 25   **24.** 18% of 50

25. 12% of 75   **26.** 22% of 200   **27.** 33% of 300

28. 45% of 200   **29.** 54% of 400   **30.** 14% of $150

31. 16% of $250   **32.** 9% of $1600   **33.** 7% of $2500

34. In a crate of 250 eggs, 12% were bad. How many eggs were good?

35. Six per cent of the oil in a cask which held 250 litres leaked out. How many litres of oil were left in the tank?

Percentages UNIT 11

Discounts

Remember: a discount is what you save when you pay less than the price marked on an article.

Very often the discount is shown as a percentage.
The advertisements below show the discounts offered in two shops.

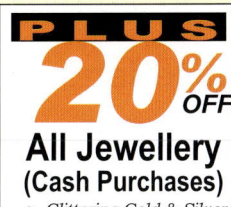

Example A student bought books which cost $600 and was given a 10% discount. How much did the student pay?

Discount = 10% of $600 = $\frac{1}{10} \times 600 = \frac{600}{10}$ = $60

Therefore the cost of books = $600 − $60 = $540.

Copy and complete the tables.

Bill	discount	amount paid
$100	15%	
$50	12%	
$150	14%	
$200	18%	
$200	9%	
$1000	15%	
$2000	16%	

Bill	discount	amount paid
$300	8%	
$120	15%	
$96	25%	
$100	8%	
$200	12%	
$1500	16%	
$2500	18%	

Assessment

Assessment 6

Solve the following:

1. 4·14 + 2·25
2. 3·45 + 2·36
3. 4·82 + 2·57
4. 6·84 − 2·41
5. 4·62 − 1·28
6. 5·35 − 2·73

Write these as decimal numbers in metres.

7. 12 m 15 cm
8. 24 m 5 cm
9. 275 cm

Round each of these lengths to the nearest metre and to the nearest tenth of a metre.

10. 4·55 m
11. 3·09 m

12. What is the sum of 5·05 m, 2·30 m and 0·75 m?

13. By how much is 10·25 m longer than 6·55 m?

Write as fractions in their lowest terms.

14. 55%
15. 64%
16. 75%

17. What per cent of 300 is 45?

18. Marlene gave away 15 of her 25 plums. What per cent did she keep?

19. What is 75% of 180?

20. In a bag of 200 mangoes 12% were spoilt. How many were unspoilt?

21. John could not sell 6% of his 300 newspapers. How many did he sell?

22. A buyer received 10% discount on a pair of shoes which was marked at $350. How much did the buyer pay?

12 Unitary method, wages and interest

Unitary method

Work out the answers to these word problems. Show all your working.

1. A school water tank holds 1800 litres of water. How many litres will eight tanks hold?

2. Thirty people can sit in each row of seats in a cinema. How many people can the cinema hold if there are 24 rows of seats?

3. How much will 15 bottles of soft drink cost if each bottle is sold for $5.95?

4. How many sacks of potatoes will a truck transport in 12 trips if it takes 60 sacks on each trip?

5. A crate of apples contains 120. How many apples are there in 16 crates?

6. An athlete runs 15 km on each of his practice runs. How many kilometres will he have travelled in going on 16 practice runs?

7. A large passenger bus seats 64 people. How many people can travel on 12 buses?

8. A crane can lift 32 boxes at a time. If each box weighs 25 kg what is the weight which the crane can lift?

Now check your answers using a calculator.

UNIT 12 Unitary method, wages and interest

Now work out the answers to these word problems. Show all your working.

9. Fifteen cans of fruit punch cost $22.50. What is the cost of 1 can?

10. Three hundred and sixty chairs are arranged in rows of 24. How many rows are there?

11. Fifteen bags of potatoes each having the same mass weigh 375 kg. How much does each bag weigh?

12. Twelve buses carry 648 people on an excursion. How many people travel in each bus if all the buses carry the same number of people?

13. A truck can transport 12 barrels of oil on a single trip. How many trips must the truck make if there are 180 barrels of oil to be transported?

14. One hundred sweets are to be shared equally among 25 children. How many sweets will each child get?

15. A man's wages for 16 weeks are $8000. What is his weekly wage?

16. Three thousand books are to be distributed among 30 school libraries. How many will each library get if all get the same number?

Now check your answers using a calculator.

Unitary method, wages and interest UNIT 12

> **Example** 12 sacks of potatoes each having the same mass weigh 300 kg.
> How much will 20 such sacks weigh?
>
> 12 sacks weigh 300 kg
> 1 sack will weigh (300 ÷ 12) kg = 25 kg
> 20 sacks will weigh (25 × 20) kg = 500 kg

Work out the answers to these word problems. Show all your working.

17. How many litres of oil will 24 casks hold if ten casks hold 2250 litres?

18. Twelve 2-litre bottles of soft drink cost $66.00. How much would 18 bottles cost?

19. Fifteen crates of tomatoes weigh 3000 kg. How much will 20 crates weigh?

20. Five buses carry 320 passengers when full. How many passengers can travel in nine buses?

21. What will 25 metres of cloth cost if I can purchase 6 metres for $90?

22. A set of six tickets for the football match cost $900. How much should I pay for 30 tickets?

Now check your answers using a calculator.

UNIT 12 Unitary method, wages and interest

Wages and salaries

> Some people are paid for the work they do on an hourly basis, some on a daily basis, some weekly and some fortnightly (every two weeks).
> These people receive **wages**.
>
> Professional people like teachers, lawyers, doctors, office managers, civil servants, nurses, policemen and many other kinds of worker are generally paid on a monthly basis.
> These people receive **salaries**.

Work out the answers to these word problems. Show all your working.

1. A household worker is paid $9.00 per hour. She works 4 hours a day for 5 days of the week. How much does she receive as wages at the end of a week?

2. A carpenter earns $250 a day. How much will he have earned after working for 24 days?

3. A store clerk works for $525 per week. How much will she earn in 5 weeks?

4. A pipefitter is paid $375 per day. He works six days a week but collects his wages fortnightly (every two weeks). How much does the worker receive every fortnight?

5. A teacher receives a salary of $7200 per month. How much is the teacher's annual salary?

Now check your answers using a calculator.

Unitary method, wages and interest UNIT 12

Percentages and interest

When you deposit money in a bank, credit union or finance company, you receive **interest** on the money after a period of time. The amount of interest you get depends on the rate which the bank, credit union or finance company is paying.

The rate of interest is always given as percentage **per annum**; per annum (p.a.) means **per year** and 5% per annum means $5 on every $100 every year.

Many people now put their money in fixed term deposits. This means they deposit a fixed sum of money for a fixed period of time at a fixed rate of interest.

For example, a person may put $10 000 in a deposit for two years at 9% per annum.

The sum you deposit is called the **principal**. Interest on a fixed term deposit is called **simple interest**.

Example How much interest will a person receive if he deposits $1000 with a bank for a period of two years at 6% per annum?

The interest on $1000 for one year is 6% of $1000

6% of $1000 is $\frac{6}{100}$ of $1000 = $1000 $\times \frac{6}{100}$.

We were not asked to find the interest for one year, so we are not required to multiply out $1000 $\times \frac{6}{100}$.

Interest for two years is $1000 $\times \frac{6}{100} \times 2 = \frac{\$6000}{100} \times 2$
$= \$120$

What do we call the $1000? What is the $\frac{6}{100}$? What does the 2 refer to?

We can therefore write:

simple interest = principal × rate × time

UNIT 12 Unitary method, wages and interest

$$200 \times \tfrac{3}{100} = \boxed{} \qquad \tfrac{200}{10} \times 3 = \boxed{}$$

$$3000 \times \tfrac{2}{100} = \boxed{} \qquad \tfrac{3000}{100} \times 2 = \boxed{}$$

What do you observe in the statements above?
See how we use this in our next examples.

Remember: simple interest = principal × rate × time (in years)

Examples Find the simple interest on:

$2000 for two years at 8% p.a.
$$\begin{aligned}\text{Interest} &= \$2000 \times \tfrac{8}{100} \times 2 \\ &= \tfrac{\$2000}{100} \times 8 \times 2 \\ &= \$20 \times 8 \times 2 \\ &= \$320\end{aligned}$$

$1200 for six months at 7% p.a.
$$\begin{aligned}\text{Interest} &= \$1200 \times \tfrac{7}{100} \times \tfrac{1}{2} \; (\tfrac{1}{2} \text{ year}) \\ &= \tfrac{\$1200}{100} \times 7 \times \tfrac{1}{2} \\ &= \$12 \times 7 \times \tfrac{1}{2} \\ &= \$42\end{aligned}$$

1. Copy and complete the table.

Principal	interest rate p.a.	time	amount = principal + interest
$1000	4%	3 years	
$1500	6%	2 years	
$2000	8%	6 months	
$2500	6%	9 months	
$3000	8%	18 months	
$4000	9%	2 years	
$10 000	8%	2 years	
$20 000	9%	3 years	

13 Measurement of length/Circumference

Centimetres and millimetres

Measure these lines to the nearest centimetre.

──────────────── Line 1

────────────────────── Line 2

You will need: a ruler.

Which is the longer line? How much longer is it?

Look at your ruler.
How many divisions are there in a centimetre?
Each of these divisions is 1 millimetre or 1 mm.
   1 centimetre = 10 millimetres, or 1 cm = 10 mm.

Now measure lines 1 and 2 again, this time in centimetres and millimetres, or, as we say, to the nearest millimetre. How long is the longer line? The shorter line?

A line 7 cm 1 mm long is 71 mm long. Can you say why we can write 7 cm 1 mm as 71 mm? We can also write 7 cm 1 mm as 7·1 cm. How do you explain this?

1. Measure the lines shown here and write the measurements in a table like the one shown.

   (a) ──────────

   (b) ──────────────

   (c) ────────────────

   (d) ──────────────

   (e) ────────────────────

Line	cm and mm	mm only	cm only
	7 cm 1 mm	71 mm	7·1 cm
(a)			
(b)			
(c)			
(d)			
(e)			

UNIT 13   Measurement of length/Circumference

Measure the sides of each of the shapes below and calculate the perimeter of each.

2.    3. 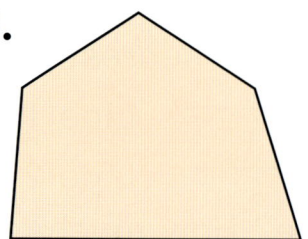   4.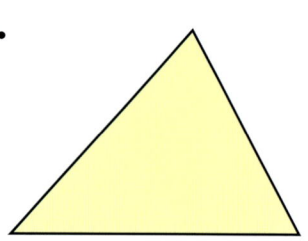

Trace around the coins on thin card and cut out as smoothly as you can.
Fold each shape in two. Open and measure the folding line.
What is the approximate width of each of the coins?

5.    6.    7.    8.

Try measuring the coins themselves and compare the results.

Draw lines of the following lengths:

9. 5 cm 4 mm   **10.** 6·3 cm   **11.** 58 mm   **12.** 9·2 cm

13. 105 mm   **14.** 12·6 cm   **15.** 10 cm 4 mm   **16.** 6·9 cm

17. 124 mm   **18.** 10 cm 2 mm

The lines drawn in red in the squares and rectangles are called diagonals. Draw the shapes and measure the diagonals.

19. 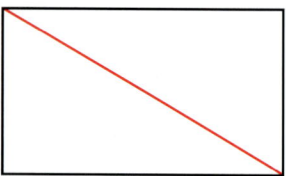   **20.** 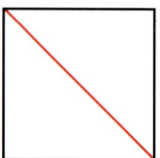   **21.** 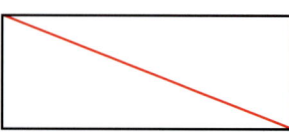   **22.**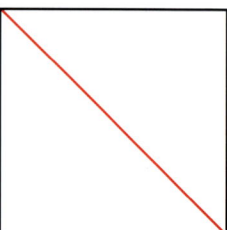

130

Measurement of length/Circumference UNIT 13

Metres and millimetres

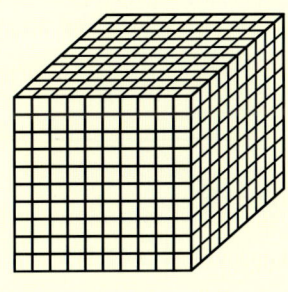

This is a block of 1000 cubes.
Each cube is $\frac{1}{1000}$, one thousandth of the block.
$\frac{1}{1000}$ is written 0·001
$\frac{12}{1000}$ is written 0·012 and $\frac{123}{1000}$ is written 0·123
Notice that in writing thousandths there are three digits to the right of the decimal point.

Remember: 10 mm = 1 cm and 100 cm = 1 m,
so that 1000 mm = 1 m
and 1 mm = $\frac{1}{1000}$ m; 10 mm = $\frac{10}{1000}$ m = $\frac{1}{100}$ m; 100 mm = $\frac{1}{10}$ m

We can write measurements in millimetres as a decimal number in metres. Look at the place value chart below.

		1000 mm 1 m	100 mm $\frac{1}{10}$ m	10 mm $\frac{1}{100}$ m	1 mm $\frac{1}{1000}$ m
	1 mm	0 ·	0	0	1
21 mm	20 mm + 1 mm	0 ·	0	2	1
321 mm	300 mm + 20 mm + 1 mm	0 ·	3	2	1
4321 mm	4000 mm + 300 mm + 20 mm + 1 mm	4 ·	3	2	1
4321 mm = 4000 mm + 300 mm + 20 mm + 1 mm =		4 ·	3	2	1 m

Write these lengths in metres using decimal numbers.

1. 425 mm
2. 2425 mm
3. 242 mm
4. 3064 mm
5. 909 mm
6. 1001 mm
7. 1010 mm
8. 4300 mm
9. 200 mm
10. 42 mm
11. 89 mm
12. 3 mm

UNIT 13 Measurement of length/Circumference

When the length is given in metres and millimetres it is safer to write it first as millimetres and then fix the decimal point.
Examples 1 m 234 mm = 1234 mm = 1·234 m
           2 m 15 mm = 2015 mm = 2·015 m

Write these lengths as metres using decimal numbers.

13. 1 m 152 mm   14. 2 m 225 mm   15. 3 m 15 mm
16. 1 m 10 mm   17. 15 m 15 mm   18. 5 m 105 mm

Kilometres and metres

Complete the following using one of the units: km, m, cm or mm.

The classroom measures 18 ___ × 20 ___ .
A 25 cents coin is about 18 ___ wide.
The distance from Port of Spain to San Fernando is about 60 ___ .
My copy book measures about 20 ___ × 15 ___ .

We can write measurements in metres as decimal numbers of kilometres.

Remember: 1 kilometre = 1000 metres; so that 1 m = $\frac{1}{1000}$ km
and 10 m = $\frac{1}{100}$ km and 100 m = $\frac{1}{10}$ km.

The place value chart will again help us.

	1000 mm 1 km	100 mm $\frac{1}{10}$ km	10 mm $\frac{1}{100}$ km	1 mm $\frac{1}{1000}$ km
7 m	0 ·	0	0	7
57 m = 50 m + 7 m	0 ·	0	5	7
257 m = 200 m + 50 m + 7 m	0 ·	2	5	7
1257 m = 1000 m + 200 m + 50 m + 7 m	1 ·	2	5	7
1257 m = 1000 m + 200 m + 50 m + 7 m =	1 ·	2	5	7 m

Measurement of length/Circumference UNIT 13

1. Copy and complete the table.

km and m	m only	km only
2 km 116 m	2116 m	2·116 km
3 km 110 m		
	5005 m	
4 km 15 m		
		0·015 km
	2022 m	
10 km 10 m		

Copy and complete.

```
2.    km   m          3.    km   m          4.    km    m
       5   35                4   90                1   250
       3  140                2  100                3   705
    +  2   65             +  1  520             +  4    65
      _____               _____              _____


5.    km   m          6.    km   m          7.    km    m
       6  200               10  255               10     0
       1  495                3   75                1   980
    +  3  310             +  1  510             +  1   720
      _____               _____              _____


8.    km   m          9.    km   m         10.    km    m
       5  450                4  250                1   500
       2  860                2  750                1   420
    +  1  375             +  1  600                2   355
      _____               _____           +  1   580
                                                  _____
```

133

UNIT 13 Measurement of length/Circumference

11.
```
   km    m
    5   40
    2   480
    2   375
+   4   515
   ─────────
```

12.
```
   km    m
    1   640
    1   505
    2   370
+   1   590
   ─────────
```

13.
```
   km    m
    4    60
    2   825
    1   755
+   1    95
   ─────────
```

14.
```
   km    m
    4   650
−   1   375
   ─────────
```

15.
```
   km    m
   10   125
−   4    95
   ─────────
```

16.
```
   km    m
    8   245
−   1   670
   ─────────
```

17.
```
   km    m
    7   430
−   5   855
   ─────────
```

18.
```
   km    m
   10   100
−   5   485
   ─────────
```

19.
```
   km    m
   20    50
−   5   275
   ─────────
```

20.
```
   km    m
   14   230
−   5   175
   ─────────
```

21.
```
   km    m
    6   300
−   2   195
   ─────────
```

22.
```
   km    m
   35    50
−  26   125
   ─────────
```

Measurement of length/Circumference   UNIT 13

Approximation to the nearest hundredth

When we write decimal numbers as approximations to the nearest tenth, we say that we write the numbers **to one decimal place**.

So if we write decimal numbers as approximations to the nearest hundredth, we say that we write the numbers **to two decimal places**.

Look at the number line in thousandths below; hundredths are written above the line.

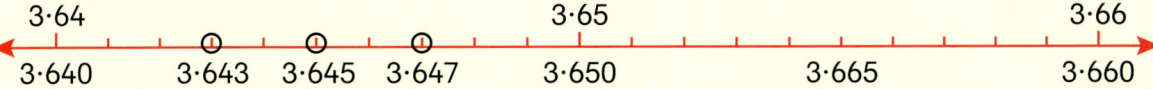

The nearest hundredth to 3·643 is 3·64; the nearest hundredth to 3·647 is 3·65.

3·643 is rounded down to 3·64 and 3·647 is rounded up to 3·65 (to the nearest hundredth).

We can also say that 3·643≈3·64 and 3·647≈3·65 (to the nearest hundredth).

We can also say that 3·643 is 3·64 to two decimal places and 3·647 is 3·65 to two decimal places.

Remember that the midway numbers 3·645 and 3·655 are rounded up.

When approximating numbers to the nearest hundredth, or when writing numbers to two decimal places, if the **thousandths** digit (the third decimal place) is 5 or more than 5, we increase the **hundreds** digit by 1.

135

UNIT 13 Measurement of length/Circumference

Round these numbers to two decimal places.

1. 1·072	**2.** 1·027	**3.** 1·720	**4.** 1·702	**5.** 2·156
6. 2·615	**7.** 2·165	**8.** 2·516	**9.** 3·007	**10.** 3·075

Approximation in lengths

In the same way as we approximate or write decimals to the nearest whole number, or tenth or hundredth, we can approximate lengths to the nearest kilometre or metre or tenth or hundredth of a kilometre or metre.

Remember: a number like 3·465 is 3 to the nearest whole number
or 3·5 to the nearest tenth
or 3·47 to the nearest hundredth.

Look at the lengths 3·465 km and 3·465 m

3·465 km	3·465 m
is 3 km to the nearest km	is 3 m to the nearest metre
or 3·5 km to the nearest tenth of a kilometre	or 3·5 m to the nearest tenth of a metre
or 3·47 km to the nearest hundredth of a kilometre	or 3·47 m to the nearest hundredth of a metre.
	Note: 3·465 m is also 347 cm to the nearest cm.

Round these lengths to the nearest km, nearest $\frac{1}{10}$ km and nearest $\frac{1}{100}$ km.

1. 2·354 km **2.** 1·925 km **3.** 4·012 km **4.** 16·231 km

Round these lengths to the nearest m, nearest $\frac{1}{10}$ m and nearest $\frac{1}{100}$ m.

5. 4·623 m **6.** 7·981 m **7.** 3·216 m **8.** 2·005 m

Measurement of length/Circumference UNIT 13

The circle

You will need: a tin, cardboard, scissors.

What is the shape of the end of a cylindrical tin?

Use a tin to draw a circle on
thin cardboard.

- Cut out the circular shape.
- Fold the shape along any two lines of symmetry.
- Open the shape and draw the lines of symmetry.

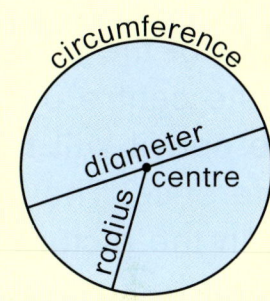

Where do the lines meet?

Any line of symmetry in a circle is called a **diameter** of the circle.
All diameters of a circle pass through the **centre** of the circle.
The distance from the centre of the circle to any point on the circle is called the **radius**.
The distance around the circle is called the **circumference**.

You will need: cardboard, scissors, drawing pin.

Here is an easy way to make an
instrument for drawing circles.

- Stick a drawing pin at one end
  of a strip of card.
- Push a pencil point through the card
  at any point on the card.
- The size of circle you make will depend
  on where you pass through the pencil point.

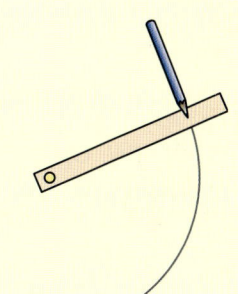

137

UNIT 13 Measurement of length/Circumference

You will need: a pair of compasses, a ruler and a pencil to draw accurate circles.

The picture shows how to set your compasses to get the radius of the circle.
The point of the compasses marks the centre of the circle, and the pencil will trace the circumference. The instrument setting in the picture will give us a circle of **radius 4 cm**.

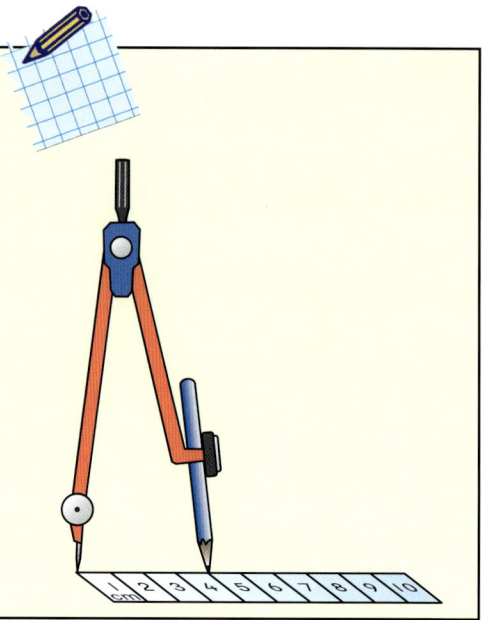

You can have some fun drawing circles with your circle maker or compasses.

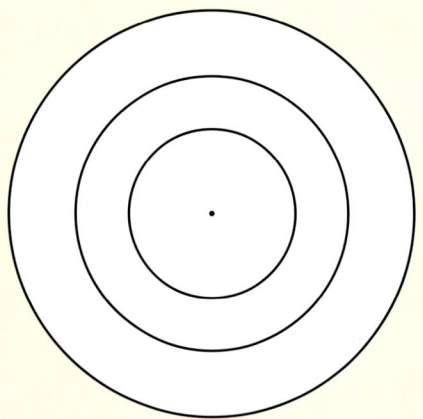

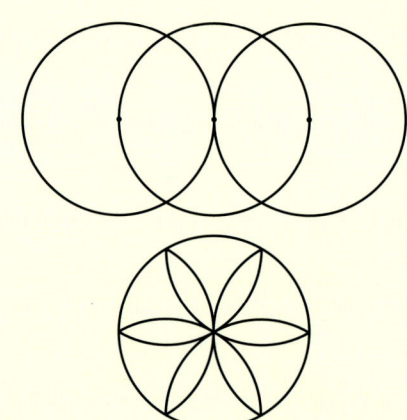

We can draw circles of smaller **radii** (plural of radius) with the **same centre** as the big circle above. Circles like this are called **concentric** circles.
Circles can also make beautiful patterns like those shown above.

Measurement of length/Circumference UNIT 13

Measuring circumference

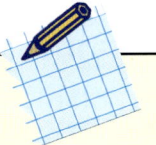

You will need: tins, paper, scissors, glue, measuring tape or string, calculator.

Use the tins to cut out circular paper shapes.
- Fold the shapes to find the centres.
- Stick the circular shapes in your book.

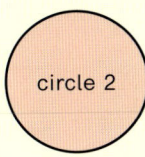
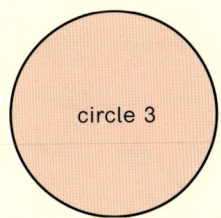

Draw a diameter in each circle and measure it as accurately as possible.
Measure the circumference at either end of the tins. Use a measuring tape or strip of paper, or a piece of string.
Make a table of the results as shown here.

	diameter	circumference	circumference ÷ diameter
circle 1			
circle 2			
circle 3			

Divide the measurement of the circumference by the measurement of the diameter in each case.
Use your calculator and give the quotient to the nearest whole number.
If you have measured as accurately as you can the quotient should be approximately 3.
In other words, the circumference is approximately 3 times the diameter, that is, circumference ≈ diameter × 3.

UNIT 13 Measurement of length/Circumference

Use the relationship circumference ≈ diameter × 3 in these questions. Measure the diameter of each of these circles and find their circumference.

1. Measure the diameter of the circle in each of these diagrams and find their circumference. What is the perimeter of the square in each?

   (a) 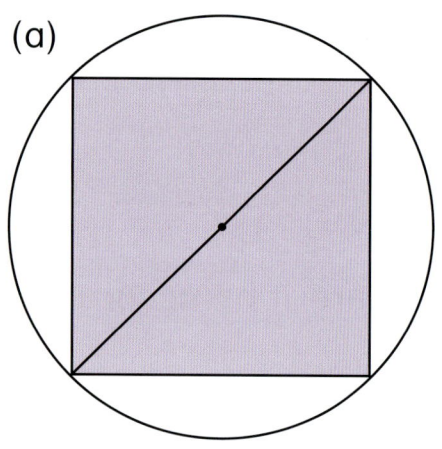   (b)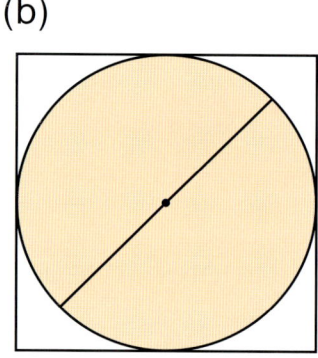

Find the circumference of the circles with these diameters:

2. 14 cm   3. 21 cm   4. 15 cm   5. 12 cm

Find the circumference of the circles with these radii (plural of radius).

6. 7 cm   7. 5 cm   8. 8 cm   9. 3 cm

10. What is the distance around a circular track of radius 63 m?

11. Which has the greater perimeter, and by how much (a) a square of side 14 cm or (b) a circle of radius 7 cm?

12. The radius of a bicycle wheel measures 30 cm. What is the circumference? How far has a cyclist travelled if the wheel has made 1000 revolutions?

Measurement of length/Circumference UNIT 13

Finding the diameter and radius

Remember: circumference ≈ diameter × 3;
therefore diameter ≈ $\frac{1}{3}$ circumference
and diameter = radius × 2;
therefore radius = $\frac{1}{2}$ diameter.

Example
Find the diameter of a circle whose circumference ≈ 45 cm
Diameter ≈ $\frac{1}{3}$ circumference = $\frac{1}{3}$ of 45 cm = 15 cm   45 × $\frac{1}{3}$
Radius = $\frac{1}{2}$ diameter = $\frac{1}{2}$ of 15 = 7$\frac{1}{2}$ cm.   15 × $\frac{1}{2}$

Find the circumference of the circles:

1. diameter 14 m
2. diameter 21 cm
3. radius 3$\frac{1}{2}$ cm
4. radius 35 m

Find the diameters and radii of the circles with these circumferences:

5. 440 m
6. 660 cm
7. 110 cm
8. 11 m

Find the diameters and radii of the circles with these circumferences:

9. 42 m
10. 80·4 cm
11. 54 cm
12. 20·5 m

Assessment 7

1. What is the cost of 15 kg of beef if 6 kg cost $150.00?
2. Mr Ali earns $16.00 an hour and twice as much if he works on Sundays. How much will Mr Ali earn if he works from 8.30 a.m to 12.30 p.m on a Sunday?
3. What is the simple interest on $25 000 invested for 3 years at 8% per annum?

Measure these lines to the nearest mm.

4. _____   5. _____

Write your measurements in (a) mm, (b) cm and mm, (c) cm only.

6. Complete this statement

   4·125 km = _____ km _____ m = _____ m.

7. 4 km 55 m + 3 km 125 m = _____ km _____ m = _____ km.

Write these lengths (a) to the nearest km, (b) to measure $\frac{1}{10}$ km and (c) to the nearest $\frac{1}{100}$ km:

8. 2·405 km   9. 10·516 km   10. 2352 m.

Use the relationship circumference ≈ diameter × 3 to calculate the circumference of the following circles:

11. circle with diameter 10·0 cm
12. circle with radius 4·5 cm

14 Area and volume

Area of a right-angled triangle

Draw a rectangle 8 cm x 4 cm.

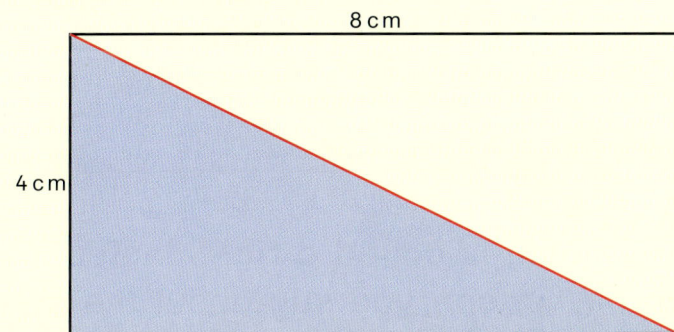

You will need: paper, ruler, scissors, coloured pencil.

- Draw one diagonal of the rectangle; ours is drawn in red.

Remember: a diagonal is a line joining opposite vertices.

- Shade the area under the diagonal.
- Cut along the diagonal.
- Match the two pieces of the shape. What do you observe about the area of the pieces?

What is the area of the rectangle?
What is the area of each piece of the rectangle?

Calculate the area of the shaded part of each rectangle.

1.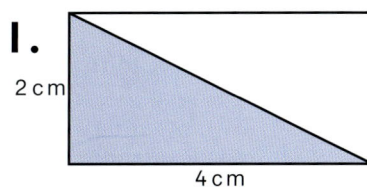

2.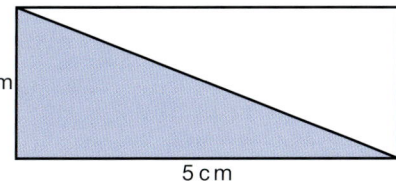

3.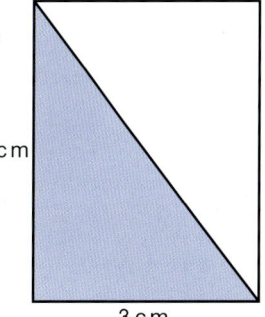

4.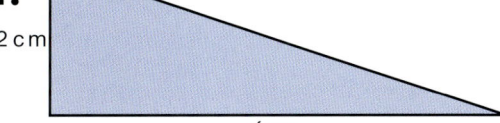

143

UNIT 14 Area and volume

When we cut along the diagonal of our rectangle, what shapes did we make?

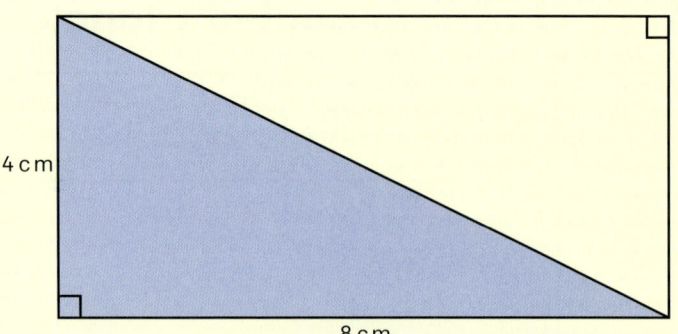

These are special triangles; each is called a right-angled triangle. Can you say why? What can you say about the area of the triangles? What can you say about the area of either triangle and the rectangle?

Area of each triangle = half the area of the rectangle.

Area of each triangle = $\frac{1}{2}$ × (length × breadth) of the rectangle.

The length and breadth of the triangle form the right angle of the rectangle.

Area of the right-angled triangle = $\frac{1}{2}$ (8 × 4) cm² = 16 cm².

Calculate the area of each of these right-angled triangles.

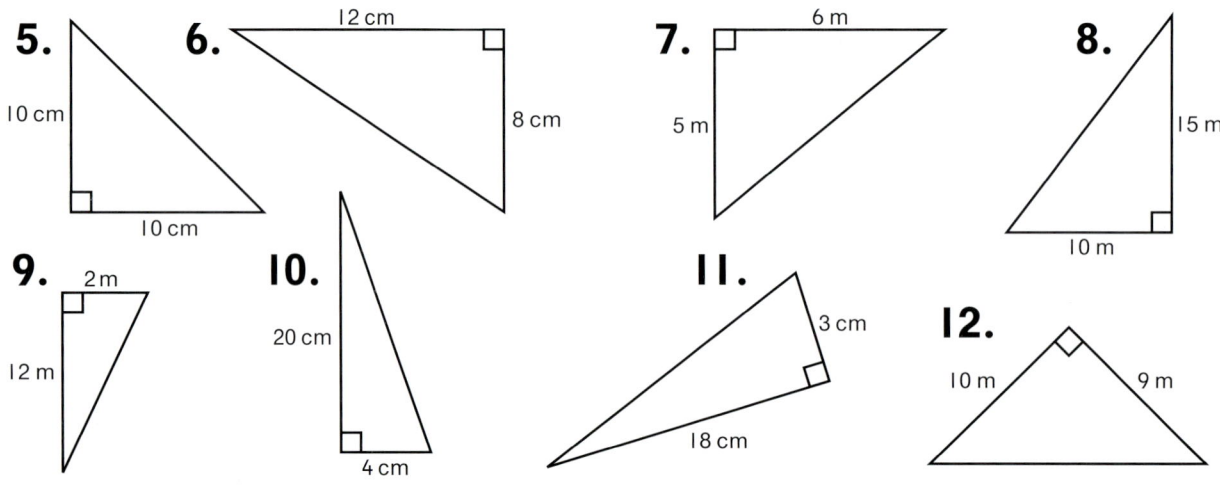

144

Area and volume   UNIT 14

Area of any triangle

Fig. 1 — rectangle with breadth and length, vertices B and C, point A on top edge, red triangle ABC inside.

Fig. 2 — triangle ABC with base BC and height from A.

- Cut out a rectangle of any size.
- Mark a point A along the length of the rectangle.
- Join A to vertices B and C.
- Cut along lines AB and AC (Fig. 1).
- Fit the green cut out triangles onto the red triangle (Fig. 2).
- The green triangles fit exactly onto the red triangle.

The area of the red triangle = $\frac{1}{2}$ (the area of the rectangle)
= $\frac{1}{2}$ (length × breadth) of the rectangle.

If we call **the length** of the rectangle **the base** of the triangle in Fig. 2, and **the width** of the rectangle **the height** of the triangle, we can write:

area of the triangle = $\frac{1}{2}$ (base × height)

You will need: paper, ruler, scissors.

Find the area of each of these triangles.

1.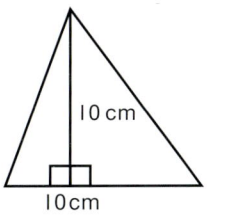
10 cm (height), 10 cm (base)

2.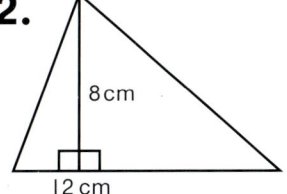
8 cm (height), 12 cm (base)

3.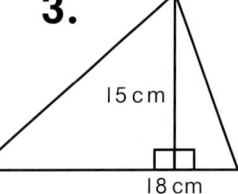
15 cm (height), 18 cm (base)

4.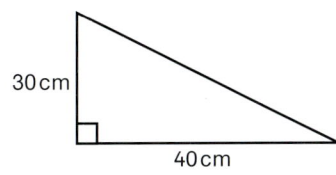
30 cm, 40 cm

5.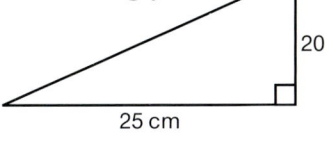
20 cm, 25 cm

6.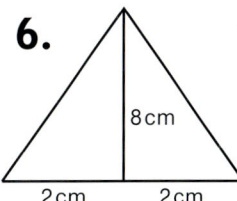
8 cm, 2 cm, 2 cm

145

UNIT 14 Area and volume

Areas of borders and paths

Example
Calculate the area of the shaded part.

Solution
Area of whole shape
= 6 × 6 = ☐ cm²
Area of unshaded part
= 2 × 2 = ☐ cm²
Area of shaded part
= ☐ − ☐ = ☐ cm²

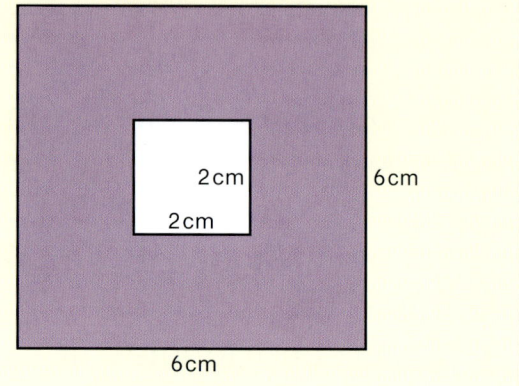

Calculate the areas of the shaded parts in these.

1.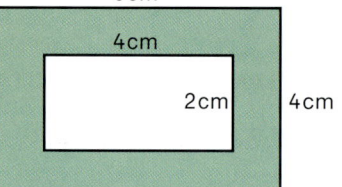

2.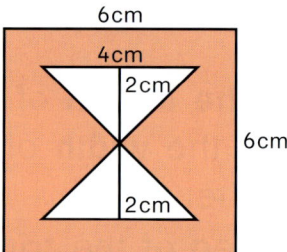

3.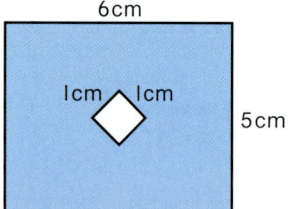

4.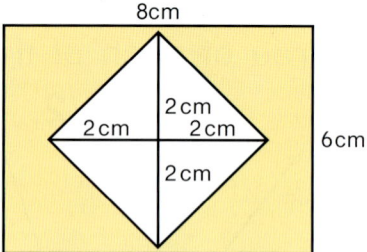

5.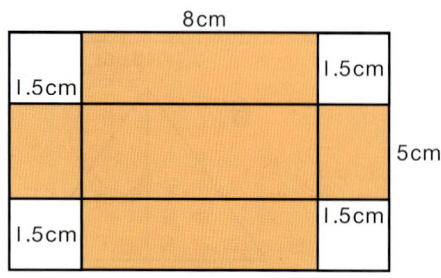

6.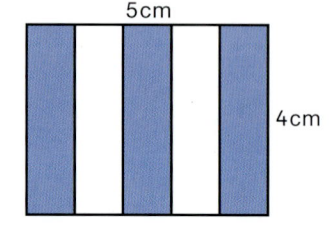

Area and volume   UNIT 14

Remember: when we measure lengths in metres, the area is computed in square metres.

A square metre is the area covered by a square of side 1 m long. If the blackboard measures 2 m by 1 m what is its area? If the classroom floor measures 10 m × 6 m what is its area?

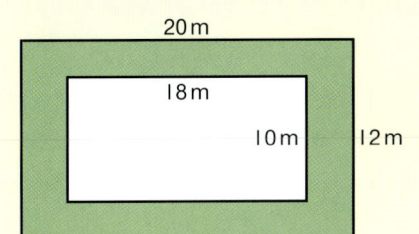

The diagram shows a path which measures 20 m × 12 m round the outside. The area in the middle is 18 m × 10 m. What is the area of the path?

area of path = area of outer rectangle − area of inner rectangle
= (20 × 12) m² − (18 × 10) m²
= 240 m² − 180 m²
= 60 m²

Find the area of the paths coloured green below.

7.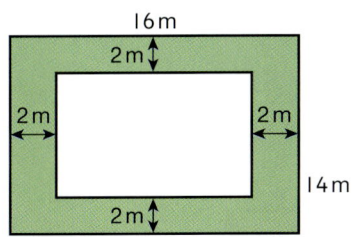

8.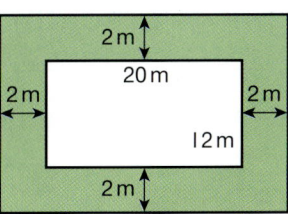

9.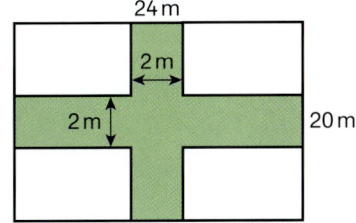

10.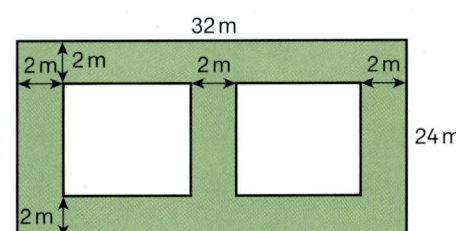

UNIT 14   Area and volume

Surface area of cuboids

Look at the box below and the net of the box. How many faces does the box have? How many faces are shown in the net?

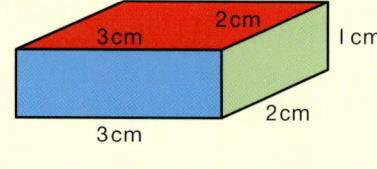
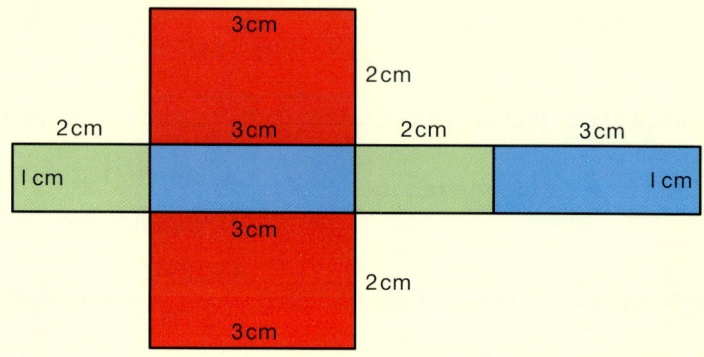

Area of red faces   = (3 × 2) × 2   = 12 cm²
Area of green faces = (2 × 1) × 2   = 4 cm²
Area of blue faces   = (3 × 1) × 2   = 6 cm²
Total area of faces = 12 + 4 + 6 = 22 cm²
This is called the **surface area** of the box.

If we wished to find the area of the sides only, we have a rectangle (2 + 3 + 2 + 3) cm long and 1 cm high.
   Area = 2 × (2 + 3) × 1 cm² = 10 cm²
   [2 (length + breadth) × height]

Find the surface area of these boxes.

1. 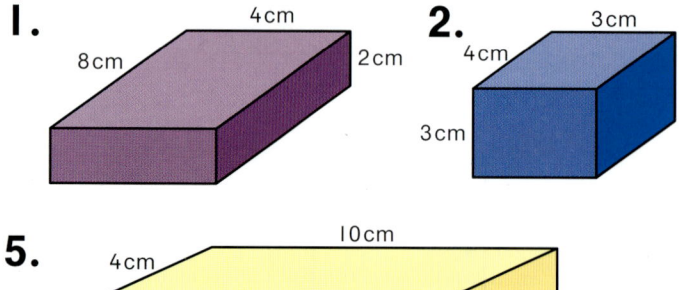   2.   3. 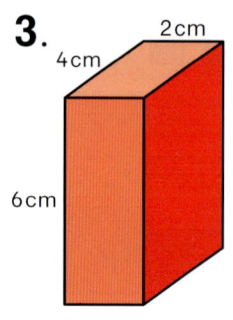   4.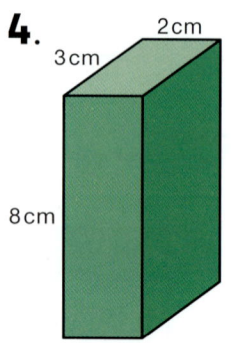

5.

Area and volume UNIT 14

Most rooms are rectangular (a cuboid) or square (a cube). A room with a flat ceiling is like a very large box with a bottom and a lid.

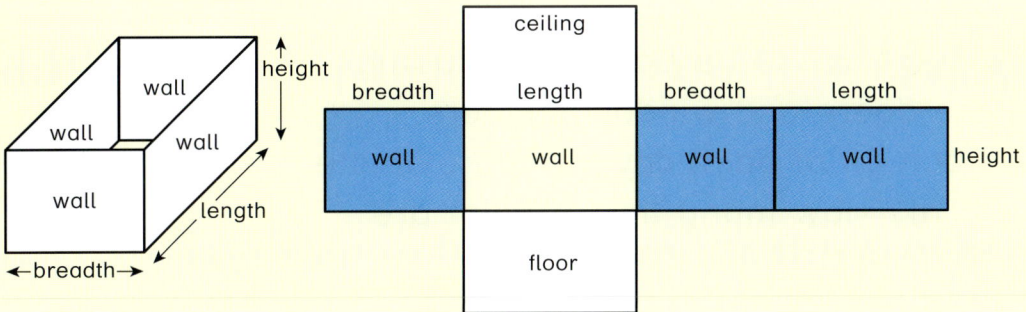

If the box on the left represents a room, the drawing on the right (the rest of the box) shows what the room would look like if we could open it out.

The four walls make a large rectangle.
The total length (2 × length and 2 × breadth) is the perimeter of the room.
The area of the four walls = (perimeter of room × height)
$= 2(L + B) \times H$.

Example
A room is 4 m long, 3 m wide and 3 m high. What is the area of its walls?
  Area = 2 (4 m + 3 m) × 3 m = 14 × 3 m³ = 42 m³

Find the area of the walls of these rooms.
  6. length 5 m   breadth 3 m   height 3 m
  7. length 10 m   breadth 6 m   height 3 m
  8. length 15 m   breadth 12 m   height 5 m
  9. length 20 m   breadth 12 m   height 6 m

UNIT 14 Area and volume

Word problems

Work out the answers to these word problems.
Show all your working.

1. (a) The inside and outside walls of this shed have to be painted, including the doors and window shutters.
Each tin of paint covers approximately 10 m². How many tins of paint are needed?

   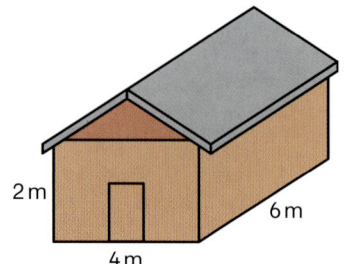

   (b) If each tin of paint costs $85.50 how much will it cost to paint the shed?

2. (a) A floor measuring 5 m × 4 m is to be tiled using tiles 20 cm × 20 cm. How many tiles are needed?

   (b) What is the cost of the tiles if they are bought at $120 per 100 tiles?

3. How much will it cost to carpet the floor of a house 15·5 m by 10 m if carpeting costs $35 per sq. metre?

4. The playground area inside the park is to be paved for basketball and netball courts.
How much will it cost if the contractors charge $55 per sq. metre?

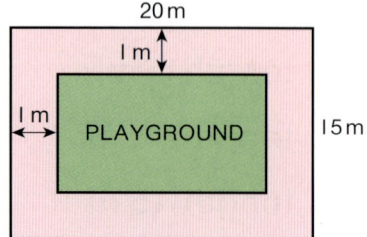

150

Area and volume UNIT 14

Volume of a cuboid

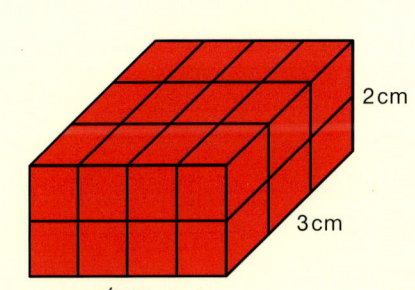

This cuboid is made up of
$(4 \times 3 \times 2)$ cm² blocks
Volume of solid is 24 cm³
4 cm × 3 cm × 2 cm = 24 cm³
Volume of solid = L × B × H

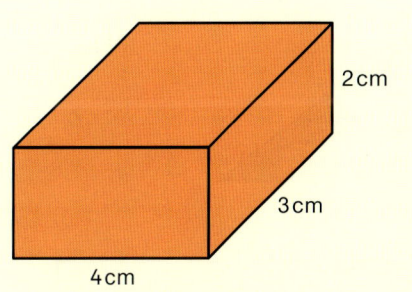

This box measures
4 cm × 3 cm × 2 cm
It can hold 24 cm³ blocks
Volume = 24 cm³
4 cm × 3 cm × 2 cm = 24 cm³
Volume = L × B × H

Remember: we can also say volume = base area × height

Find the volume of these cuboids.

1. 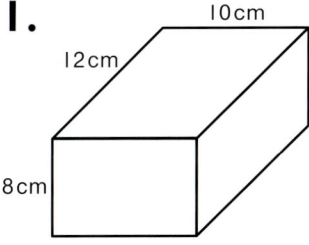   2. 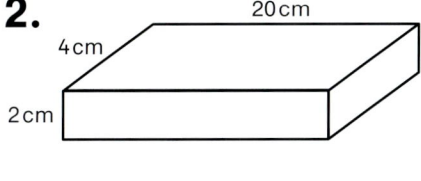   3.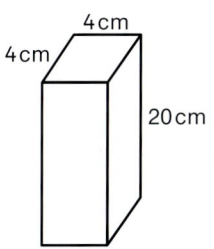

In the following questions L = length B = breadth, H = height,
A = base of area of several cuboids. Find their volumes.

4. L 25 cm   B 20 cm   H 20 cm
5. L 8 m   B 2 m   H 1 m
6. L 12 m   B 4 m   H 4 m
7. A = 40 m²   H 6 m
8. L 3·5 m   B 2·4 m   H 6 m
9. A = 24·5 m²   H 2·5 m

151

Assessment 8

Find the areas of the following triangles.

1.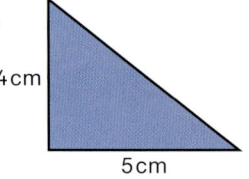

2.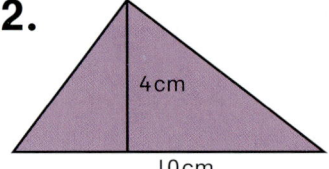

3. The path around this playing field is 2 m wide. How much will it cost to have the path paved at $120 per m²?

4. Find the surface area of this gift box. How many sheets of wrapping paper ½ m × 1 m will you need to buy to cover the box?

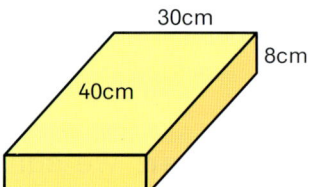

5. How many buckets of paint will be needed to paint the inside and outside walls of this shed? The doors and windows, area 60 m², are not to be painted. 1 bucket of paint will cover 10 m².

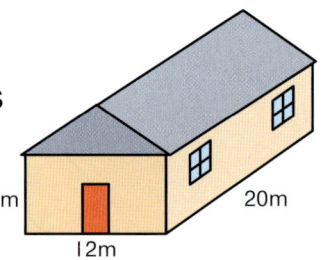

6. Which of these boxes will hold the most? Which the least?

(a) 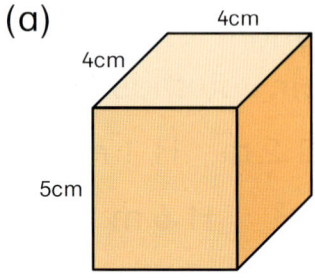   (b) 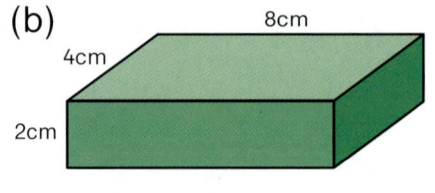   (c)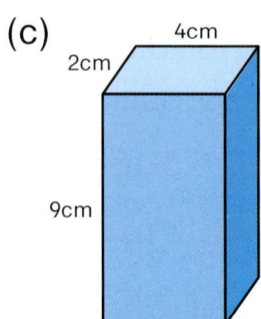

15 Mass and weight

Kilograms and grams

Say whether you would weigh the following in kilograms or grams.

1. a cricket bat
2. a tennis ball
3. your pet
4. a leg of beef
5. a tea bag
6. a packed suitcase
7. a box of cookies
8. a sack of potatoes
9. a bag of cement
10. a packet of curry powder

> We can write weights in grams as a decimal number of kilograms.
>
> **Remember:** 1 kilogram = 1000 grams and $1\,g = \frac{1}{1000}\,kg$
> $10\,g = \frac{1}{100}\,kg$ and $100\,g = \frac{1}{10}\,kg$

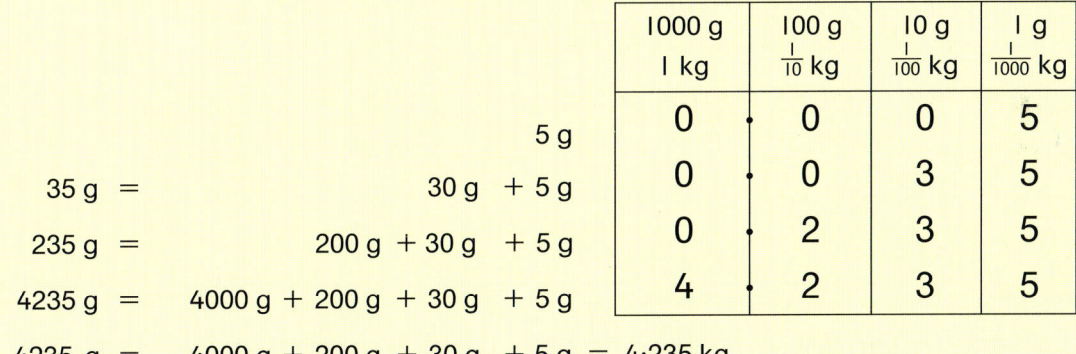

	1000 g 1 kg	100 g $\frac{1}{10}$ kg	10 g $\frac{1}{100}$ kg	1 g $\frac{1}{1000}$ kg
5 g	0	0	0	5
35 g = 30 g + 5 g	0	0	3	5
235 g = 200 g + 30 g + 5 g	0	2	3	5
4235 g = 4000 g + 200 g + 30 g + 5 g	4	2	3	5

4235 g = 4000 g + 200 g + 30 g + 5 g = 4·235 kg

Write these as grams:

11. 1 kg 245 g
12. 3 kg 195 g
13. 2 kg 250 g
14. 5 kg 90 g
15. 4 kg 555 g
16. 20 kg 55 g
17. 13 kg 5 g
18. 22 kg 100 g
19. 6 kg 600 g
20. 20 kg 20 g

UNIT 15 Mass and weight

Write these as kilograms and grams:
21. 2345 g   **22.** 1985 g   **23.** 6075 g   **24.** 5008 g
25. 14 215 g **26.** 1900 g   **27.** 2750 g   **28.** 12 040 g

Write as a decimal number in kilograms:
29. 2 kg 152 g   **30.** 3 kg 180 g   **31.** 2 kg 75 g
32. 5 kg 50 g   **33.** 20 kg 45 g   **34.** 23 kg 205 g

Write as a decimal number in kilograms:
35. 3245 g   **36.** 1890 g   **37.** 5045 g   **38.** 2002 g
39. 10 125 g **40.** 15 080 g **41.** 30 040 g **42.** 5050 g

Approximation in weight

> 4·375 kg ≈ 4 kg to the nearest kg   (the tenth digit 3 is less than 5)
>
> 4·375 kg ≈ 4·4 kg to the nearest $\frac{1}{10}$ kg   (the hundredth digit is more than 5)
>
> 4·375 kg ≈ 4·38 kg to the nearest $\frac{1}{100}$ kg (the thousandth digit is 5)

Round these quantities to the nearest kg, tenth of a kg and hundredth of a kg.
1. 1·525 kg   **2.** 4·371 kg   **3.** 5·640 kg   **4.** 2·825 kg
5. 6·320 kg   **6.** 4·605 kg   **7.** 8·975 kg   **8.** 7·985 kg
9. 15·010 kg **10.** 12·312 kg **11.** 10·055 kg **12.** 10·008 kg

Mass and weight UNIT 15

Adding kilograms and grams

Example

```
   kg    g
    1  1 1 5      Adding grams, we get
    2  2 7 5      195 g = 1 kg 195 g
+   1  8 0 5
   ─────────
    5  1 9 5   = 5·195 kg
```

If we add the numbers 1115, 2275 and 1805 we get the same digits 5195. Check this on your calculator. Adding kilograms and grams is simply adding 4-digit numbers.

Copy and complete these calculations.

1.
```
   kg    g
    2  5 1 5
    1  1 7 5
+   2  1 0 5
   ─────────
```

2.
```
   kg    g
    1  2 2 5
    1  4 1 5
+   2  6 5 0
   ─────────
```

3.
```
   kg    g
    1  3 0 5
    1  6 2 5
+   2  2 0 0
   ─────────
```

4.
```
   kg    g
    2  4 2 5
    1  7 5 5
+   2  3 0 0
   ─────────
```

5.
```
   kg    g
    5    4 5
    1  6 5 5
+      7 5 0
   ─────────
```

6.
```
   kg    g
    3    7 5
    1  2 1 5
+   2  1 0 0
   ─────────
```

7.
```
   kg    g
    2  1 5 0
    2  8 0 5
+   1  7 0 5
   ─────────
```

8.
```
   kg    g
    4  2 2 0
    1    9 5
+   2  1 0 5
   ─────────
```

9.
```
   kg    g
    1  7 5 0
    2  1 9 5
+   1  2 2 0
   ─────────
```

Now check your answers using a calculator.

UNIT 15   **Mass and weight**

Subtracting kilograms and grams

Examples

```
    kg   g              kg    g
   4  7⁴5̶¹0           1⁴5̶  ¹4⁷8̶¹0
 - 2  1 4 5         - 4  6 4 5
   ───────           ─────────
   2  6 0 5          10  8 3 5
```

Write these two problems. Use your calculator to subtract.

    4 750   and   15 480
  - 2 145   - 4 645
   ───────   ───────

What do you notice about the digits in the result and those in the examples above?

Copy and complete these calculations.

1. kg   g
    9 2 4 5
  - 2 1 3 4
    ───────

2. kg   g
   10 5 3 0
  - 2 3 6 4
    ───────

3. kg   g
    5 7 2 5
  - 1 4 7 5
    ───────

4. kg   g
    4 6 4 0
  - 1 3 5 5
    ───────

5. kg   g
    5 3 6 5
  - 2 7 4 0
    ───────

6. kg   g
    6 2 0 5
  - 1 4 5 5
    ───────

7. kg   g
   10 1 4 0
  - 2 3 7 5
    ───────

8. kg   g
   12 2 5 0
  - 6 4 6 5
    ───────

9. kg   g
    4 2 0 0
  - 1 5 2 5
    ───────

156

Mass and weight   UNIT 15

10.
```
   kg    g
    5  3 0 5
 -  1  2 6 0
   _____
```

11.
```
   kg    g
    6  7 5 0
 -  2  5 8 5
   _____
```

12.
```
   kg    g
   10    6 0
 - 1  2 5 5
   _____
```

Now check your answers using a calculator.

Multiplying kilograms and grams

Example

```
   kg    g
    2  4 1 5
 ×         3
   _____
    7  2 4 5
   _____
```

Multiplying grams: $5 × 3 = 15$
$1 × 3 = 3 + 1 = 4$
$4 × 3 = 12$, this is 1200 g
1200 g = 1 kg 200 g
Multiplying kilograms: $2 × 3 = 6$ $6 + 1 = 7$

Copy and complete these calculations.

1. 1 kg 215 g × 4
2. 2 kg 154 g × 3
3. 1 kg 45 g × 5

4. 2 kg 105 g × 4
5. 6 kg 95 g × 5
6. 3 kg 20 g × 6

7. 4 kg 215 g × 3
8. 3 kg 345 g × 3
9. 4 kg 120 g × 6

10. 2 kg 145 g × 8
11. 3 kg 145 g × 10
12. 4 kg 225 g × 10

UNIT 15 Mass and weight

Dividing kilograms and grams

Examples

```
        kg   g
         3  105
      ┌─────────
   5  │15  5²25
      │15   5
      ├─────────
      │ 0  025
      │    25
      │     0
```

15 kg 525 g ÷ 5 = 3 kg 105 g

```
        kg    g
         2   848
      ┌──────────
   5  │14   240
      │10  4000
      ├──────────
      │ 4  4²2⁴40
      │    40        8 × 5
      │    24
      │    20        4 × 5
      │    40
      │    40        8 × 5
      │     0
```

14 kg 240 g ÷ 5 = 2 kg 848 g

Copy and complete these calculations.

1. 3 kg 246 g ÷ 3

2. 5 kg 160 g ÷ 5

3. 4 kg 264 g ÷ 4

4. 3 kg 140 g ÷ 2

5. 3 kg 144 g ÷ 4

6. 4 kg 245 g ÷ 5

7. 2 kg 145 g ÷ 3

8. 1 kg 800 g ÷ 2

9. 10 kg 355 g ÷ 5

10. 15 kg 450 g ÷ 6

11. 20 kg 70 g ÷ 9

12. 6 kg 120 g ÷ 8

Mass and weight UNIT 15

Word problems

Work out the answers to these word problems. Show all your working.

1. In her shopping basket Devi carried $2\frac{1}{2}$ kg of fish, 3 kg 200 g of meat, 4 kg of potatoes and 250 g of cheese. How much did her groceries weigh?

2. How much heavier is a bag of potatoes weighing 15 kg than one weighing 12 kg 500 g?

3. (a) After using some of the potatoes from a 100 kg sack, Ram had 53·25 kg left. How much was used?

   (b) Ram divided the 53·25 kg equally into five smaller bags. How much was in each bag?

4. How much will you pay for $2\frac{1}{2}$ kg of fish at $15 per kg?

5. Curry powder is sold in packets of 100 g. How many packets can be made from 15 kg of curry powder?

16 Time

Reviewing five-minute intervals in time

Write the time shown on the clock faces.

1.
2.
3.
4.
5.
6.

Draw the hands of the clock to show the times on the digital watches.

7.
8.
9.
10.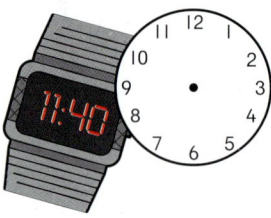
11.
12.

Time   UNIT 16

Reading the time to one-minute intervals

A digital watch   An analogue clock

They show the same time.

Write the times shown on these analogue clocks.

1.
2.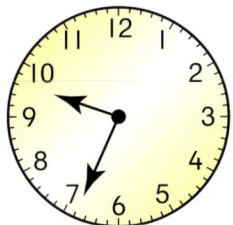
3.
4.
5.
6.

Draw the hands of the clock to show the time on the digital clocks.

7.
8.
9.
10.
11.
12.

UNIT 16 Time

Word problems

Remember: 6.34 a.m. means 34 minutes past 6 in the morning
or 26 minutes to 7 in the morning
and 6.34 p.m. means 34 minutes past 6 in the evening
or 26 minutes to 7 in the evening

Problem 1
A film show began at 1.15 p.m. and ended at 3.56 p.m. How long was the show?

    1.15 p.m. to 3.15 p.m. — 2 hours
    3.15 p.m. to 3.56 p.m. — 41 minutes
    The show lasted 2 hours 41 minutes.

Problem 2
A bus left the terminus at 11.15 a.m. and arrived at its final stop at 2.26 p.m. How long did the journey take?

		hours	minutes
11.15 a.m to 12 noon	— 45 minutes	0	45
12 noon to 2.26 p.m.	— 2 hours 26 minutes	2	26
Time for journey 45 minutes + 2 hours 26 minutes			
= 3 hours 11 minutes		3	11

(note: 60 minute = 1 hour)

Problem 3
The school display began at 10.15 a.m. and lasted for 3 hours 12 minutes. When did it end?

    3 hours from 10.15 a.m. is 1.15 p.m.
    12 minutes from 1.15 p.m. is 1.27 p.m.
    The display ended at 1.27 p.m.

Time UNIT 16

Work out the answers to these word problems. Show all your working.

1. How many hours and minutes are there between:
   (a) 9.15 a.m. and 11.26 a.m.?
   (b) 6.50 a.m. and 9.15 a.m.?
   (c) 10.20 a.m. and 2.12 p.m.?

2. A show began at 10.15 a.m. and finished at 1.28 p.m. How long did it last?

3. Molly and her parents left for the beach at 10.45 a.m. and returned home at 5.40 p.m. How long were they away from home?

4. A plane which left Port of Spain at 11.20 a.m. took 2 hours 42 minutes to reach Kingston. At what time did the plane arrive in Kingston?

5. A walking race began at 5.30 a.m. The times taken by the first five walkers to finish the race were:

   7 hours 10 minutes; 7 hours 22 minutes; 7 hours 59 minutes; 8 hours 30 minutes; 8 hours 40 minutes. Write the time when each arrived at the finish.

6. Ronnie left home at 7.05 a.m. and arrived at school at 7.45 a.m. Val left home at 7.45 a.m. and took 15 minutes less than Ronnie. What time did Val get to school?

Assessment

Assessment 9

1. Complete the table below.

g	kg g	kg
2455 g		
	1 kg 5 g	
		3·015 kg

Round each of the weights in questions 2–4 to (a) the nearest kg, (b) the nearest $\frac{1}{10}$ kg, (c) the nearest $\frac{1}{100}$ kg.

2. 2·516 kg   3. 1·340 kg   4. 12·125 kg

5. 5 kg 115 g + 1 kg 920 g = _____ kg _____ g = _____ kg.

6. By how much is 4 kg 250 g heavier than 1 kg 730 g?

7. A bag of corn weighs 55·2 kg. How much will six bags weigh?

8. How much should you pay for $3\frac{1}{2}$ kg of beef at $24 per kg?

9. Draw the hands of the clock to show the same time as the digital clock.

10. An Express bus left Port of Spain at 11.26 a.m. and arrived in San Fernando at 12.41 p.m. How long did the bus take to complete the trip?

11. A BWIA plane which left Piarco at 10.30 a.m. took 2 hours 42 minutes to reach Kingston, Jamaica. At what time did the aircraft arrive in Kingston?

17 Handling data

Average or mean

> The following table shows the number of girls wearing red ribbons to school during a week.
>
> | Monday | Tuesday | Wednesday | Thursday | Friday |
> |--------|---------|-----------|----------|--------|
> | 5 | 7 | 8 | 7 | 3 |
>
> The number of girls wearing red ribbons for the 5 days was 30. If we divide 30 by 5 the result is 6.
> 6 is called the **average** or **mean** of the five numbers 5, 7, 8, 7 and 3. To calculate the average or mean of a set of numbers we add all the numbers and divide the total by the number of numbers.

Find the mean or average of the following:

1. 62, 46, 79, 122, 81, 32
2. $15.00, $25.00, $18.00, $23.00, $9.00
3. 215 m, 192 m, 239 m, 82 m
4. 21, 39, 42, 28, 40, 37, 56
5. 36 kg, 28 kg, 33 kg, 26 kg, 27 kg

6. The attendance in class during one week was as follows: Monday – 28, Tuesday – 30, Wednesday – 30, Thursday – 27, Friday – 25.
   What was the average daily attendance?

7. The marks made in a test by 20 children were: 5, 7, 7, 4, 8, 9, 10, 10, 7, 6, 6, 4, 5, 8, 9, 7, 8, 5, 8, 7.
   What was the average mark made by a child?

UNIT 17 Handling data

Mode

> Let us look back to page 165 at the girls wearing red ribbons. The number which appears most often is 7. We say the **mode** of the set is 7.
>
> Let us look at the marks made by the 20 students in the test on page 165. We can make a count of the number of students making different marks.
>
> | Score on test | 4 | 5 | 6 | 7 | 8 | 9 | 10 |
> |---|---|---|---|---|---|---|---|
> | Number of students | 2 | 3 | 2 | 5 | 4 | 2 | 2 |
>
> The score which appears most often is 7. We say the mode of the scores is 7.

Write down the mode of each of these sets.

1. 3, 5, 1, 3, 2, 1, 3, 4, 5

2. 30, 27, 30, 25, 28, 27, 26, 25, 30

3. 14, 11, 10, 12, 16, 12, 15, 12, 13

4. 200, 300, 300, 100, 100, 400, 300

Write down the mode for each set of information.

5. Class size
- Infants 1   25
- Infants 2   25
- Standard 1   30
- Standard 2   28
- Standard 3   30
- Standard 4   30
- Standard 5   35

6. Newspapers delivered
- Monday   25
- Tuesday   25
- Wednesday   24
- Thursday   22
- Friday   25
- Saturday   35
- Sunday   35

Handling data UNIT 17

The pie chart

This percentage chart was shown earlier on page 117. It shows the results of a survey of people's favourite types of TV programmes.

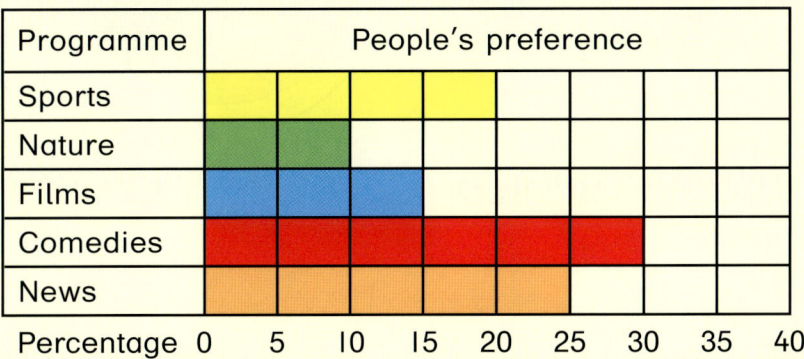

We can show the same information on a pie chart.

- Draw a circle of radius about 5 cm.

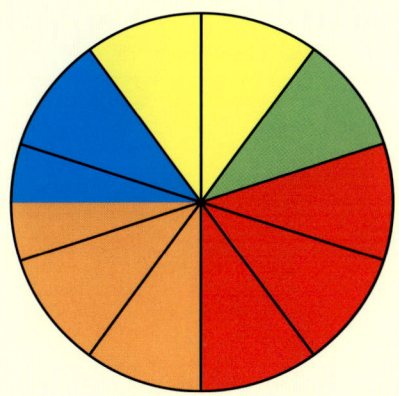

You will need: a pair of compasses, ruler, coloured pencils.

- Divide the circle into tenths, since we are showing percentages.
- Colour in the chart to show the choices.
- Write in the choices and the percentages.

167

UNIT 17 Handling data

Look at the pie chart on the right.
It shows a class of 24 children of
whom 12 liked red, six green and
six yellow. We did not divide this
circle into tenths.

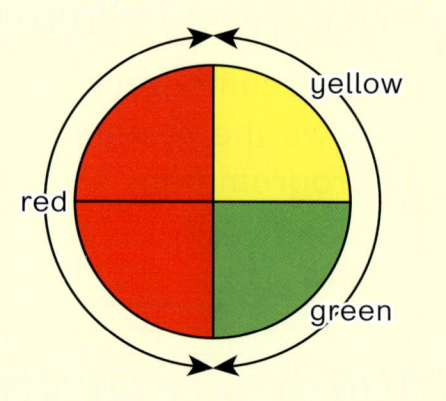

12 is $\frac{1}{2}$ of 24 and 6 is $\frac{1}{4}$ of 24.
We need to divide the circle into
halves and quarters only.
Our circle or pie is therefore coloured
$\frac{1}{2}$ red, $\frac{1}{4}$ green and $\frac{1}{4}$ yellow.

Here is another pie chart.
This one is divided into eighths.
It shows a class of 40 children and
their choice of ice cream.

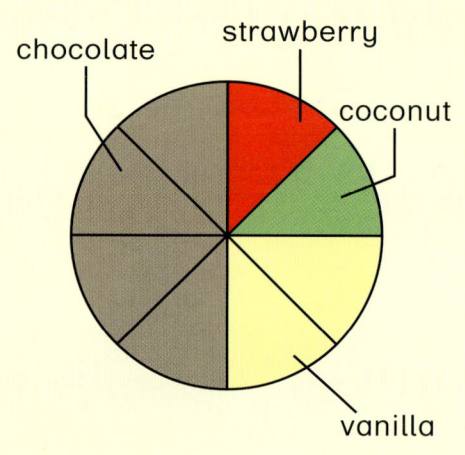

What fraction liked chocolate?
How many liked chocolate?
What fraction like vanilla?
How many liked vanilla?
What fraction liked coconut?
How many liked coconut?
What fraction liked strawberry?
How many liked strawberry?

1. In a class of 32 girls, 16 wore yellow ribbons, eight wore red, four green and four blue.

   Draw a pie chart to show this information.

Handling data UNIT 17

A man spends his weekly wages as shown in the pie chart.
He spends $200 on food.
How much does he spend on travel and rent?
How much does he save?

The pie chart is divided into halves and quarters.
He spends $\frac{1}{4}$ on food, $\frac{1}{2}$ on travel and rent and he saves $\frac{1}{4}$.

$\frac{1}{4}$ of his weekly wage is $200.
Therefore $\frac{1}{2}$ of his weekly wage will be $400.

So, the man spends $400 on travel and rent, and he saves $200.

2. The chart below shows how a man spends his monthly salary.
   (a) If he pays $300 income tax every month, how much does he spend on each of the other items?
   (b) How much does he save?
   (c) What is his total salary for the month?

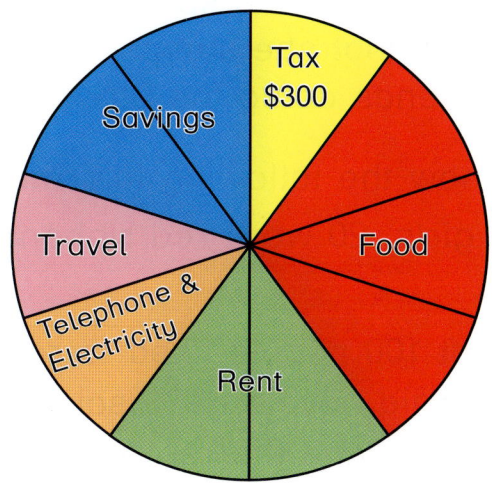

169

UNIT 17 Handling data

3. Look at the circle below. It is divided into 24 parts. Count the parts. Each part represents 1 hour a day.

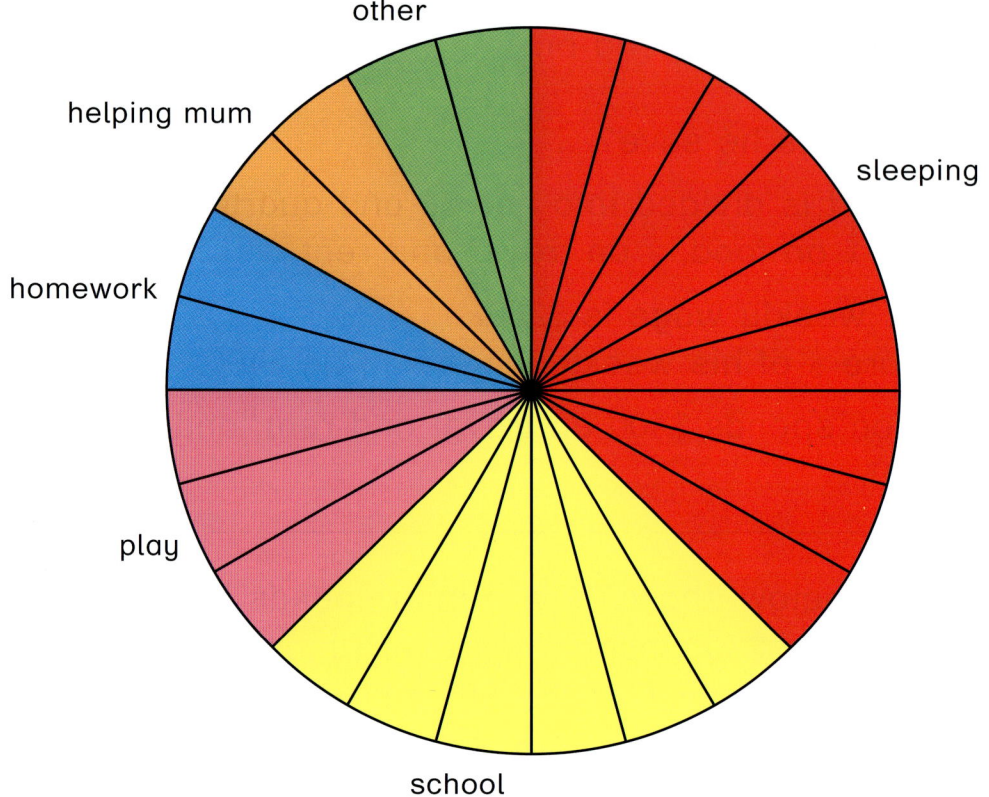

This diagram shows how Mala spends her day. If you count the sections you see that she sleeps for 9 hours. Say how many hours she spends doing the other things.

Draw pie charts to show the following information:

4. In a count of 100 girls, 20 wore red ribbons, 25 blue, 40 white and the rest pink.

5. In a survey of what 100 people liked to read, 25% said newspapers, 40% said novels, 10% science fiction, 15% adventure stories and the rest sports magazines.

End-of-year test – Standard 4

1. Write in words:

   (a) 5050   (b) 105 501

2. Write numerals for:

   (a) ten thousand and fifteen,
   (b) one million, five thousand and fifty.

3. 19 515 people attended the World Cup qualifying match at the stadium.
   Write this number (a) to the nearest thousand,
   (b) to the nearest ten thousand.

4.
   A
   | 1 | 5 | 0 | 4 | 2 | 3 |

   B

   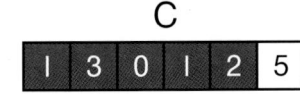
   C

   The meters show the distances in kilometres travelled by three cars A, B and C.

   (a) Which of these cars has travelled most?
   (b) How much further did car C travel than car B?

5. There are 132 seats in each row at the football stadium. How many people can sit in 25 rows?

6. Soft drinks are sold in crates of 24 bottles. How many crates must the school buy for each of the 600 students to get a drink?

7. Arrange these fractions in ascending order:

   $\frac{3}{5}, \frac{1}{2}, \frac{3}{4}, \frac{7}{10}$

End-of-year test

8. What fraction of (a) 60 is 36 (b) 10 m is 200 cm?

9. One quarter of Sammy's weekly allowance was $1.50. What was Sammy's full allowance?

10. Find (a) $3\frac{1}{2} + 1\frac{2}{5}$ (b) $5\frac{1}{2} - 2\frac{2}{5}$

11. How many litres are there in $\frac{2}{5}$ of 40 litres?

12. A cake weighing $1\frac{1}{2}$ kg was divided into 10 equal pieces. How much did each piece weigh?

13. Through what angle do you turn when you change direction from facing West to facing East?

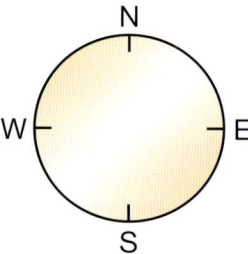

14. The perimeter of a triangle is 20·0 cm. One side is 5·8 cm long; another is 6·4 cm. What is the length of the third side?

15. Round 21·59

    (a) to the nearest whole number,
    (b) to the nearest tenth.

16. Copy and fill in the blank spaces

    115 cm = _____ m _____ cm = _____ m

17. Mavis cut off 2·75 m from a piece of ribbon 5·60 m long. What length of ribbon was left?

End-of-year test

18. Write as fractions in their lowest terms:
(a) 15%   (b) 75%

19. In a class of 40 children, 22 are girls. What per cent are boys?

20. Fifteen sacks of potatoes weigh 450 kg. What would 24 sacks weigh?

21. A household worker is paid $9.00 per hour. She works 5 hours a day for 6 days of the week. How much money does she earn in a week?

22. How much interest will my money earn if I invest $5000 in Regal Bank for 2 years at 5% per annum?

23.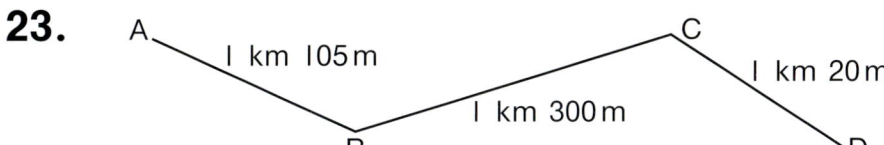

What is the distance travelled in going from A to D?

24. Use the relationship circumference = diameter × 3 to find the circumference of a circle of radius 4·2 cm.

25. Find the area of this triangle.

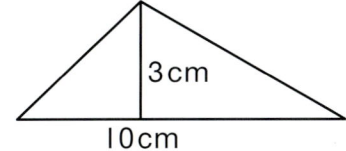

End-of-year test

26. Find the volume of this box.

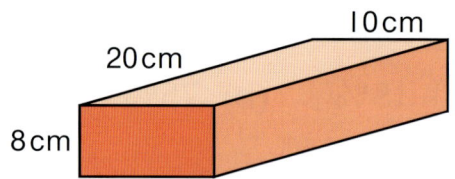

27. What is the cost of paving the pathway around the playing field at $25 per square metre?
The pathway is 2 m wide.

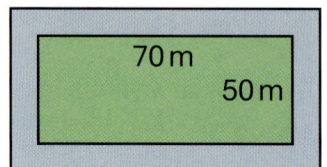

28. Draw the hands of the clock to show the time on the radio clock.

29. The numbers shown here represent the number of children in each of eight different families: 5, 3, 3, 7, 4, 5, 2, 3.
What is the average number of children in a family?

30. The pie chart shows children's choices of milkshake.

(a) Which flavour was the most popular choice?
(b) What fraction of the children chose the most popular flavour?
(c) Which flavours were chosen by the same number of children?
(d) There were 40 children in the class. How many chose strawberry?

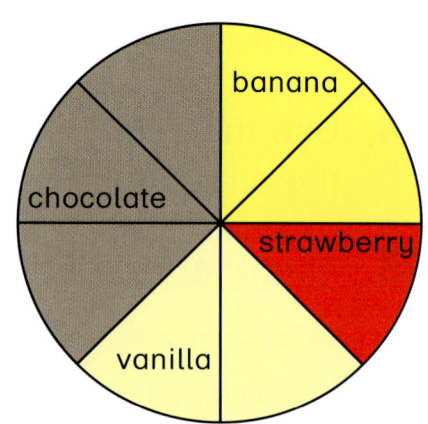

174

18 Angles/Triangles/Polygons

Measuring angles

Remember that your set square and your circle folded in quarters can be used to measure right angles (see page 84).

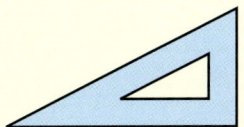 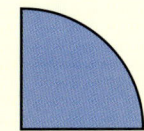

You will need: a set square, paper circle.

The shape on the right is a quadrilateral.
Use your set square or folded circle to find out which angles are smaller than a right angle and which are larger.
The dotted lines show the position of the set square and the quarter circle when measuring the angles.

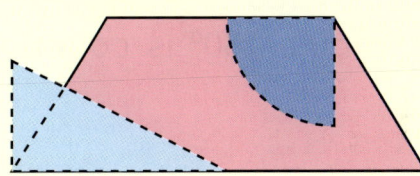

Copy or trace the shapes below.
Use your set square or quarter circle to measure the angles in the shapes below (1–6).
Draw a tiny square, □, in the angles that are right angles.
Put a small dot, •, in the angles that are less than a right angle.
Put a small × in the angles that are larger than a right angle.

1.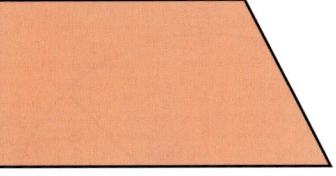

2.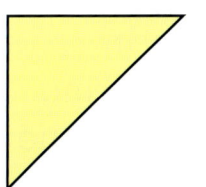

3.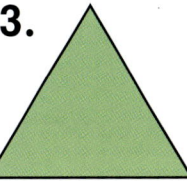

4.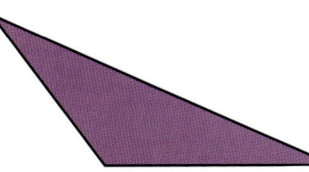

5.

6.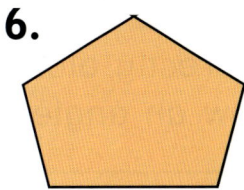

UNIT 18 Angles/Triangles/Polygons

Using a paper protractor

Remember: a complete turn is four right angles or 360°

$\frac{1}{2}$ a turn is two right angles or 180°

$\frac{1}{4}$ turn is one right angle or 90°

$\frac{1}{2}$ a right angle is 45°

A turn from East to West or from West to East is a turn through 180°.
The angle 180° is called a **straight angle**. Can you say why?

You will need: card, ruler, scissors.

- Cut a circle from a piece of card. The circle should measure about 6 cm across.
- Fold the shape in half, then in quarters, and then eighths.
- Draw along the folding lines and cut the shape in two halves.
- Each half should now look like this.

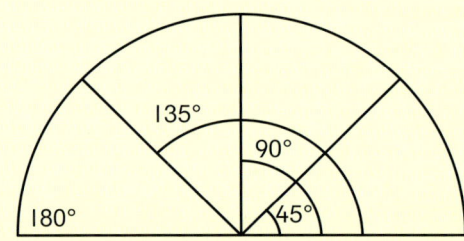

We can now use this shape to measure and draw angles of 45°, 90°, 135° and 180°.

Measure the angle drawn in red on the right. Place your measuring shape exactly as is shown in the picture. The two red lines which make the angle you are measuring fit directly along the lines which show an angle of 90° on your shape.

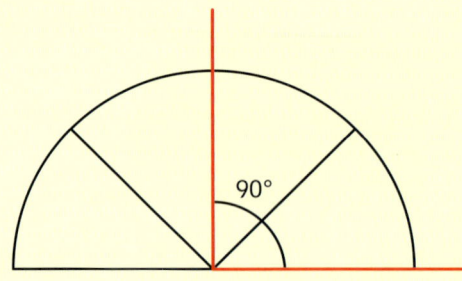

Angles/Triangles/Polygons   UNIT 18

Remember: The lines which form an angle are called the **arms** of the angle. The point where the **arms** meet is called the **vertex** of the angle.

We can also measure angles in an anti-clockwise direction.
What do the angles in this drawing measure?

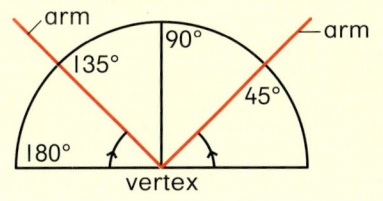

Use your shape to measure these angles.

1.
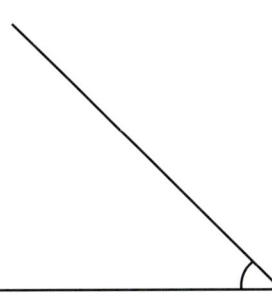

2.
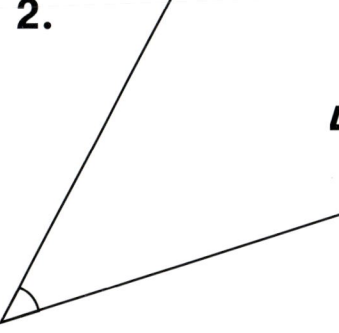

3.
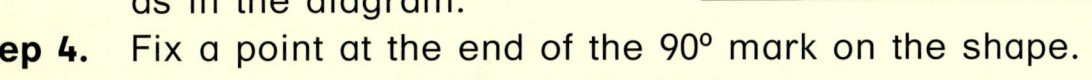

4.
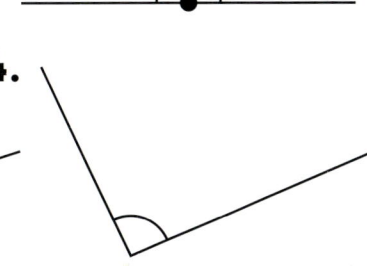

We can also use our shape to draw angles.
To draw an angle of 90°, follow these steps:

Step 1. Fix any point which will be the vertex of the angle.
Step 2. Draw one arm from the vertex.
Step 3. Place your shape exactly as in the diagram.
Step 4. Fix a point at the end of the 90° mark on the shape.
Step 5. Remove the shape and draw the line through the point and the vertex.

Use your shape to draw other angles of:

5. 90°   **6.** 45°   **7.** 180°

177

UNIT 18 Angles/Triangles/Polygons

Using the protractor

We measure angles with a **protractor**. Your card shape is a simple protractor.
The protractor you use will look like the one in the picture.

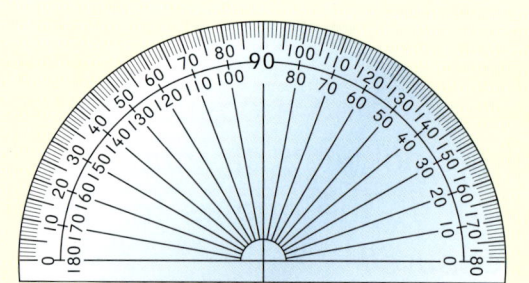

The protractor allows you to measure in a clockwise or an anti-clockwise direction.
You can see this from the drawings below.

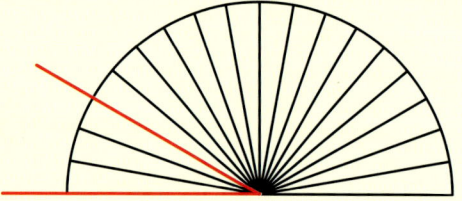   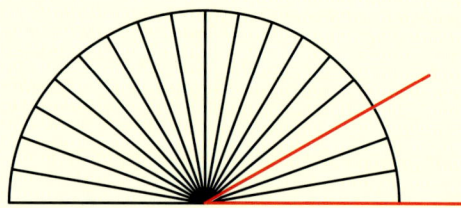

Use a protractor to measure these angles. Try clockwise and anti-clockwise measurements for each angle.

1.
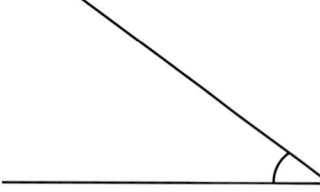

2.
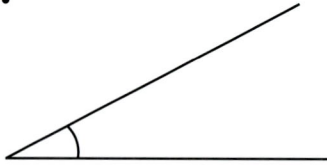

3.
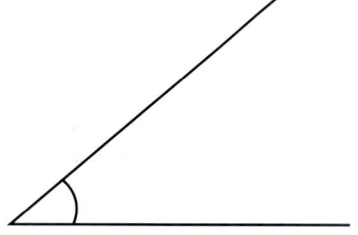

4.
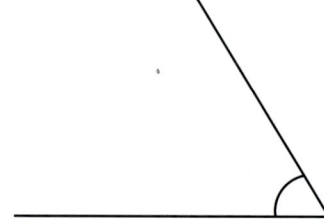

Angles/Triangles/Polygons UNIT 18

Obtuse and acute angles

> Angles which are less than 90° are called **acute angles**.
> Angles which are greater than 90° but less than 180° are called **obtuse angles**.

Measure each of these angles with your protractor and write whether it is a right angle, acute angle or obtuse angle.

1.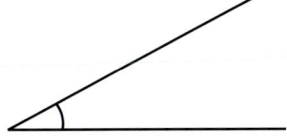

2.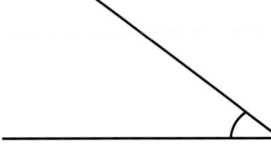

3.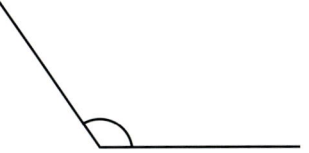

4.

5.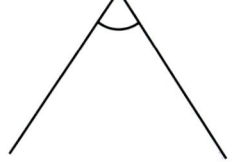

6.

7.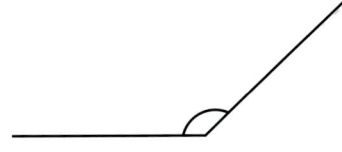

8.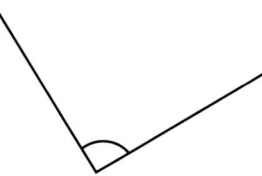

9.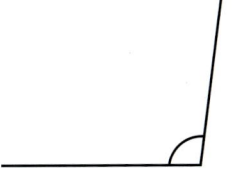

10.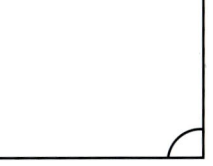

179

UNIT 18 Angles/Triangles/Polygons

Reviewing angles

> **Remember:** a right angle measures 90 degrees (90°)
> an acute angle is less than 90°
> an obtuse angle is more than 90° and less than 180°
>
> 90° — a right angle
> 180° — a straight angle
> 360° — a complete turn, four right angles

Use your protractor to measure these angles.

1.
2.
3.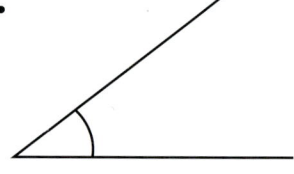
4.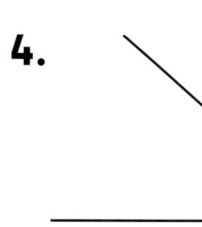
5.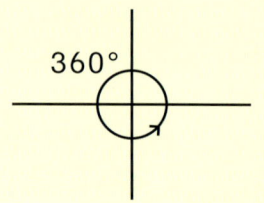

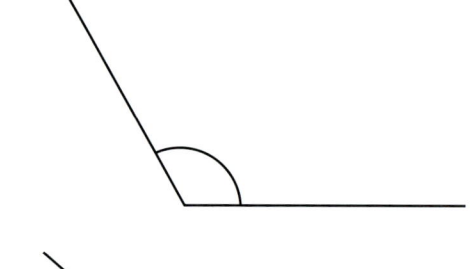

> Lines which make right angles are **perpendicular** to each other.

6. Which pairs of lines in the questions above are perpendicular?

7. Which angles in the questions above are (a) obtuse, (b) acute?

Angles/Triangles/Polygons UNIT 18

More about angles

You will need: a protractor.

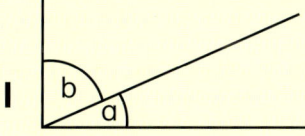

Fig. 1

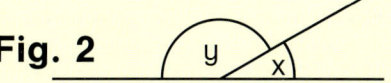

Fig. 2

In Fig. 1 a + b = 90°
Angles a and b are called **complementary angles**; they **add up to 90°**.

In Fig. 2 x + y = 180°
Angles x and y are called **supplementary angles**; they **add up to 180°**.

Remember: angles a, b and x are **acute angles**; they measure **less than 90°**. Angle y is an **obtuse angle**; it measures **more than 90° but less than 180°**.

Look at Fig. 3.

Remember: a complete turn measures 360°.

There are two angles p and q.
Measure p. Calculate the size of q.
An angle like q which measures **more than 180°** is called a **reflex angle**.

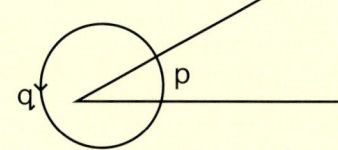

Fig. 3

Look at Fig. 4.
Two lines when they cut each other make four angles.
Measure the angles a, b, c and d.
What do you notice?
The angles a and c are called **vertically opposite** angles.
The angles b and d are also **vertically opposite** angles.

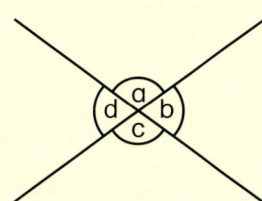

Fig. 4

181

UNIT 18 Angles/Triangles/Polygons

1. (a) Draw any two lines cutting each other.
   (b) Measure the vertically opposite angles.

In the diagrams below **measure** x and **calculate** y.

2.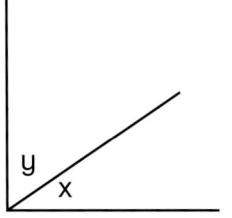

3.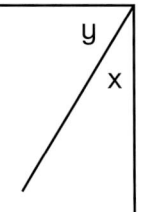

4.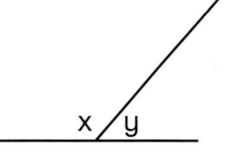

5.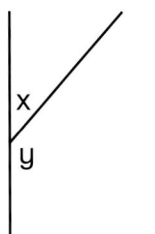

6.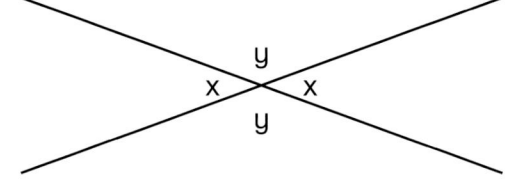

7.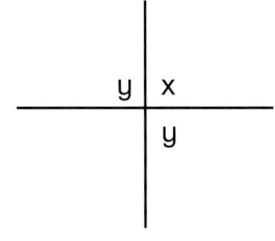

8.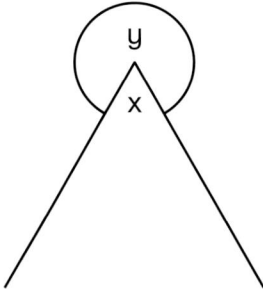

9. What angles are complementary to these?
   15°, 30°, 45°, 50°, 75°.

10. What angles are supplementary to these?
    15°, 45°, 60°, 105°, 150°

Angles/Triangles/Polygons   UNIT 18

Perpendicular and parallel lines

Remember: when two lines make a right angle with each other these lines are **perpendicular**.

Look at lines AB and CD below; they will never meet.
They are called **parallel lines**.

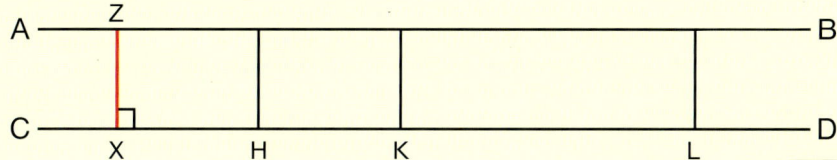

Draw a perpendicular line at X on the bottom line CD.
Let the perpendicular touch the top line at Z. What angle is made at Z?
The distance ZX shown in red is the distance between the parallel lines.
What can you say about the distance between the parallel lines at positions H, K, L? Measure these distances.

The distance between two parallel lines never changes.

Lines drawn on level or flat ground are **horizontal lines**.
A surface like a table top when standing normally is a **horizontal** surface; it is **parallel** to the ground.
Lines drawn upright from the ground are **vertical lines**.
Vertical lines are **perpendicular** to lines on the ground or horizontal lines.

Look around the classroom. List things which are examples of perpendicular lines and parallel lines.

183

UNIT 18 Angles/Triangles/Polygons

Drawing squares and rectangles

Remember we have been using a set square to measure right angles.
We can also use it to draw right angles, especially when constructing squares or rectangles.

To draw a rectangle 6 cm by 2 cm:
- Draw a horizontal line 6 cm long.
- Use your set square to draw a perpendicular line at each end of the line.
- Mark off the lengths 2 cm on both perpendicular lines (at **a** and **b**).
- Join **a** and **b**.

You will need: a set square, a ruler.

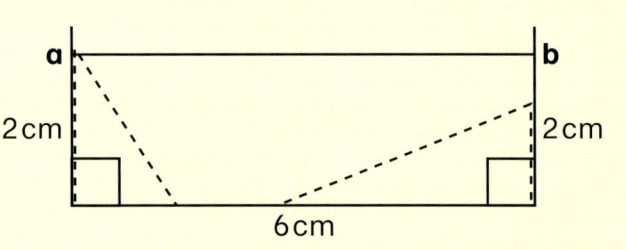

Use a ruler and set square to measure and copy these rectangles.

1.

2.

3.

4.

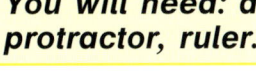 

Angles/Triangles/Polygons UNIT 18

Triangles and their angles

Measure the lengths of the sides of the triangles A, B and C below.
Measure the angles of the triangles.
Make a table of the results as shown.

You will need: a protractor, ruler.

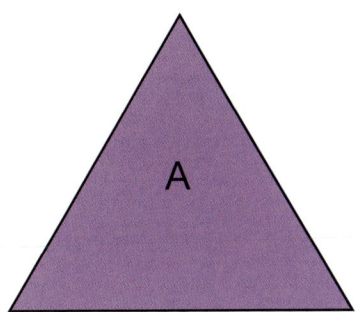 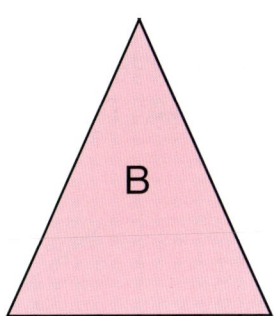 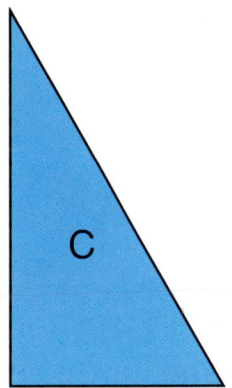

Triangle	lengths of sides	angles	sum of angles
A			
B			
C			

Triangle A has three equal sides; it is called an **equilateral triangle**. What do you notice about the angles of an equilateral triangle?

Triangle B has two equal sides; it is called an **isosceles triangle**. What can you say about the angles of an isosceles triangle?

Triangle C is called a **right-angled triangle**; one of its angles is a right angle. What statement can you make about the other two angles of the right-angled triangle?

Remember: when two angles add up to 90° these angles are called **complementary angles**.

Make a statement that is true for the angles of all three triangles.

185

UNIT 18 Angles/Triangles/Polygons

Drawing right-angled triangles

You will need: a ruler, set square or protractor.

Draw a right-angled triangle with perpendicular sides 8 cm and 6 cm.

Usually when we are drawing a right-angled triangle we draw one of the perpendicular sides in the horizontal position and draw the other in the vertical position. Suppose we choose the horizontal side to be 8 cm.

- Draw a horizontal line 8 cm long.
- With your set square or protractor draw the perpendicular line 6 cm long.
- Join the end points of both lines.

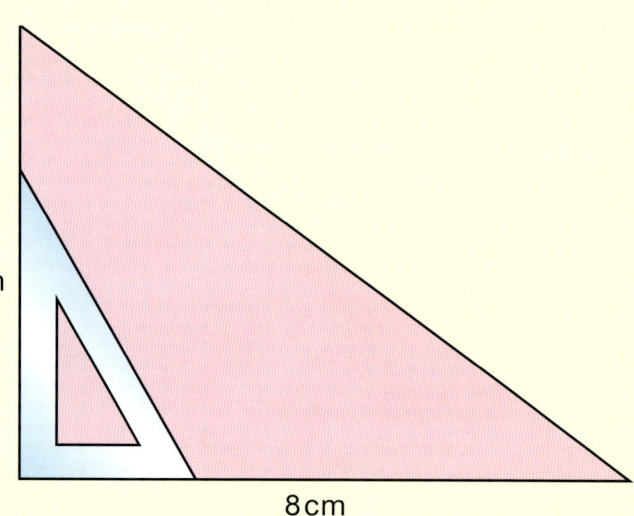

The horizontal side of the triangle is called the **base**, the vertical side the **perpendicular** or **height** or **altitude** and the third side the **hypotenuse**.

Draw right-angled triangles using these measurements. Write the length of the hypotenuse.

1. base 3 cm, perpendicular 4 cm
2. base 5 cm, height 12 cm
3. base 4 cm, altitude 6 cm
4. base 2·5 cm, height 3 cm
5. base 5·5 cm, height 4 cm
6. base 4·5 cm, height 3·5 cm

186

Angles/Triangles/Polygons UNIT 18

Draw the right-angled triangles shown below. Begin with the horizontal lines and then draw the vertical lines. Finally draw the red line. The red line is called the **hypotenuse**.

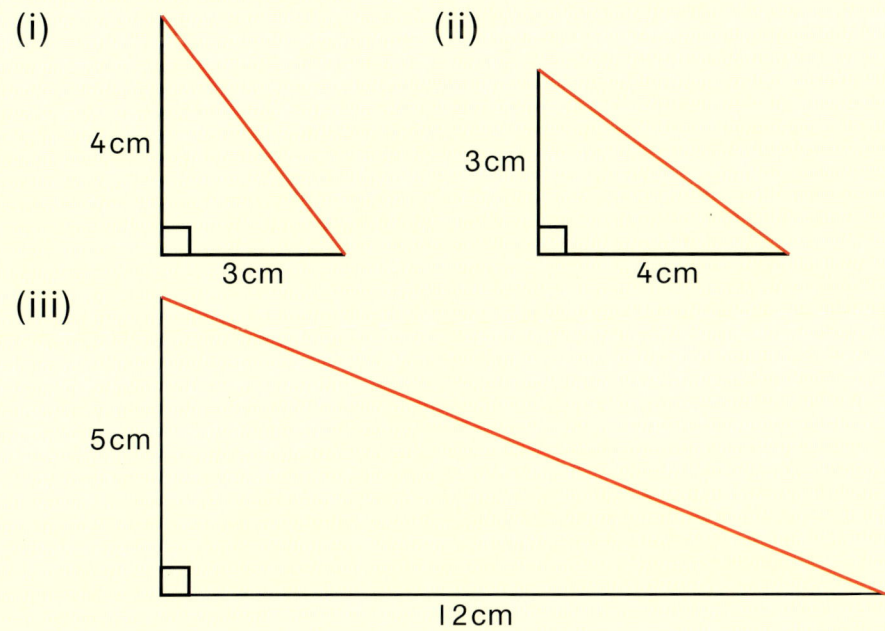

Measure the lengths of the red lines.
In every case you will see that if you square the lengths of the sides making the right angle, the squares add up to the square of the hypotenuse.

(i) $4^2 + 3^2 = 25 = 5^2$ (ii) $3^2 + 4^2 = 25 = 5^2$
(iii) $5^2 + 12^2 = 25 + 144 = 169 = 13^2$

This is known as **Pythagoras' rule** for the right-angled triangle.

Say which of these triangles are right-angled triangles. The numbers given are the unit lengths of the sides.

7. 7, 24, 25   **8.** 6, 8, 9   **9.** 8, 5, 17   **10.** 10, 8, 6

UNIT 18 Angles/Triangles/Polygons

Find the hypotenuse in these triangles. Use your calculator to work out the square roots.

11. base 4 cm, perpendicular 6 cm
12. base 5 cm, perpendicular 6 cm

Scalene triangles

The triangle below is called a **scalene triangle**.
Measure the length of its sides.

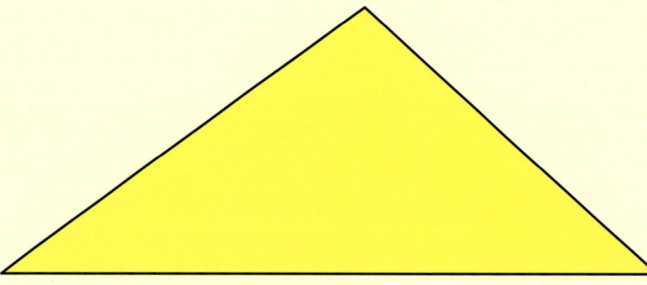

In a scalene triangle all the sides are different lengths.
Measure the angles of the triangle.
Find the sum of the angles.
How does it compare with the sum of the angles of other triangles?

In any triangle the sum of the angles is 180°.

Calculate the size of the angles marked in these triangles.

1. 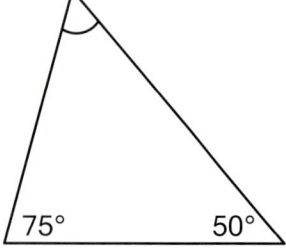   2. 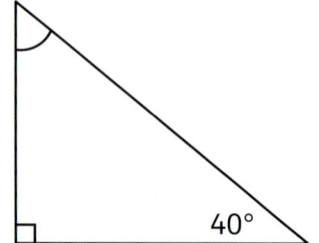   3.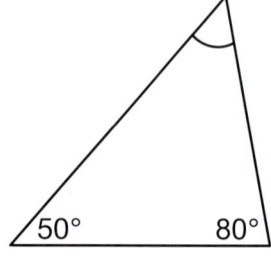

188

Angles/Triangles/Polygons UNIT 18

4.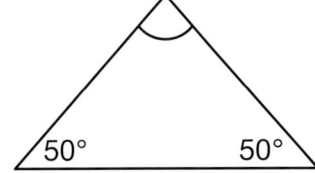

5.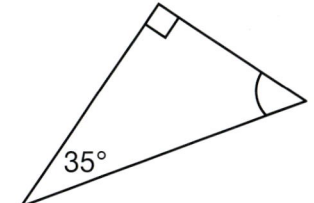

6.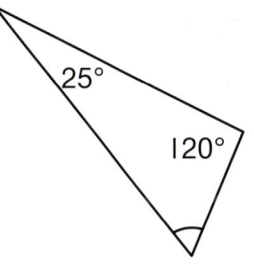

Drawing other triangles

If you know two sides of a triangle and the angle between those sides you can draw the triangle.

Example
- Draw the base (horizontal side) 6 cm long.
- Draw an angle 50° and mark off 5 cm along the line.
- Join the end points of the base and 50° line.
- You can now measure the remaining side and angles of the triangle.

You will need: a ruler, protractor.

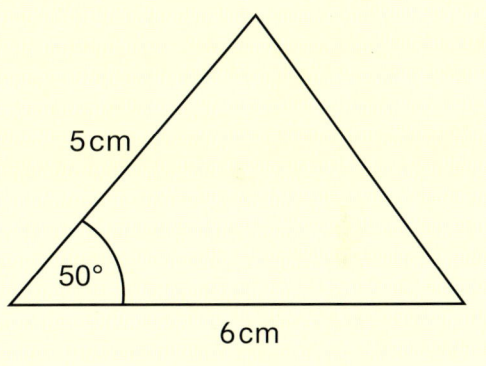

Draw the triangles with the following sides and angles between the sides.
Measure the remaining side and angles of the triangles.

1. 3 cm, 5 cm, 30°
2. 4 cm, 5 cm, 40°
3. 6 cm, 2 cm, 60°
4. 4 cm, 6 cm, 45°
5. 3·2 cm, 4·5 cm, 30°
6. 4·2 cm, 3·6 cm, 45°

UNIT 18 Angles/Triangles/Polygons

We can also draw triangles when we know two angles and any side.

You will need: a ruler, protractor.

Example
- Draw the base 6 cm long.
- Draw angles 40° and 70° and let the angle lines meet.
- The angle lines meet at the third vertex of the triangle.

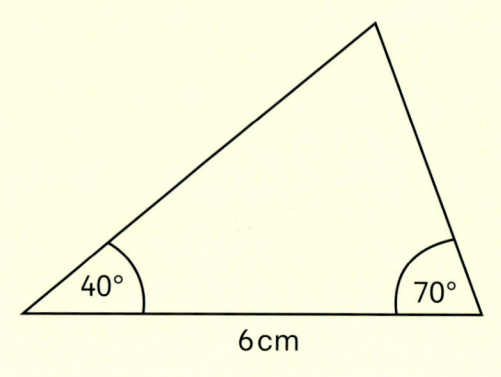

Draw the following triangles and measure the remaining sides and angle.

7. 5 cm, 30°, 50°

8. 6 cm, 50°, 70°

9. 4·5 cm, 75°, 60°

10. 4 cm, 50°, 70°

11. 5·5 cm, 45°, 75°

12. 6·5 cm, 45°, 55°

Calculate the third angle of each triangle as a check on your measurements.

Angles/Triangles/Polygons UNIT 18

Polygons

> Closed shapes which are made by straight lines are called **polygons**.
> A regular polygon has all its sides equal in length and all its angles equal in size.

Copy and complete the table below.
Use a sketch of the shapes below for your table.
Measure sides and angles from the shapes. Measure sides to the nearest millimetre and angles to the nearest degree.

Sketch of polygon	name of polygon	number of sides	number of angles	number of vertices	length of sides	size of angles

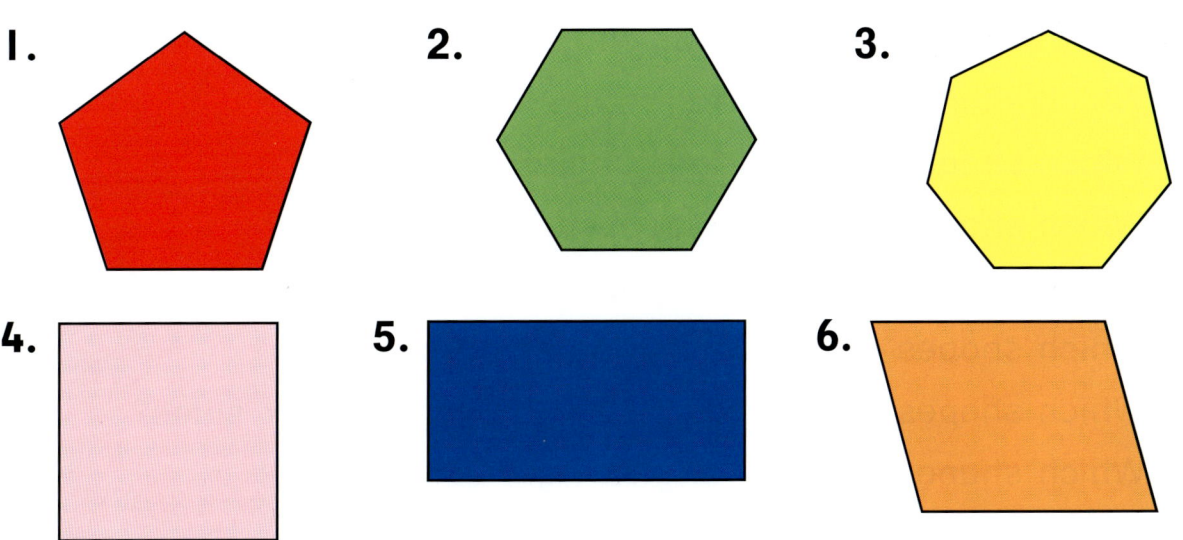

7. Say which of the polygons are not regular polygons.

UNIT 18   Angles/Triangles/Polygons

Special quadrilaterals

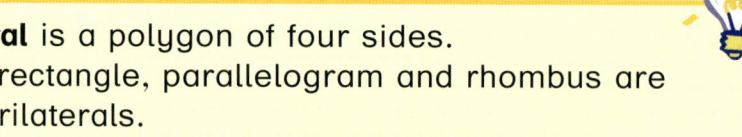

> **Remember:** a **quadrilateral** is a polygon of four sides.
> The square, rectangle, parallelogram and rhombus are special quadrilaterals.

(a)    (b)

(c)    (d)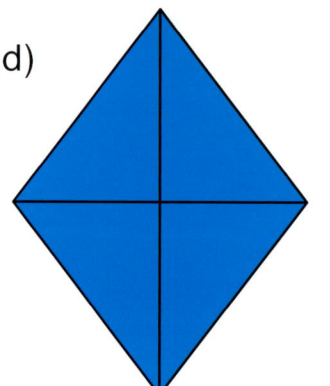

Draw the shapes (a–d) and name them.

Measure the sides of all four shapes.
Measure the angles of all four shapes.

1. Which shapes have all four sides equal?
2. Which shapes have all four angles equal?
3. Which shapes have only opposite angles equal?
4. Which shapes have only opposite sides equal?
5. Which shapes have opposite sides parallel?
6. Which shapes have sides perpendicular to other sides?
7. Which shapes have all angles right angles?
8. Which shapes have both diagonals equal?
9. Which shapes have diagonals at right angles to each other?

Angles/Triangles/Polygons   UNIT 18

Nets

Which of these nets make pyramids?

1.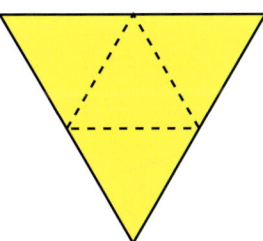

2.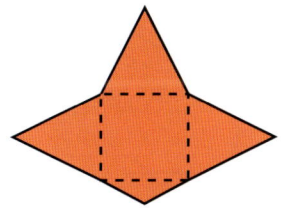

3.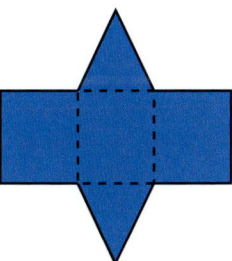

4.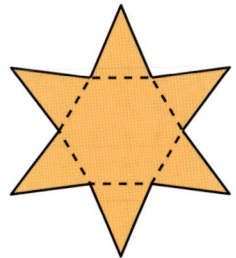

5.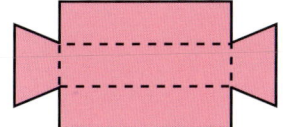

6.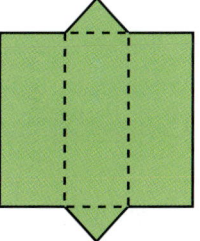

Draw the solids which these nets represent.

7.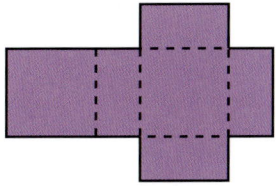

8.

9.

10.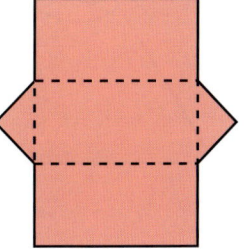

11.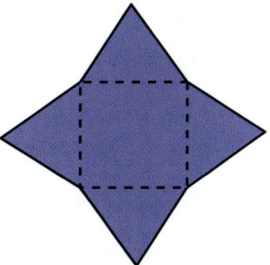

193

Assessment

Assessment 10

Measure angle x and calculate angle y.

1.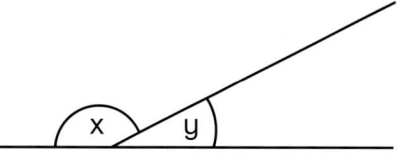

2.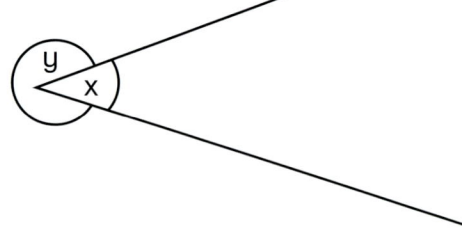

3. What is the size of the angles marked with the 0?

   (a)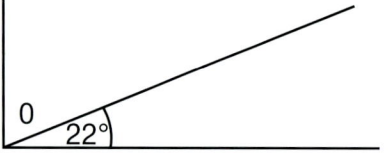

   (b)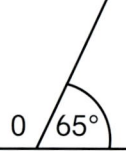

4. What is the size of the angles marked with the x?

   (a)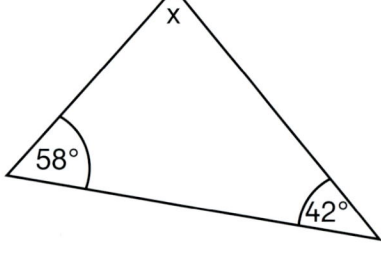

   (b)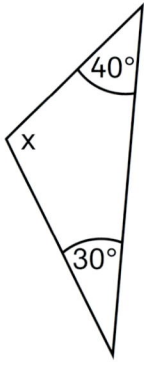

5. This triangle on the right is an isosceles triangle. What is the size of each angle at the base of the triangle?

   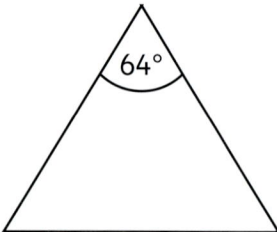

6. Draw a right-angled triangle with base 6 cm and perpendicular height 5 cm. Measure the hypotenuse and the other angles.

19 Multiplication and division of fractions

Multiplying a fraction by a fraction

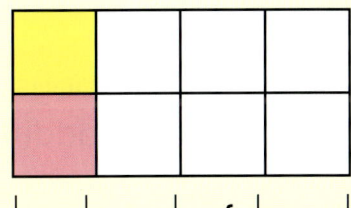

$\frac{1}{4} \times \frac{1}{2} = \frac{1}{2}$ of $\frac{1}{4} = \frac{1}{8}$

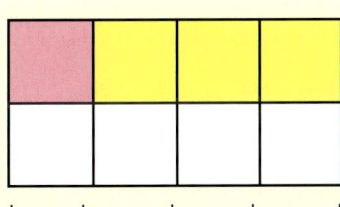

$\frac{1}{2} \times \frac{1}{4} = \frac{1}{4}$ of $\frac{1}{2} = \frac{1}{8}$

$\frac{1}{4} \times \frac{1}{2} = \frac{1}{2} \times \frac{1}{4}$

$\frac{2}{3} \times \frac{1}{4} = \frac{1}{4}$ of $\frac{2}{3}$

$\frac{2}{3} \times \frac{1}{4} = \frac{2}{12}$ or $\frac{1}{6}$

$\frac{1}{4} \times \frac{2}{3} = \frac{2}{3}$ of $\frac{1}{4}$

$\frac{1}{4} \times \frac{2}{3} = \frac{2}{12}$ or $\frac{1}{6}$

$\frac{2}{3} \times \frac{1}{4} = \frac{1}{4} \times \frac{2}{3}$

$\frac{3}{4} \times \frac{2}{3} = \frac{2}{3}$ of $\frac{3}{4} = \frac{6}{12}$ or $\frac{1}{2}$

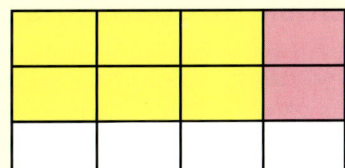

$\frac{2}{3} \times \frac{3}{4} = \frac{3}{4}$ of $\frac{2}{3} = \frac{6}{12}$ or $\frac{1}{2}$

$\frac{3}{4} \times \frac{2}{3} = \frac{2}{3} \times \frac{3}{4}$

Let us look at our results.

$\frac{1}{4} \times \frac{1}{2} = \frac{1}{8}$ $\frac{1}{2} \times \frac{1}{4} = \frac{1}{8}$

$\frac{2}{3} \times \frac{1}{4} = \frac{2}{12}$ $\frac{1}{4} \times \frac{2}{3} = \frac{2}{12}$

$\frac{3}{4} \times \frac{2}{3} = \frac{6}{12}$ $\frac{2}{3} \times \frac{3}{4} = \frac{6}{12}$

Look at the numerator of the fractions we are multiplying and look at the numerator of the product. What do you observe? Look at the denominators now. What do you observe?

UNIT 19 Multiplication and division of fractions

When multiplying fractions we must multiply the numerators to get the numerator of the product fraction, and we must multiply the denominators to get the denominator.

You should note also that multiplication of fractions obeys the commutative law just as with addition of fractions or addition and multiplication of whole numbers.

$$\tfrac{1}{4} \times \tfrac{1}{2} = \tfrac{1}{2} \times \tfrac{1}{4} \text{ just as } \tfrac{1}{4} + \tfrac{1}{2} = \tfrac{1}{2} + \tfrac{1}{4}$$

or $2 + 3 = 3 + 2$ and $2 \times 3 = 3 \times 2$

Example $\tfrac{4}{5} \times \tfrac{2}{3} = \tfrac{4 \times 2}{5 \times 3} = \tfrac{8}{15}$

Copy and complete.

1. $\tfrac{1}{2} \times \tfrac{1}{3}$
2. $\tfrac{1}{3} \times \tfrac{1}{4}$
3. $\tfrac{1}{4} \times \tfrac{1}{5}$
4. $\tfrac{1}{5} \times \tfrac{1}{6}$
5. $\tfrac{2}{3} \times \tfrac{3}{4}$
6. $\tfrac{2}{5} \times \tfrac{1}{3}$
7. $\tfrac{3}{4} \times \tfrac{4}{5}$
8. $\tfrac{5}{6} \times \tfrac{3}{4}$

Look back at questions 7 and 8 in the exercise above.

7. $\tfrac{3}{4} \times \tfrac{4}{5} = \tfrac{3 \times 4}{4 \times 5} = \tfrac{12}{20} = \tfrac{3}{5}$, dividing both numerator and denominator by 5.

We did not have to multiply out to get the product; we could have divided by 4 before multiplying, so that $\tfrac{3 \times 4}{4 \times 5} = \tfrac{3}{5}$

In the same way

8. $\tfrac{5}{6} \times \tfrac{3}{4} = \tfrac{5 \times \overset{1}{3}}{\underset{2}{6} \times 4} = \tfrac{5}{8}$

Copy and complete.

9. $\tfrac{1}{2} \times \tfrac{2}{3}$
10. $\tfrac{1}{3} \times \tfrac{3}{4}$
11. $\tfrac{4}{5} \times \tfrac{1}{4}$
12. $\tfrac{5}{6} \times \tfrac{1}{5}$
13. $\tfrac{1}{3} \times \tfrac{3}{5}$
14. $\tfrac{4}{9} \times \tfrac{1}{4}$
15. $\tfrac{5}{12} \times \tfrac{1}{5}$
16. $\tfrac{1}{6} \times \tfrac{6}{7}$
17. $\tfrac{2}{3} \times \tfrac{3}{10}$
18. $\tfrac{3}{4} \times \tfrac{11}{12}$
19. $\tfrac{3}{5} \times \tfrac{2}{3}$
20. $\tfrac{3}{4} \times \tfrac{7}{12}$

Multiplication and division of fractions UNIT 19

Multiplying a mixed number by a fraction

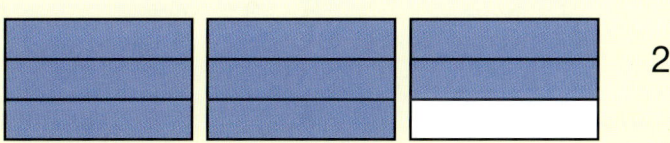

$$2\tfrac{2}{3} \times \tfrac{3}{4} = \tfrac{24}{12} = 2$$

The diagram above shows $2\tfrac{2}{3} \times \tfrac{3}{4}$

Remember $2\tfrac{2}{3} \times \tfrac{3}{4}$ means $\tfrac{3}{4}$ of $2\tfrac{2}{3}$ which we see is $\tfrac{24}{12}$

So that $2\tfrac{2}{3} \times \tfrac{3}{4}$ which is $\tfrac{8}{3} \times \tfrac{3}{4} = \tfrac{24}{12} = 2$

The rule for multiplying fractions also applies when multiplying a mixed number by a fraction or an improper fraction by a proper fraction. And, since the commutative law holds for multiplication of fractions, the rule for multiplying fractions also applies for multiplying a fraction by a mixed number or by an improper fraction.

Examples

$$3\tfrac{2}{3} \times \tfrac{3}{5} = \tfrac{11}{3} \times \tfrac{3}{5} = \tfrac{11 \times \cancel{3}}{\cancel{3} \times 5} = \tfrac{11}{5} = 2\tfrac{1}{5}$$

$$\tfrac{3}{4} \times 3\tfrac{1}{3} = \tfrac{3}{4} \times \tfrac{10}{3} = \tfrac{\cancel{3} \times \cancel{10}^{5}}{{}_{2}\cancel{4} \times \cancel{3}} = \tfrac{5}{2} = 2\tfrac{1}{2}$$

UNIT 19 Multiplication and division of fractions

Copy and complete.

1. $1\frac{1}{4} \times \frac{4}{9}$
2. $2\frac{1}{3} \times \frac{3}{5}$
3. $3\frac{3}{4} \times \frac{2}{3}$
4. $1\frac{1}{2} \times \frac{7}{12}$

5. $2\frac{1}{5} \times \frac{5}{12}$
6. $4\frac{2}{5} \times \frac{5}{6}$
7. $2\frac{2}{9} \times \frac{4}{5}$
8. $4\frac{2}{3} \times \frac{9}{10}$

9. $6\frac{2}{5} \times \frac{5}{8}$
10. $5\frac{2}{5} \times \frac{5}{9}$
11. $8\frac{3}{4} \times \frac{3}{5}$
12. $3\frac{1}{3} \times \frac{3}{10}$

13. $9\frac{1}{3} \times \frac{9}{10}$
14. $2\frac{1}{12} \times \frac{4}{5}$
15. $6\frac{1}{4} \times \frac{7}{10}$
16. $2\frac{5}{8} \times \frac{2}{3}$

Copy and complete.

17. $\frac{1}{3} \times 4\frac{1}{5}$
18. $\frac{3}{8} \times 5\frac{1}{3}$
19. $\frac{4}{5} \times 3\frac{1}{3}$
20. $\frac{1}{6} \times 2\frac{2}{5}$

21. $\frac{5}{12} \times 4\frac{4}{5}$
22. $\frac{2}{3} \times 2\frac{1}{4}$
23. $\frac{3}{4} \times 1\frac{1}{2}$
24. $\frac{5}{8} \times 2\frac{2}{3}$

25. $\frac{3}{10} \times 2\frac{2}{3}$
26. $\frac{5}{6} \times 2\frac{1}{10}$
27. $\frac{2}{9} \times 1\frac{1}{2}$
28. $\frac{2}{3} \times 1\frac{3}{4}$

29. $\frac{5}{8} \times 2\frac{2}{5}$
30. $\frac{5}{12} \times 1\frac{3}{10}$
31. $\frac{4}{9} \times 3\frac{1}{2}$
32. $\frac{5}{6} \times 2\frac{1}{4}$

Copy and complete.

33. $1\frac{1}{4} \times 4\frac{1}{5}$
34. $2\frac{1}{3} \times 1\frac{1}{3}$
35. $3\frac{3}{4} \times 3\frac{1}{3}$
36. $1\frac{1}{2} \times 2\frac{2}{5}$

37. $2\frac{2}{5} \times 2\frac{1}{4}$
38. $4\frac{2}{3} \times 2\frac{1}{4}$
39. $2\frac{2}{9} \times 6\frac{3}{4}$
40. $4\frac{2}{3} \times 1\frac{1}{2}$

41. $6\frac{2}{5} \times 1\frac{1}{8}$
42. $2\frac{1}{10} \times 3\frac{1}{3}$
43. $1\frac{1}{2} \times 1\frac{5}{6}$
44. $1\frac{3}{4} \times 3\frac{1}{5}$

45. $2\frac{2}{5} \times 1\frac{5}{12}$
46. $1\frac{3}{10} \times 6\frac{2}{3}$
47. $3\frac{1}{2} \times 1\frac{1}{9}$
48. $2\frac{1}{4} \times 1\frac{3}{5}$

Multiplication and division of fractions   UNIT 19

Division of fractions by whole numbers

When dividing a whole number by a fraction we **invert** the divisor and multiply.

Example $4 \div \frac{2}{3} = 4 \times \frac{3}{2} = \frac{\overset{2}{\cancel{4}} \times 3}{\cancel{2}} = 6$

Instead of saying invert the divisor and multiply, we sometimes say multiply by the **inverse** or **reciprocal** of the divisor.

$\frac{3}{2}$ is the inverse or reciprocal of $\frac{2}{3}$;

$\frac{5}{4}$ is the inverse or reciprocal of $\frac{4}{5}$.

$\frac{1}{4}$ is the reciprocal of 4,

$\frac{1}{5}$ is the reciprocal of 5 and so on.

Look at these pictures:

This shows $\frac{1}{2} \div 3$, that is, $\frac{1}{2}$ divided into three equal parts.
Each part is $\frac{1}{6}$.
So $\frac{1}{2} \div 3 = \frac{1}{6}$.
$\frac{1}{2} \div 3$ also means $\frac{1}{3}$ of $\frac{1}{2}$.

This picture shows $\frac{1}{3}$ of $\frac{1}{2}$, that is $\frac{1}{2} \times \frac{1}{3}$.
This is also $\frac{1}{6}$.
So $\frac{1}{2} \div 3$ gives the same result as $\frac{1}{2} \times \frac{1}{3}$.
Therefore we can write $\frac{1}{2} \div 3 = \frac{1}{2} \times \frac{1}{3}$.

UNIT 19 Multiplication and division of fractions

Look now at these pictures:

$\frac{2}{3} \div 4$

Each part is $\frac{2}{12}$ or $\frac{1}{6}$

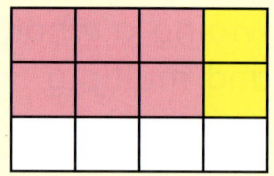

$\frac{1}{4}$ of $\frac{2}{3}$ or $\frac{2}{3} \times \frac{1}{4}$

$\frac{2}{12}$ or $\frac{1}{6}$

$\frac{2}{3} \div 4$ gives the same result as $\frac{1}{4}$ of $\frac{2}{3}$ or $\frac{2}{3} \times \frac{1}{4}$

Therefore $\frac{2}{3} \div 4 = \frac{2}{3} \times \frac{1}{4}$

If we have to divide a fraction by a whole number we must multiply the fraction by the **inverse** (or **reciprocal**) of the whole number.
If the whole number is 2 the inverse or reciprocal is $\frac{1}{2}$.
If the whole number is 3 the inverse or reciprocal is $\frac{1}{3}$, and so on.

Write the reciprocals or inverses of the following:

1. $\frac{2}{3}$ 2. $\frac{3}{4}$ 3. $\frac{4}{5}$ 4. $\frac{5}{6}$ 5. $\frac{7}{10}$
6. 4   7. 5   8. 6   9. 7   10. 8
11. $\frac{5}{9}$ 12. $\frac{4}{15}$ 13. $\frac{8}{7}$ 14. $\frac{14}{3}$ 15. $\frac{1}{12}$

Example $\frac{4}{9} \div 12 = \frac{4}{9} \times \frac{1}{12} = \frac{\cancel{4}^1 \times 1}{9 \times \cancel{12}_3} = \frac{1}{27}$

Copy and complete.

16. $\frac{1}{2} \div 3$ 17. $\frac{1}{4} \div 4$ 18. $\frac{2}{5} \div 4$ 19. $\frac{2}{5} \div 3$
20. $\frac{3}{4} \div 2$ 21. $\frac{1}{2} \div 5$ 22. $\frac{3}{5} \div 5$ 23. $\frac{5}{8} \div 4$
24. $\frac{5}{12} \div 3$ 25. $\frac{4}{9} \div 3$ 26. $\frac{7}{8} \div 7$ 27. $\frac{3}{10} \div 3$

Multiplication and division of fractions   UNIT 19

Division of a fraction by a fraction

$$\frac{1}{2} \div 16 = \frac{1}{2} \times \frac{1}{16} = \frac{1}{32}$$
$$\frac{1}{2} \div 8 = \frac{1}{2} \times \frac{1}{8} = \frac{1}{16}$$
$$\frac{1}{2} \div 4 = \frac{1}{2} \times \frac{1}{4} = \frac{1}{8}$$
$$\frac{1}{2} \div 2 = \frac{1}{2} \times \frac{1}{2} = \frac{1}{4}$$
$$\frac{1}{2} \div 1 = \frac{1}{2} \times \frac{1}{1} = \frac{1}{2}$$
$$\frac{1}{2} \div \frac{1}{2} = \frac{1}{2} \times \square = 1$$
$$\frac{1}{2} \div \frac{1}{4} = \frac{1}{2} \times \square = 2$$

$$\frac{2}{3} \div 16 = \frac{2}{3} \times \frac{1}{16} = \frac{1}{24}$$
$$\frac{2}{3} \div 8 = \frac{2}{3} \times \frac{1}{8} = \frac{1}{12}$$
$$\frac{2}{3} \div 4 = \frac{2}{3} \times \frac{1}{4} = \frac{1}{6}$$
$$\frac{2}{3} \div 2 = \frac{2}{3} \times \frac{1}{2} = \frac{1}{3}$$
$$\frac{2}{3} \div 1 = \frac{2}{3} \times \frac{1}{1} = \frac{2}{3}$$
$$\frac{2}{3} \div \frac{1}{2} = \frac{2}{3} \times \square = \frac{4}{3}$$
$$\frac{2}{3} \div \frac{1}{4} = \frac{2}{3} \times \square = \frac{8}{3}$$

Study the number patterns above very carefully. What fractions must be put in the boxes to make true statements?

If you followed the patterns then you would have seen that the missing numbers are $\frac{2}{1}$ and $\frac{4}{1}$, because

$$\frac{1}{2} \times \frac{2}{1} = 1 \text{ and } \frac{1}{2} \times \frac{4}{1} = 2.$$

Also $\frac{2}{3} \times \frac{2}{1} = \frac{4}{3}$ and $\frac{2}{3} \times \frac{4}{1} = \frac{8}{3}$

We can conclude therefore that

$$\frac{1}{2} \div \frac{1}{2} = \frac{1}{2} \times \frac{2}{1} \text{ and } \frac{1}{2} \div \frac{1}{4} = \frac{1}{2} \times \frac{4}{1};$$

also $\frac{2}{3} \div \frac{1}{2} = \frac{2}{3} \times \frac{2}{1}$ and $\frac{2}{3} \div \frac{1}{4} = \frac{2}{3} \times \frac{4}{1}.$

Can you state the rule for dividing one fraction by another fraction? The following examples should help you.

Examples $\frac{2}{3} \div \frac{3}{4} = \frac{2}{3} \times \frac{4}{3} = \frac{2 \times 4}{3 \times 3} = \frac{8}{9}$

$$1\frac{1}{2} \div 2\frac{1}{4} = \frac{3}{2} \div \frac{9}{4} = \frac{3}{2} \times \frac{4}{9} = \frac{\overset{1}{\cancel{3}} \times \overset{2}{\cancel{4}}}{\underset{1}{\cancel{2}} \times \underset{3}{\cancel{9}}} = \frac{2}{3}$$

UNIT 19 Multiplication and division of fractions

Copy and complete.

1. $\frac{2}{3} \div \frac{4}{5}$
2. $\frac{1}{3} \div \frac{2}{5}$
3. $\frac{5}{6} \div \frac{3}{4}$

4. $\frac{2}{5} \div \frac{2}{3}$
5. $\frac{3}{5} \div \frac{1}{3}$
6. $\frac{2}{3} \div \frac{3}{4}$

7. $\frac{1}{4} \div \frac{1}{2}$
8. $\frac{1}{2} \div \frac{1}{4}$
9. $\frac{3}{4} \div \frac{2}{3}$

10. $\frac{1}{3} \div \frac{3}{5}$
11. $\frac{2}{3} \div \frac{2}{5}$
12. $\frac{3}{4} \div \frac{5}{6}$

13. $\frac{5}{12} \div \frac{3}{8}$
14. $\frac{7}{10} \div \frac{5}{6}$
15. $\frac{4}{9} \div \frac{2}{3}$

16. $\frac{1}{12} \div \frac{5}{6}$
17. $\frac{1}{8} \div \frac{1}{2}$
18. $\frac{2}{3} \div \frac{1}{4}$

Copy and complete.

19. $2\frac{1}{2} \div 1\frac{1}{4}$
20. $3\frac{1}{5} \div 1\frac{1}{10}$
21. $5\frac{1}{3} \div 1\frac{5}{6}$

22. $4\frac{1}{2} \div 2\frac{1}{3}$
23. $1\frac{4}{5} \div 1\frac{1}{10}$
24. $2\frac{5}{8} \div 1\frac{1}{5}$

25. $3\frac{1}{6} \div 2\frac{2}{5}$
26. $4\frac{3}{8} \div 2\frac{4}{5}$
27. $6\frac{1}{4} \div 2\frac{1}{4}$

28. $1\frac{1}{2} \div 1\frac{4}{5}$
29. $3\frac{1}{8} \div 3\frac{3}{4}$
30. $7\frac{1}{2} \div 2\frac{3}{4}$

31. $5\frac{1}{3} \div 2\frac{2}{9}$
32. $2\frac{2}{3} \div 1\frac{3}{4}$
33. $2\frac{1}{10} \div 1\frac{2}{5}$

34. $5\frac{1}{2} \div 3\frac{1}{4}$
35. $9\frac{1}{2} \div 5\frac{1}{4}$
36. $8\frac{1}{7} \div 3\frac{2}{7}$

20 Multiplication and division of decimals

Fractions and decimal numbers

Remember: $\frac{1}{100} = 0.01 \quad \frac{11}{100} = 0.11 \quad \frac{1}{5} = \frac{20}{100} = 0.20$ or 0.2

Write these fractions as decimal numbers:
1. $\frac{2}{5}$
2. $\frac{3}{10}$
3. $\frac{3}{5}$
4. $\frac{7}{10}$
5. $\frac{3}{20}$
6. $\frac{9}{20}$
7. $\frac{13}{20}$
8. $\frac{17}{20}$
9. $\frac{11}{25}$
10. $\frac{13}{25}$
11. $\frac{17}{50}$
12. $\frac{19}{50}$

Write these decimal numbers as fractions in their lowest terms.
13. 0·10
14. 0·12
15. 0·15
16. 0·35
17. 0·40
18. 0·44
19. 0·49
20. 0·50
21. 0·56
22. 0·64
23. 0·72
24. 0·76

Remember: $3.1 = 3 \times 1 + 1 \times \frac{1}{10}$
and $13.24 = 1 \times 10 + 3 \times 1 + 2 \times \frac{1}{10} + 4 \times \frac{1}{100}$

Write these decimal numbers in expanded form:
25. 1·5
26. 3·7
27. 2·6
28. 4·8
29. 11·9
30. 24·3
31. 52·7
32. 28·5
33. 23·18
34. 19·37
35. 24·65
36. 37·29

Write the decimal numbers for:
37. $4\frac{3}{10}$
38. $5\frac{7}{10}$
39. $16\frac{1}{10}$
40. $22\frac{9}{10}$
41. $3\frac{13}{100}$
42. $2\frac{23}{100}$
43. $14\frac{21}{100}$
44. $30\frac{3}{100}$

45. twenty-four and one tenth
46. thirteen and seven hundredths
47. one hundred and six and three tenths
48. two hundred and two and two hundredths

UNIT 20 Multiplication and division of decimals

Multiplying tenths by whole numbers

See how quickly you can do these. Leave your answers as tenths or whole numbers and tenths.

Example $\frac{3}{10} \times 4 = \frac{12}{10} = 1\frac{2}{10}$

1. $\frac{1}{10} \times 4$
2. $\frac{3}{10} \times 5$
3. $\frac{1}{10} \times 6$
4. $\frac{3}{10} \times 8$
5. $\frac{9}{10} \times 3$
6. $\frac{7}{10} \times 12$
7. $\frac{1}{10} \times 9$
8. $\frac{3}{10} \times 12$
9. $\frac{2}{10} \times 6$
10. $\frac{4}{10} \times 5$
11. $\frac{5}{10} \times 7$
12. $\frac{6}{10} \times 9$
13. $\frac{3}{10} \times 7$
14. $\frac{7}{10} \times 8$
15. $\frac{9}{10} \times 8$
16. $\frac{4}{10} \times 12$

Let us now replace our fractions in tenths by decimal numbers.

Examples $0.4 \times 6 = \frac{4}{10} \times 6 = \frac{24}{10} = 2\frac{4}{10} = 2.4$

$0.3 \times 10 = \frac{3}{10} \times 10 = \frac{30}{10} = 3.0$

17. 0·2 × 3
18. 0·3 × 4
19. 0·4 × 5
20. 0·5 × 6
21. 0·6 × 7
22. 0·7 × 8
23. 0·8 × 9
24. 0·9 × 10
25. 0·2 × 4
26. 0·3 × 5
27. 0·4 × 6
28. 0·5 × 7
29. 0·8 × 12
30. 0·9 × 9
31. 0·7 × 9
32. 0·4 × 12

Let us now multiply decimal numbers greater than 1 by whole numbers.

Example $2.3 \times 5 = 2\frac{3}{10} \times 5 = \frac{23}{10} \times 5 = \frac{115}{10} = 11\frac{5}{10} = 11.5$

33. 2·1 × 4
34. 4·3 × 5
35. 2·6 × 6
36. 3·2 × 8
37. 5·4 × 3
38. 4·5 × 3
39. 3·8 × 4
40. 4·3 × 9
41. 6·2 × 2
42. 2·8 × 4
43. 1·6 × 5
44. 2·4 × 4

Multiplication and division of decimals   UNIT 20

Multiplying hundredths by whole numbers

> **Examples** $0.03 \times 7 = \frac{3}{100} \times 7 = \frac{21}{100} = 0.21$
> $0.12 \times 8 = \frac{12}{100} \times 8 = \frac{96}{100} = 0.96$
> $0.15 \times 7 = \frac{15}{100} \times 7 = \frac{105}{100} = 1\frac{5}{100} = 1.05$

Copy and complete.

1. 0.06×4
2. 0.05×9
3. 0.09×8
4. 0.07×5
5. 0.15×5
6. 0.24×3
7. 0.36×2
8. 0.46×2
9. 0.12×12
10. 0.25×5
11. 0.44×3
12. 0.54×4
13. 0.42×8
14. 0.55×9
15. 0.32×6
16. 0.95×6

Multiplying two decimal numbers

> **Examples** $0.4 \times 0.6 = \frac{4}{10} \times \frac{6}{10} = \frac{24}{100} = 0.24$
> $1.2 \times 0.4 = 1\frac{2}{10} \times \frac{4}{10} = \frac{12}{10} \times \frac{4}{10} = \frac{48}{100} = 0.48$

Copy and complete.

1. 0.2×0.3
2. 0.4×0.6
3. 0.7×0.8
4. 0.3×0.9
5. 0.5×0.9
6. 0.4×0.9
7. 0.8×0.9
8. 0.5×0.6
9. 0.8×0.8
10. 0.2×0.8
11. 0.3×0.5
12. 0.2×0.1
13. 0.7×0.6
14. 0.1×0.9
15. 0.6×0.8
16. 0.2×0.7

Copy and complete.

17. 1.6×0.4
18. 2.4×0.4
19. 3.5×0.5
20. 3.6×0.4
21. 0.2×4.8
22. 0.3×3.2
23. 0.4×2.3
24. 0.6×1.6
25. 3.6×0.6
26. 2.4×0.8
27. 0.6×2.4
28. 0.5×3.4
29. 4.2×0.4
30. 5.4×0.5
31. 3.1×0.6
32. 5.1×0.8

UNIT 20   **Multiplication and division of decimals**

Remember: $\frac{1}{1000} = 0.001$; $\frac{12}{1000} = 0.012$; $\frac{123}{1000} = 0.123$

Examples $0.12 \times 0.1 = \frac{12}{100} \times \frac{1}{10} = \frac{12}{1000} = 0.012$

$0.24 \times 0.8 = \frac{24}{100} \times \frac{8}{10} = \frac{192}{1000} = 0.192$

Copy and complete.

33. 0.14×0.2 **34.** 0.18×0.3 **35.** 0.24×0.4 **36.** 0.34×0.2

37. 0.18×0.4 **38.** 0.26×0.3 **39.** 0.32×0.3 **40.** 0.22×0.4

41. 0.24×0.6 **42.** 0.36×0.6 **43.** 0.24×0.7 **44.** 0.14×0.9

45. 0.42×0.4 **46.** 0.28×0.5 **47.** 0.26×0.8 **48.** 0.84×0.8

Example $2.16 \times 0.6 = 2\frac{16}{100} \times \frac{6}{10} = \frac{216}{100} \times \frac{6}{10} = \frac{1296}{1000} = 1\frac{296}{1000} = 1.296$

Copy and complete.

49. 1.24×0.4 **50.** 2.18×0.3 **51.** 4.06×0.6 **52.** 2.16×0.4

53. 1.45×0.5 **54.** 1.42×0.6 **55.** 2.32×0.4 **56.** 1.51×0.6

57. 2.34×0.4 **58.** 3.28×0.3 **59.** 2.41×0.6 **60.** 1.34×0.8

61. 3.36×0.4 **62.** 2.56×0.6 **63.** 1.72×0.9 **64.** 1.58×0.7

Multiplication and division of decimals — UNIT 20

Finding a rule for multiplying decimals

Look at the products in columns A and B on the right.

A	B
0·2 × 3 = 0·6	0·2 × 0·3 = 0·06
0·3 × 4 = 1·2	0·5 × 0·9 = 0·45
1·2 × 3 = 3·6	1·6 × 0·4 = 0·64
2·3 × 5 = 11·5	3·1 × 0·6 = 1·26

Check the products on your calculator.

Count the number of digits to the right of the decimal point in the numbers you are multiplying and in the product.
What do you notice?

Look back at the products in columns A and B.
Look at the digits in the numbers you are multiplying and the digits in the product.
What conclusion can you come to?

Copy and complete.

1. 2 × 3 = ☐
   0·2 × 3 = ☐
   2 × 0·3 = ☐
   0·2 × 0·3 = ☐

2. 4 × 2 = ☐
   0·4 × 2 = ☐
   4 × 0·2 = ☐
   0·4 × 0·2 = ☐

3. 3 × 4 = ☐
   0·3 × 4 = ☐
   3 × 0·4 = ☐
   0·3 × 0·4 = ☐

4. 5 × 3 = ☐
   0·5 × 3 = ☐
   5 × 0·3 = ☐
   0·5 × 0·3 = ☐

5. 12 × 4 = ☐
   1·2 × 4 = ☐
   12 × 0·4 = ☐
   1·2 × 0·4 = ☐

6. 23 × 3 = ☐
   2·3 × 3 = ☐
   23 × 0·3 = ☐
   2·3 × 0·3 = ☐

UNIT 20 Multiplication and division of decimals

Look at these products on the right:

Can you discover the rule for finding the products?
Count the digits to the right of the decimal point in the numbers you are multiplying and in the product.
Notice the digits which make up the numbers in the product and the digits in the numbers you are multiplying.

0·05 × 9	= 0·45
0·24 × 3	= 0·72
0·42 × 4	= 1·68
0·14 × 0·2	= 0·0028
0·24 × 0·6	= 0·144
1·24 × 0·4	= 0·496

Copy and complete.

7. 6 × 9 = ☐
    0·06 × 9 = ☐
    6 × 0·09 = ☐
    0·06 × 0·9 = ☐

8. 25 × 3 = ☐
    0·25 × 3 = ☐
    25 × 0·03 = ☐
    0·25 × 0·03 = ☐

9. 36 × 4 = ☐
    0·36 × 4 = ☐
    36 × 0·04 = ☐
    0·36 × 0·04 = ☐

10. 0·48 × 0·6   **11.** 1·24 × 0·8   **12.** 2·54 × 0·06   **13.** 5·12 × 0·3

Multiplication and division of decimals — UNIT 20

Remember: to multiply decimal numbers, we multiply as ordinary numbers and fix the decimal point in the product by counting the number of decimal places in the numbers we multiply.

Example
$$45 \times 23 = 1035$$
So $4·5 \times 2·3 = 10·35$; $45 \times 2·3 = 103·5$; $4·5 \times 0·23 = 1·035$

Use your calculator to write the products of the numbers below as the product of whole numbers. See the example above. Fix the decimal point for the product of the decimal numbers.

Now check the product on your calculator.

14. 1·5 × 1·6

15. 1·4 × 1·8

16. 2·4 × 2·1

17. 2·5 × 3·2

18. 4·51 × 5·4

19. 4·22 × 1·6

20. 12·8 × 2·6

21. 15·3 × 1·7

22. 2·19 × 1·4

23. 2·8 × 1·9

24. 3·5 × 0·24

25. 20·2 × 1·25

26. 14·8 × 2·12

27. 5·48 × 1·6

28. 20·1 × 1·42

29. 0·62 × 2·3

UNIT 20 Multiplication and division of decimals

Estimating products of decimal numbers

> Look at the calculation: 4·8 × 2·7
> $$48 \times 27 = 1296$$
> The product of 4·8 × 2.7 is one of these (0·1296, 1·296, 12·96, 129·6)
> $$4\cdot8 \approx 5 \text{ and } 2\cdot7 \approx 3$$
> $$\text{So } 4\cdot8 \times 2\cdot7 \approx 5 \times 3 \text{ which is } 15$$
> The nearest number to 15 from those in the brackets is 12·96
> $$\text{Therefore } 4\cdot8 \times 2\cdot7 = 12\cdot96$$
> Estimating the product is a **very useful way of checking** your answer after multiplying and counting decimal places.

Choose the correct answer from the brackets.

1. 4·2 × 2·4 (10·08, 1·008, 100·8)
2. 3·6 × 5·2 (1·872, 18·72, 187·2)
3. 15·3 × 3·2 (48·96, 4·896, 489·6)
4. 12·8 × 4·4 (56·32, 563·2, 5·632)
5. 16·2 × 2·4 (388·8, 38·88, 3·888)
6. 15·2 × 3·5 (53·2, 5·32, 0·532)

Estimate the products to these first. Then find the true product and check with your calculator.

7. 19·5 × 14·2
8. 18·3 × 2·5
9. 16·1 × 2·1
10. 22·4 × 4·4
11. 19·2 × 3·4
12. 17·8 × 9·4
13. 20·12 × 2·3
14. 15·24 × 1·5
15. 13·81 × 2·6
16. 12·08 × 2·4

Multiplication and division of decimals   UNIT 20

Put in the decimal point in the product in the brackets.

17. 15·2 × 3·9 (5928)
18. 2·12 × 3·6 (7632)
19. 17·6 × 8·2 (14432)
20. 1·65 × 5·4 (8910)
21. 9·9 × 8·8 (8712)
22. 17·2 × 0·8 (1376)
23. 4·3 × 29 (1247)
24. 5·5 × 4·5 (2475)
25. 12·4 × 36 (4464)
26. 108 × 3·6 (3888)

Word problems

Work out the answers to these word problems. Show all your working.

1. A litre of super unleaded gasoline costs $2.95. How much will 24·5 litres cost?
2. A race track is 1·5 km around. If an athlete runs around the track 24 times, how many kilometres has he run?
3. A square measures 9·5 cm along its side. What is its area?
4. What is the area of a rectangle which measures 10·4 cm × 6·8 cm?
5. Beef is sold in the grocery at $32.99 per kg. What will a piece weighing 4·2 kg cost?
6. A car can run for about 7·5 km on 1 l of petrol. How far will it go on 20·2 l of petrol?

UNIT 20   Multiplication and division of decimals

Changing money

Many West Indians living abroad send money to their families in the West Indies. The families may receive US or Canadian dollars or British pounds or other currencies. They exchange these at the banks for local currency. The rate of exchange may vary from day to day and from one bank to another. Here is a sample of the rates of exchange on a particular day.

FOREIGN EXCHANGE RATES — FEBRUARY 16TH 2005 — REGAL BANK

CURRENCY	CASH	BUY	SELL
US$	6.0000	6.1150	6.2999
CAN$	4.7302	4.9792	5.2033
£STG	10.8918	11.4650	12.0728
YEN	*****	0.0577	0.0612
EURO	7.5613	7.9593	8.3573
EC$	2.0617	2.2410	2.3531
BDOS$	2.8139	*****	3.1939

The rates you see under the column BUY are used when you are cashing cheques in foreign currency. If you are changing foreign notes the rates are those under the column CASH. If you are buying foreign currency the rates are under the column SELL. Do you know which countries use the Euro or the Yen?

Answer the following questions. The amounts are Trinidad and Tobago dollars and cents. Round off rates to two decimal places.

1. (a) How much would you get from the bank for US $500 cash?
   (b) How much would you pay the bank for US $500?
   (c) How much would you get if you cashed a cheque for Can $500?
   (d) How much would a visitor from Barbados get for Bdos $500?
   (e) How much would you have to pay for EC $500?
   (f) If you want to buy £200 sterling, how much would you pay?

Multiplication and division of decimals UNIT 20

Multiplying decimals by multiples of 10

Do these multiplications and check the results with your calculator.

1·4 × 10 = ☐   2·6 × 10 = ☐
3·82 × 10 = ☐   5·56 × 10 = ☐

What do you notice about the products above?

Now write the answers to these calculations.

1. 2·4 × 10   **2.** 3·9 × 10   **3.** 4·1 × 10   **4.** 5·2 × 10
5. 2·32 × 10 **6.** 3·91 × 10 **7.** 14·12 × 10 **8.** 15·22 × 10

To multiply by 20 or 30 or 40 etc. we can multiply by 2 and 10, 3 and 10, 4 and 10.
   So 1·4 × 20 = 2·8 × 10 = 28
   and 5·2 × 30 = 15·6 × 10 = 156

Now work out these products.

9. 1·8 × 20   **10.** 3·4 × 30   **11.** 2·5 × 40   **12.** 6·7 × 50
13. 1·32 × 20 **14.** 2·43 × 30   **15.** 12·09 × 40 **16.** 10·01 × 70

The product 2·14 × 100 is the same as 2·14 × 10 × 10
   So 2·14 × 100 = 21·4 × 10 = 214
   and 2·14 × 200 = 2·14 × 2 × 100 = 4·28 × 100 = 428

Work out these products.

17. 3·52 × 100   **18.** 4·61 × 100   **19.** 11·23 × 100
20. 12·22 × 500   **21.** 13·01 × 200   **22.** 14·19 × 300

Say what happens to decimal numbers when you multiply them by 100.

UNIT 20   Multiplication and division of decimals

Dividing decimal numbers by whole numbers

Remember: we can always add zeros at the end of decimal numbers since this does not change their value.

Example
$$2·4 = 2 \text{ ones} + 4 \text{ tenths} + 0 \text{ hundredths} + 0 \text{ thousandths}$$
$$= 2·400$$

Look at these problems.

```
        ones | tenths | hundredths
          0  .   4       2
       ┌─────────────────
     4 │  1  .   6       8
 1÷4      1
16÷4     ─────
         1 6
         1 6
 8÷4     ─────
             0   8
                 8      2 × 4 = 8
             ─────
                 0
```
1 one = 10 tenths
4 × 4 = 16

$1·68 \div 4 = 0·42$

```
         tens | ones | tenths | hundredths
           0  .  8  .   5        2
        ┌──────────────────────
      5 │  4  .  2  .   6        0
42÷5       4  0
          ─────
           4  2
           4  0
26÷5      ─────
              2    20
                   2 6
                   2 5
10÷5              ─────
                      1   10
                          1 0
                         ─────
                              0
```
4 tens = 40 ones
8 × 5 = 40
2 ones = 20 tenths
5 × 5 = 25
1 tenth = 10 hundredths

$42·6 \div 5 = 8·52$

We can carry out all these steps mentally just as we did when dividing whole numbers.

```
        0·42                        8·52
     ┌──────                     ┌────────
   4 │ 1̶·68                    5 │ 4̶4̶2̶·2̶1̶60
```

214

Multiplication and division of decimals — UNIT 20

Copy and complete.

1. 14·5 ÷ 5
2. 13·6 ÷ 2
3. 17·4 ÷ 3
4. 1·68 ÷ 4
5. 15·63 ÷ 3
6. 20·64 ÷ 4
7. 13·75 ÷ 5
8. 18·72 ÷ 6
9. 3·6 ÷ 5
10. 4·3 ÷ 2
11. 2·8 ÷ 5
12. 6·2 ÷ 4
13. 19·0 ÷ 4
14. 16·4 ÷ 5
15. 23·4 ÷ 4
16. 18·6 ÷ 5
17. 14·2 ÷ 4
18. 12·8 ÷ 4

19. If I divide 14·4 kg of bananas equally into five bags, how much will each bag hold?

20. A container holds 25 litres of petrol. One quarter of the petrol was used. How many litres were left?

21. The perimeter of a square field is 50 m. What is the length of one side?

22. A rope 16 m long is cut into five equal pieces. What is the length of each piece?

23. If I put 15 litres of squash into four bottles of the same size how much will each hold?

UNIT 20 Multiplication and division of decimals

Expressing a fraction as a decimal

- Cut out two strips 5 cm × 1 cm each.
- Divide each strip into five parts.
- Put them together end to end.

You will need: paper, ruler, scissors.

How much will the two strips measure to the nearest cm?
Divide this 10 cm length into five equal parts.
Shade one of these equal parts in red.
What fraction of one of the small strips is this red portion?
This means that $2 \div 5 = \frac{2}{5}$
Any fraction can be taken to mean the numerator ÷ the denominator.

Draw a picture to show that if we divide three cakes equally among four students each will get $\frac{3}{4}$ of a cake.
We can now use our knowledge of decimal numbers to divide fractions like $\frac{3}{4}$.
Remember that 3 can be written as
3 ones + 0 tenths + 0 hundredths = 3·00

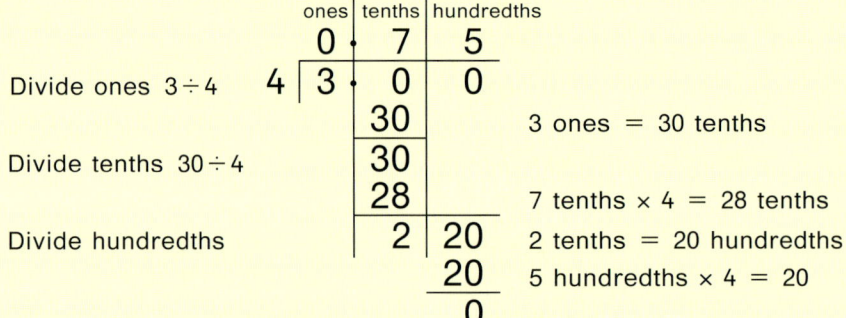

Divide ones 3 ÷ 4

3 ones = 30 tenths

Divide tenths 30 ÷ 4

7 tenths × 4 = 28 tenths

Divide hundredths

2 tenths = 20 hundredths
5 hundredths × 4 = 20

The fraction $\frac{3}{4} = 0.75$

Multiplication and division of decimals UNIT 20

Use the process of division to convert the following to decimals:

1. $\frac{1}{5}$
2. $\frac{2}{5}$
3. $\frac{3}{5}$
4. $\frac{4}{5}$
5. $\frac{3}{10}$
6. $\frac{7}{10}$
7. $\frac{9}{10}$
8. $\frac{1}{2}$
9. $\frac{1}{4}$
10. $\frac{1}{8}$
11. $\frac{3}{8}$
12. $\frac{8}{10}$

Try converting $\frac{1}{3}$ to a decimal by division.

$$3\overline{)1{\cdot}000\ldots}^{\,0{\cdot}333\ldots}$$ We can go forever.

Check the value on your calculator.

0·333... is called a recurring decimal and is written **0·3̇**.

Find decimals for $\frac{2}{3}$, $\frac{1}{9}$, $\frac{1}{6}$ and $\frac{5}{6}$ on your calculator.

UNIT 20   Multiplication and division of decimals

Dividing two decimal numbers

Remember: we do not change the value of a fraction when we multiply both numerator and denominator by the same factor.

Example $\dfrac{2}{5} = \dfrac{2 \times 10}{5 \times 10} = \dfrac{2 \times 10 \times 10}{5 \times 10 \times 10} = \dfrac{2 \times 100}{5 \times 100}$

Multiplying both numerator and denominator by multiples of 10 will help us to divide by a decimal.

Example $1.6 \div 0.2 = \dfrac{1.6}{0.2} = \dfrac{1.6 \times 10}{0.2 \times 10} = \dfrac{16}{2} = 8$

We chose to multiply by 10 to make the denominator a whole number.

Copy and complete.

1. $1.8 \div 0.3$
2. $2.4 \div 0.4$
3. $3.5 \div 0.5$
4. $4.2 \div 0.6$
5. $16.8 \div 0.7$
6. $19.2 \div 0.8$
7. $21.6 \div 0.9$
8. $12.0 \div 0.2$
9. $3.36 \div 0.5$
10. $4.34 \div 0.4$
11. $3.21 \div 0.6$
12. $2.42 \div 0.4$

Example $0.18 \div 0.03 = \dfrac{0.18}{0.03} = \dfrac{0.18 \times 100}{0.03 \times 100} = \dfrac{18}{3} = 6$

Can you say why we chose to multiply by 100 in this problem?

Copy and complete.

13. $0.24 \div 0.03$
14. $0.28 \div 0.04$
15. $0.45 \div 0.05$
16. $0.48 \div 0.06$
17. $1.54 \div 0.07$
18. $1.76 \div 0.08$
19. $1.62 \div 0.09$
20. $2.46 \div 0.03$
21. $3.42 \div 0.05$
22. $4.34 \div 0.04$
23. $6.21 \div 0.06$
24. $2.82 \div 0.04$
25. $15.06 \div 0.03$
26. $21.06 \div 0.06$
27. $27.36 \div 0.09$

Assessment 11

1. (a) $\frac{3}{8} \times \frac{4}{5}$ (b) $\frac{2}{3}$ of $\frac{3}{10}$
2. (a) $2\frac{3}{4} \times \frac{1}{2}$ (b) $3\frac{1}{3} \times 1\frac{1}{5}$
3. (a) $\frac{2}{5} \div 4$ (b) $6 \div \frac{2}{5}$
4. (a) $\frac{5}{12} \div \frac{1}{3}$ (b) $1\frac{4}{5} \div 1\frac{2}{3}$
5. (a) 4.5×4 (b) 12.3×6
6. (a) 2.14×5 (b) 14.25×8
7. (a) 15.1×10 (b) 1.51×100
8. (a) 12.4×20 (b) 3.02×300
9. (a) 5.2×4.3 (b) 2.42×3.6

10. Without multiplying, choose the correct answer from the brackets.
    (a) 5.4×2.8 (10.32, 15.12, 8.12)
    (b) 12.3×5.2 (60.06, 17.06, 63.96)

11. Write the answers to these:
    (a) $17.5 \div 5$ (b) $12.84 \div 4$

12. A piece of string measures 2·25 m. What length will six pieces measure if put end to end?

13. If 6 litres of punch is poured into five bottles of the same size, how much will each bottle hold?

14. A packet of butter weighs 0·25 kg. What is the weight of 20 packets?

15. Four girls share 5 kg of grapes equally among themselves. How much will each girl get?

21 Transformations/Symmetry

Translation

Look at the diagram on the right:

The square was in position A. It was moved to position P1, P2 and P3 from position A at different times.

What can you say about the direction of the motion shown by the red arrows?

When you slide a shape along a straight line without turning the shape, the movement is called a **translation**.

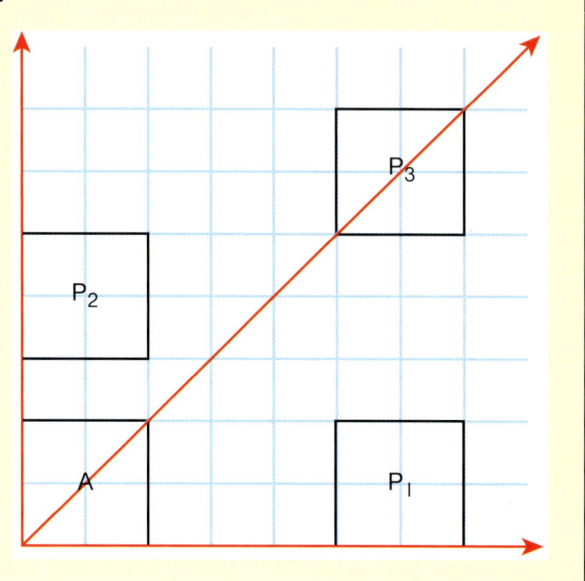

Draw the shapes on squared paper and show the direction of each translation or slide. Describe the translation by the number of blocks the shape has moved and the direction.

You will need: squared paper, ruler.

1.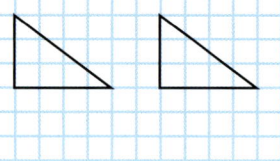

2.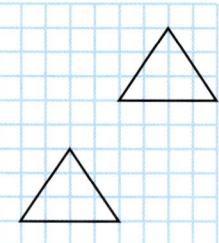

3.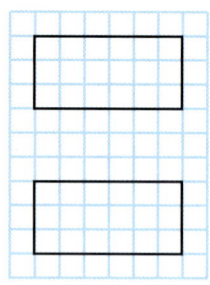

4.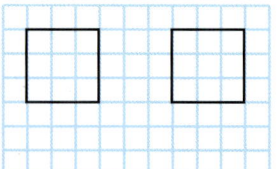

5.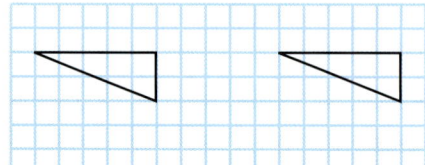

6.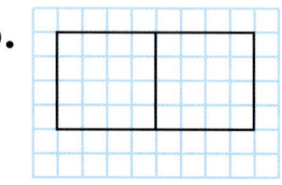

Transformations/Symmetry UNIT 21

Flips and reflections

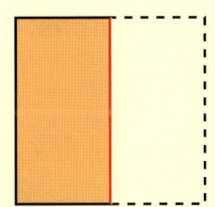 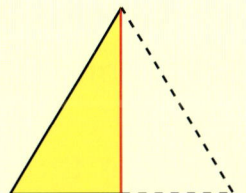 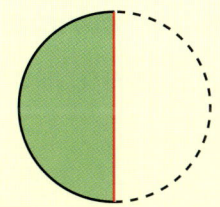

If we place a mirror along the red lines we will see the image or reflection of the shapes in the mirror. If we flip the shapes on the red line they will fit exactly on to the mirror image or reflection of the shapes.

The mirror or flip lines are lines of symmetry of the new shapes made by reflections, or flips.

Copy the shapes. Use a mirror along the red line to study carefully the image or reflection of the shapes.

You will need: a mirror, squared paper.

Now complete the drawings to show a flip along the red line. Use squared paper to help you.

1.    2. 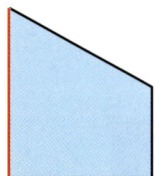   3. 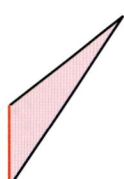   4.

Follow the same procedure as above, and complete the shapes after a flip along the dotted lines.

5. 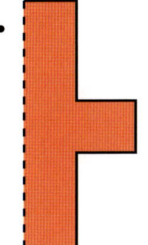   6. 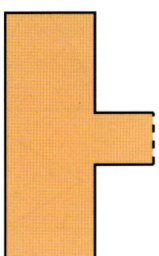   7. 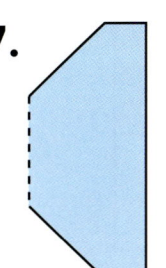   8.

221

UNIT 21 Transformations/Symmetry

Rotation

You will need: card, protractor, ruler, scissors, coloured pencils.

- Cut out an equilateral triangle and draw around it.
- Rotate about a vertex each time through 90° until you come back to the original position.
- Draw the position after each rotation.
- Colour the shape you have created.

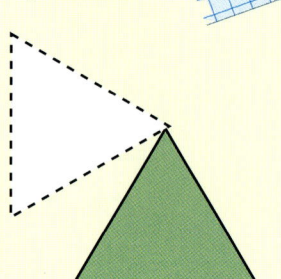

Remember: each angle of the equilateral triangle measures 60°.

Rotate about a vertex through 60°.
Draw the new position. What shape have you created?
Continue rotating through 60° each time until you get back to the original position.
Draw the new position after each rotation.

What shape do you now have? Colour it.

Describe the rotations. The original position of the shape is shaded.

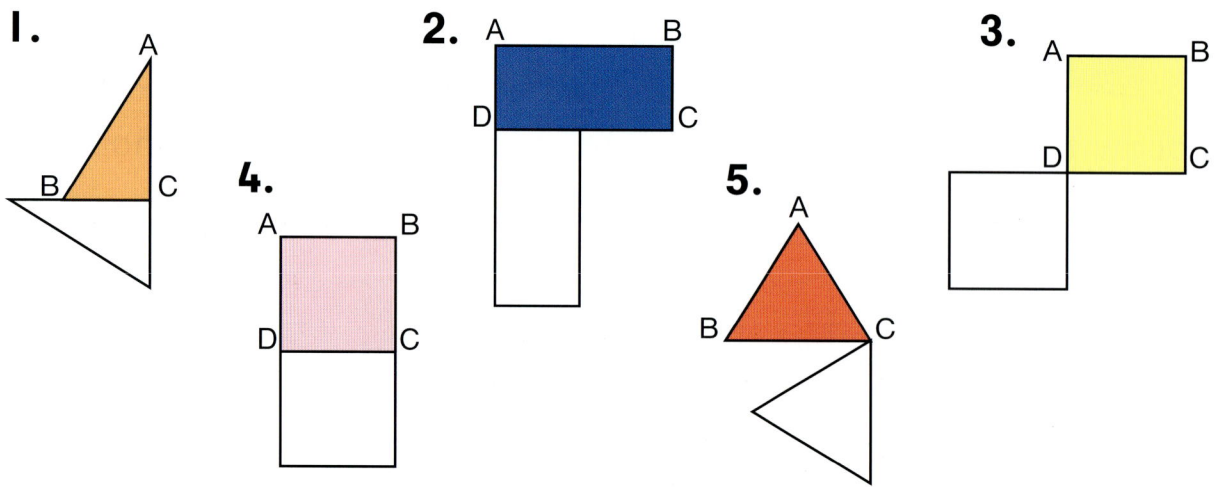

222

Transformations/Symmetry UNIT 21

More transformations

You will need: squared paper, ruler.

1.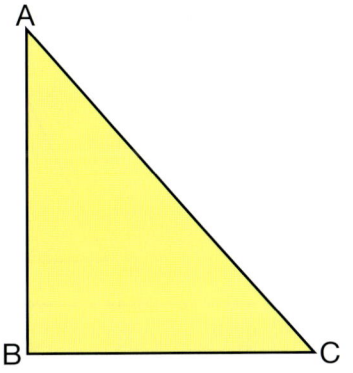

   Triangle ABC is flipped about the line BC. Draw the new position of the triangle.

2.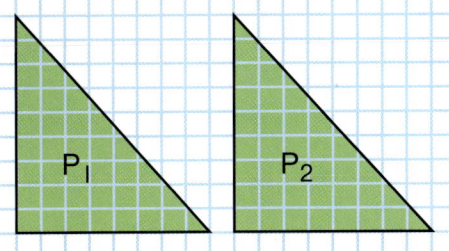

   The diagram shows the positions of P1 and P2 of a triangle. Describe the movement of the triangle from P1 to P2.

3.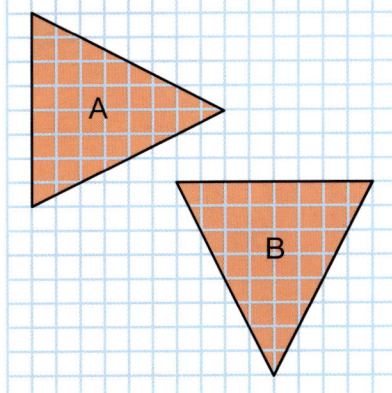

   Describe completely the movement of the triangle from position A to position B.

4.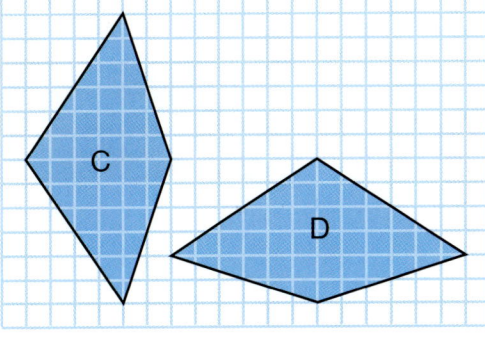

   Which two movements are used to move the shape from C to D? Describe these movements completely.

223

UNIT 21 Transformations/Symmetry

Symmetry

Name each shape.
How many lines of symmetry does each shape have?
Use your ruler to draw each shape and dotted lines that show the lines of symmetry.

Example
Isosceles triangle.
1 line of symmetry

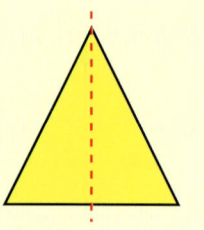

1. 
2. 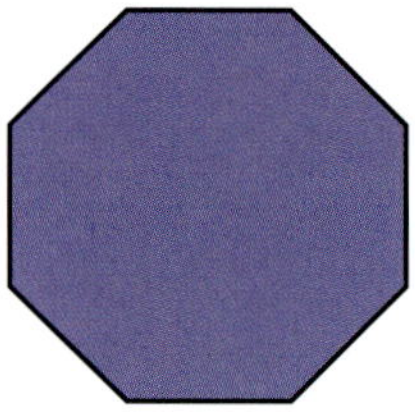
3. 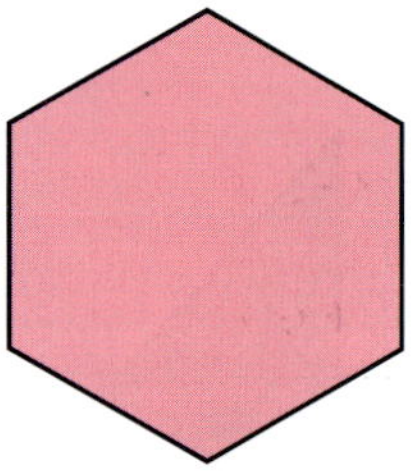
4. 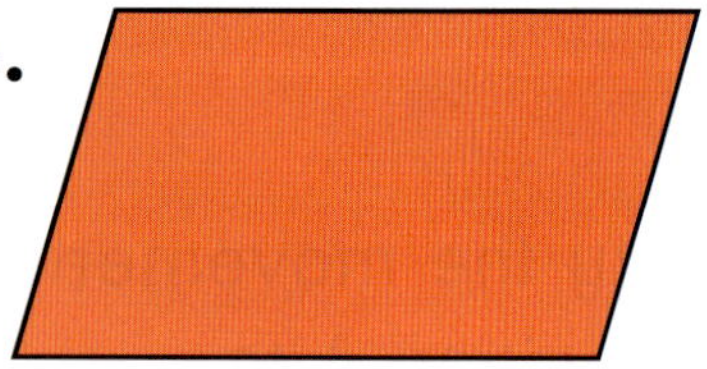
5. 
6. 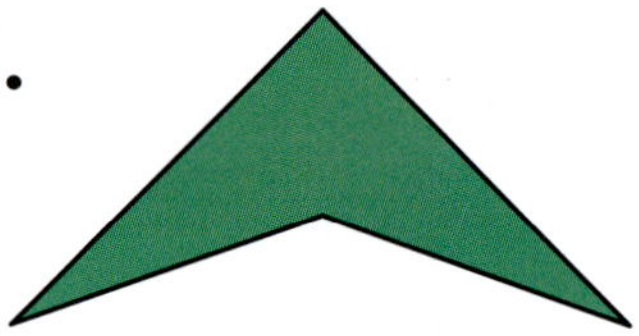
7. 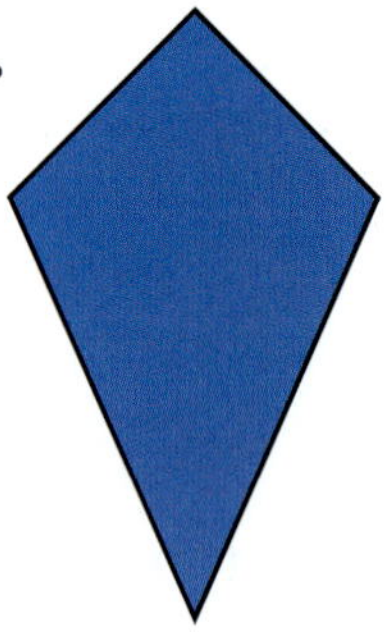
8. 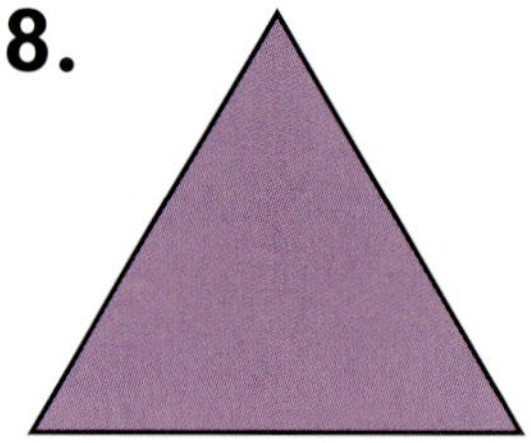
9.
10. 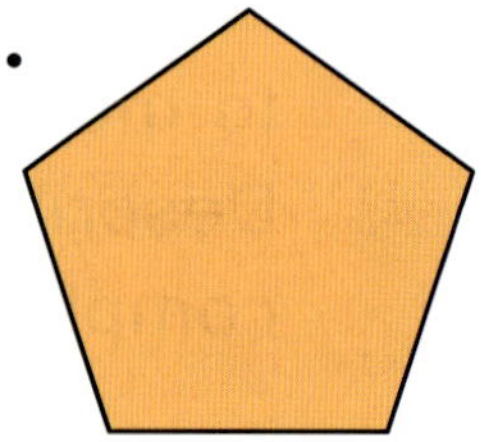
11.

22 Percentages

Fractions, decimals and per cent

Remember: **per cent** means **out of a hundred**.
The symbol we use for per cent is %

1 per cent, 1% = $\frac{1}{100}$; 2 per cent, 2% = $\frac{2}{100}$; 15 per cent, 15% = $\frac{15}{100}$

Remember: $\frac{1}{100}$ = 0·01, $\frac{2}{100}$ = 0·02, $\frac{15}{100}$ = 0·15
so that 1% = 0·01, 2% = 0·02, 15% = 0·15

1. Copy and complete the table below.

Percentage	fraction as hundredths	decimal
4%	$\frac{4}{100}$	0·04
6%	$\frac{6}{100}$	0.06
10%	$\frac{10}{100}$	0.1
11%	$\frac{11}{100}$	0.11
15%		0.15
20%		0.2
25%		0.25
28%		0.28
42%		0.42
50%		0.5
55%		0.55
75%		0.75
88%		0.88
95%		0.95

UNIT 22 Percentages

We can convert a fraction to a decimal number and rewrite the decimal number as a percentage.

$$\frac{1}{4} = 4\overline{)1.00}^{\ 0.25} \qquad \frac{2}{5} = 5\overline{)2.00}^{\ 0.40}$$

$$\frac{1}{4} = 0.25 = 25\% \text{ and } \frac{2}{5} = 0.40 = 40\%$$

2. The table includes some fractions which can conveniently replace their equivalent percentages in computations.
Copy and complete the table. Convert each fraction to a decimal first and then write the equivalent percentage.

Fraction	decimal	percentage
$\frac{1}{10}$	0.1	10%
$\frac{1}{5}$	0.2	20%
$\frac{1}{4}$	0.25	25%
$\frac{3}{10}$		30%
$\frac{2}{5}$		40%
$\frac{1}{2}$		50%
$\frac{3}{5}$		60%
$\frac{3}{4}$	0.75	75%
$\frac{4}{5}$		80%

We can also convert a fraction to a percentage without writing the decimal number.
I whole = 100% $\frac{1}{4} = \frac{1}{4}$ of 100% = 25%
and $\frac{1}{5} = \frac{1}{5}$ of 100% = 20%

Write the equivalent percentages for these fractions:

3. $\frac{1}{8}$ **4.** $\frac{1}{3}$ **5.** $\frac{3}{8}$ **6.** $\frac{2}{3}$ **7.** $\frac{5}{8}$ **8.** $\frac{7}{8}$

Percentages UNIT 22

Percentages of quantities

Example 1 Find 75% of 600 kg.
This is a case where it is more convenient to use the fraction $\frac{3}{4}$, the equivalent of 75%.

$$75\% \text{ of } 600 \text{ kg} = \frac{3}{4} \text{ of } 600 \text{ kg} = \overset{150}{\cancel{600}} \times \frac{3}{\cancel{4}_1} = 450 \text{ kg}$$

Use your calculator to check your computations.
You can also use the per cent key % on the calculator to work out the answer.
Try this [6][0][0] [×] [7][5] [%] [=]   450

Example 2 Find 15% of 350 grams.

$$15\% \text{ of } 350 \text{ g} = \frac{15}{100} \text{ of } 350 \text{ g} = \overset{3}{\cancel{350}} \times \frac{15}{\cancel{100}_2} = \frac{105}{2} = 52.5 \text{ g}$$

Calculate the following:
1. 10% of $900
2. 25% of 900 grams
3. 45% of 1 litre
4. 90% of 360 children
5. 15% of $700
6. 88% of 700 marks
7. 75% of 2 metres
8. 100% of $300
9. 60% of 200 kilograms
10. 0% of $300
11. At a football match in Trinidad $25 000 was collected at the gates. Fifty per cent was given to a Hurricane Fund and 30% to the Society for the Poor. How much was given to:
    (a) The Hurricane Fund?   (b) The Society for the Poor?
12. Sandra had $60. If she spent 20% of her money. How much did she have left?
13. Maria scored 72 marks in her mathematics test. Her teacher wants her to improve her score by 25%. How many marks does Maria have to score?
    Now check your answers using a calculator.

UNIT 22 Percentages

> **Problem** 45% of a man's weekly wage is $1350. What is his full weekly wage?
>
> **Solution**   45% = $1350
> 1% = $\frac{1}{45}$ of $1350
> = $1350 × $\frac{1}{45}$ = $30
> total weekly wage = $30 × 100
> = $3000
>
> $\dfrac{\cancel{1350}^{\,270} \times 1}{\cancel{45}_{9}} = \dfrac{270}{9} = 30$
>
> $\dfrac{\cancel{1350}^{\,\cancel{270}^{\,30}} \times 1 \times 100}{\cancel{45}_{\cancel{9}}} = 3000$
>
> In these problems you could leave all your multiplication and division to the end.

Work out the answers to these word problems. Show all your working.

14. Ten per cent of Roy's weekly allowance was 50 cents. What was Roy's full allowance?

15. Thirty per cent of the audience at a show was 540. How many people attended the show?

16. In a crate of eggs 180 or 15% of the eggs were bad. What was the total number of eggs in the crate?

17. Joey scored 540 marks which was 60% of the total number of marks for the test. What was the total for the test?

18. Fifty-four students, which was 30% of a group on an outing, wore jeans. How many students went on the outing?

19. Forty-five per cent of the students in a school were boys. There were 180 boys. How many were girls?

Now check your answers using a calculator.

Percentages **UNIT 22**

> Look back at question 19.
> How did you solve it?
> Did you find out the total number of students, that is 100%?
> What did you do then? Subtract boys from the total to get girls? Well, that is one approach.
>
> Here is another. If 45% were boys what per cent were girls?
> $$45\% = 180$$
> $$1\% = \frac{180}{45}$$
> $$55\% = \frac{180}{45} \times 55 = 220$$
>
> $$\frac{180 \times 55}{45} = 55 \times 4 = 220$$
>
> Number of girls = 220

Try to solve these problems without having to find 100%.

20. Sanjeev spent 75% of his weekly allowance and saved the remainder. He spent $3. How much did he save?

21. Sixty per cent of patrons, or 900, at a show were males. How many were females?

22. Thirty toys, which was 6% of the number in a crate, were broken. How many were in good condition?

23. Cintra scored 70%, or 560 marks, in her term test. How many marks did she lose?

24. Thirty per cent of students, or 45, travel by car to come to school. The others either walk or travel by bus. How many students either walk or travel by bus?

Now check your answers using a calculator.

UNIT 22 Percentages

Finding percentages

> **Remember:** when we multiply a fraction by 100 the answer gives the percentage equivalent of the fraction.

Look at this problem.
What percentage of 40 is 24?

24 out of 40 is the fraction $\frac{24}{40}$

Percentage $= \frac{24}{40} \times 100 = 60\%$

$$\frac{\overset{6}{\cancel{24}}}{\underset{1}{\cancel{40}}} \times \overset{10}{\cancel{100}}$$

$6 \times 10 = 60$

Here is another problem.
From a tank holding 5000 litres of water children in a school used 1500 litres on Monday and 1350 litres on Tuesday. What percentage was used on each of the two days?

Fraction used on Monday $= \frac{1500}{5000} = \frac{15}{50}$

Percentage used $= \frac{15}{50} \times 100 = 30\%$

$$\frac{\overset{3}{\cancel{15}} \times \overset{10}{\cancel{100}}}{\underset{\underset{1}{\cancel{5}}}{\cancel{50}}}$$

$3 \times 10 = 30$

Fraction used on Tuesday $= \frac{1350}{5000} = \frac{135}{500}$

Percentage used $= \frac{135}{500} \times 100 = 27\%$.

$$\frac{\overset{27}{\cancel{135}} \times \overset{1}{\cancel{100}}}{\underset{\underset{1}{\cancel{5}}}{\cancel{500}}}$$

Calculate the following percentages.
1. 30 out of 50
2. 24 out of 200
3. $2.00 out of $20.00
4. $500 out of $2000
5. 6 litres out of 30 litres
6. 500 millilitres out of 4 litres
7. 500 cm out of 4 metres
8. 70 m out of 1 kilometre
9. 200 gm out of 2 kilograms
10. 490 marks out of 500 marks

11. In a football competition a team won seven matches, lost three and drew two. What percentage of the matches played did it win?

12. If I spent $60 from my allowance of $480, what percentage of my money did I keep?

13. There are 16 boys in a class of 24. What per cent are girls?

23 Discount/Profit and loss/Interest

Discount

When there are SALES in stores prices are reduced on the articles on sale. The reduction in the price is called the **discount**. Discounts are usually shown in percentages.

Power Tools **10% OFF**
Hand Tools **20% OFF**

15% DISCOUNT
ON ALL PRINTING
to the end of September

PVC FITTING 20% DISCOUNT

Remember: 10% or 15% or 20% discount means a reduction in the cost by 10% or 15% or 20%.

Example
A buyer gets 25% discount on an article marked $480.
How much does he pay?

Solution If the buyer's discount was 25% he paid 75%.

Amount paid = 75% of $480 = $480 × $\frac{3}{4}$ 75% = $\frac{3}{4}$

= $360 $\frac{\cancel{480}^{120} \times 3}{\cancel{4}}$ = 360

How much did the buyer save?
We can subtract $360 from $480 or we could find
25% of $480 = $\frac{1}{4}$ of $480 = $120 $\cancel{480}^{120} \times \frac{1}{4}$

In each of these problems calculate how much a buyer would pay after discount and how much he/she would save.

1. Marked price $300; discount 5%
2. Marked price $650; discount 6%

UNIT 23 Discount/Profit and loss/Interest

3. Marked price $1200; discount $12\frac{1}{2}\%$

4. Marked price $900; discount $33\frac{1}{3}\%$

5. Marked price $450; discount 20%

> **Example**
> A buyer pays $240 for an article usually sold for $300; what was his percentage discount?
>
> **Solution**
> The percentage discount means finding what per cent of the marked price is the discount.
> $$\text{Discount} = \$300 - \$240 = \$60$$
> $$\text{Percentage discount} = \tfrac{60}{300} \times 100 = 20\%$$
>
> $\dfrac{\cancel{60} \times 100}{\cancel{300}} \; {}_{20}{}^{\cancel{300}}$

Calculate the percentage discount in each case.

6. Normal price $500; sale price $425.

7. Normal price $250; sale price $220.

8. Normal price of one shirt $60; sale price two for $100.

9. Normal price for a TV set $4000; sale price $3400.

10. The marked price of a table was $1200. A customer obtained it for $750 cash. What was his percentage discount?

11. Adam bought two jerseys each with a marked price of $60. If he paid $100 for them in a sale what was his percentage discount?

232

Discount/Profit and loss/Interest UNIT 23

Profit and loss

People buy and sell things to make a **profit**.
When you sell (the selling price or S.P.) an article for more than it cost (the cost price or C.P.) you make a profit; when you sell it for less than it cost you suffer a loss.
Percentage profit or loss means finding what per cent of the cost price is the profit or loss.

Example
A bicycle which cost the store owner $600 was being sold for $720. What percentage profit was being made?

Solution

Remember: percentage profit is always calculated on the basis of the cost price. One must find what per cent of the cost price is the profit.

Cost price of the bicycle = $600
The selling price of the bicycle = $720
  Profit = $720 − $600 = $120

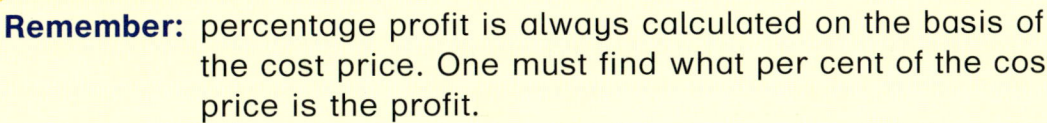

Percentage profit = $\frac{120}{600} \times 100 = 20\%$

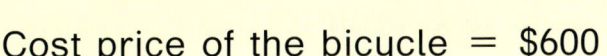

Find the percentage profit in each of the following:

1. C.P. of a pocket radio $120, S.P. $150.
2. C.P. of a CD player $500, S.P. $650
3. C.P. of a TV set $3200, S.P. $3600
4. C.P. of a refrigerator $8500, S.P. $10 000. Give your answer to the nearest per cent.
5. Oranges were bought at 100 for $50.00 and sold at four for $3.00. What percentage profit was made after selling the entire box?

UNIT 23 Discount/Profit and loss/Interest

Calculate the loss % in each of the following transactions.

6. C.P. $500.00, S.P. $475.00
7. C.P. $850.00, S.P. $700.00
8. C.P. $250.00, S.P. $210.00
9. C.P. $1000.00, S.P. $840.00
10. C.P. $300.00, S.P. $2700.00

Example
How much should an article costing $300 be sold for to make a profit of 20%?

Solution
20% of C.P. = $\frac{1}{5}$ of $300 = $60   20% = $\frac{1}{5}$
S.P. must be $300 + $60 = $360

Work out the answers to these word problems. Show all your working.

11. An article costing $400 was sold at a profit of $12\frac{1}{2}$%. What did the buyer pay for it?

12. What price should the store manager put on a TV set if he needs to make a profit of $33\frac{1}{3}$%? The set cost $3000?

13. A vendor bought fish at $12 per kg. At what price should he sell if he must make a profit of 25%?

14. The owner of the snackette bought soft drinks at $36.00 per case of 24 bottles. At what price should she sell a bottle to make a profit of $33\frac{1}{3}$%?

15. Pencils are bought at $24.00 per box of 12. What should the store owner charge for each pencil if he needs to make a profit of 25%?

Discount/Profit and loss/Interest — UNIT 23

Percentages and taxes

> In many countries you pay a tax when you buy some kinds of goods. The tax is called by different names in different countries – purchase tax, sales tax, value added tax or VAT. In Trinidad and Tobago you pay a VAT of 15%.
>
> **Example**
> An article is marked $300. How much will a person pay if 15% VAT is added to the cost?
>
> Marked price = $300
> VAT = 15% of $300 = $\frac{15}{100} \times 300$
> = $45
>
> $\dfrac{15 \times \overset{3}{\cancel{300}}}{\underset{1}{\cancel{100}}}$
> 15×3
>
> Cost of article = $300 + $45 = $345

1. Work out the price you pay for the articles below after you have added VAT (value added tax) at 15%.

Article	marked price	15% VAT	price with VAT included
Pen	$20		
Stationery	$50		
Bicycle	$300		
Radio	$500		
Airline ticket	$1500		
Video player	$2200		

2. Tyres are sold at $450 each. VAT is charged at 15% of the selling price. How much will I have to pay for four tyres?

3. My motor car cost $3000 for some repair work. VAT is charged at 15% for these services. How much will I be required to pay in total?

235

UNIT 23 Discount/Profit and loss/Interest

Interest on loans and hire purchase

> Interest on an **investment** is money you earn by keeping your money in an account in a bank or other financial organisation. **Interest on a loan** is money charged by a bank or other financial organisation for borrowing money. **Hire purchase** is a method of paying for something where the buyer pays part of the cost immediately then makes smaller regular payments until the debt is repaid. Interest is usually calculated as a per cent per annum (p.a.).

Work out the answers to these word problems. Show all your working.

1. Regal Bank charges interest at the rate of 6% on loans up to $10 000 for 1 year. How much interest will I have to pay if I borrow $4 500?

2. The Farmer's Credit Union pays 7% interest when you invest up to $50 000 for 1 year. How much interest will I get if I invest $30 000?

3. Furniture King Ltd charges interest at 12% p.a. if you buy furniture or appliances on hire purchase. How much will I have to pay altogether after a period of 2 years if I wish to buy a refrigerator for $9000 and the down payment is $1000?

4. If I have to pay the total amount for the refrigerator above in 24 monthly instalments how much will I have to pay each month?

5. How much interest will I have to pay if I borrow $5000 for 2 years if the bank interest charges are $4\frac{1}{2}$% p.a.?

Discount/Profit and loss/Interest UNIT 23

6. Regal Bank wants a loan repaid by monthly instalments. How much will I have to repay each month if I borrow $4000 for 1 year at 5% p.a. interest?

7. Farmer's Credit Union lowered their interest rate from 7% to $6\frac{1}{2}$% p.a. How much less interest would I get for an investment of $30 000 for 1 year?

Find the interest payable on the following loans:

8. $1000 for 2 years at 9% p.a.
9. $600 for 6 months at 10% p.a.
10. $5000 for $2\frac{1}{2}$ years at 10% p.a.
11. $10 000 for 3 years at 9% p.a.
12. $2500 for 18 months at 12% p.a.
13. $7500 for 2 years at 9% p.a.
14. $20 000 for 2 years at 12% p.a.
15. $50 000 for 5 years at 10% p.a.

Work out the HP (hire purchase) charge and total cost on these times. The down payment in each case is 10% of the cash price.

16. Cash price $500; HP 10% p.a.; period 2 years
17. Cash price $900; HP 12% p.a.; period 2 years
18. Cash price $1200; HP 10% p.a.; period 3 years
19. Cash price $1500; HP 10% p.a.; period 18 months
20. Cash price $10 000; HP 15% p.a.; period 30 months
21. Cash price $50 000; HP 15% p.a.; period 5 years

237

UNIT 23 Discount/Profit and loss/Interest

Word problems

Work out the answers to these word problems. Show all your working.

1. An article is sold for $500 and VAT is charged at 15% of the marked price. How much does the buyer pay for the article?

2. A man borrows $1000 and pays back $1100 one year later.
   (a) How much interest does he pay?
   (b) What percentage interest does he pay?

3. A person invests $10 000 in a fixed term deposit at the bank for 2 years at a rate of interest of 10% per annum. How much interest does the person receive after 2 years?

4. A borrower is charged 12% per annum interest on a loan of $1500 for 3 years. How much interest does he pay?

5. A buyer purchases a refrigerator priced at $3000. He signs a hire purchase agreement to pay over a period of 30 months at an interest rate of 15% per annum. How much will he have paid altogether after the 30 months?

6. Amy borrows $10 000 and pays back $12 000 after two years.
   (a) How much interest does she pay?
   (b) How much interest does she pay each year?
   (c) What percentage interest does she pay each year?

Assessment 12

1. Write these percentages as fractions and decimals.
   (a) 11%   (b) 20%   (c) 48%

2. Write these fractions as percentages and decimals.
   (a) $\frac{2}{5}$ (b) $\frac{1}{4}$ (c) $\frac{9}{100}$

3. Calculate the following:
   (a) 5% of 80   (b) 15% of 120 kg

4. (a) What per cent of 40 is 24?
   (b) What per cent of $2.00 is 40 cents?

5. Thirty per cent of John's marbles is 18. What is 40%?

6. What will I pay for a fan if I get 10% discount on the marked price which is $250?

7. Pens which were bought by the storeowner for $6.00 each were sold for $7.50. What percentage profit did the owner make?

8. How much VAT will you pay on a TV set which cost $2500 and VAT is 15%?

9. Calculate the interest payable on a loan of $5000 for 3 years when the rate of interest is 9% per annum.

10. A person invests $10 000 with a Credit Union where the interest payable is 7% p.a. How much interest will he receive after 3 years?

24 Unequal sharing

> **Problem:** If you had eight marbles and your friend had 12, how many more marbles did your friend have than you?
> If your friend put away four marbles, how many would each of you then have?
>
> This should give you a clue to solve this problem.
> How many marbles would your friend get if you shared 20 marbles with him and he got four more than you?
> If you subtract the 4 you then have 16 to share equally.
> Each will get 8 from the 16; your friend will then have
> 8 + 4 = 12.

Work out the answers to these word problems. Show all your working.

1. Mr Ram wishes to share $20 between Ravi and Ray so that Ravi would get $2 more than Ray. How much would each get?

2. Bobby wanted to share 30 marbles between Larry and Sunil so that Larry would get six more than Sunil. How many would each get?

3. Teacher wanted to share 24 house points out to the first three girls in the test. The first girl would get two house points more than the second and the second girl would get two more than the third. How many more house points would the first girl get than the third? How many house points would each of the girls get?

4. Share $10 among two boys so that one gets $1 more than the other. How much would each get?

Unequal sharing UNIT 24

The paint from the 5 litre bucket A was put into two smaller buckets, B holding 1 l and C holding 4 l. In this case we say that we have divided the paint in the ratio 1 to 4 or 4 to 1.

We write the ratio 1 to 4 as 1:4 and the ratio 4 to 1 as 4:1

The ratio 4:1 says that bucket C has 4 times the amount as bucket B. What does the ratio 1:4 mean in this case? Observe that bucket B now has $\frac{1}{5}$ of bucket A and bucket C has $\frac{4}{5}$.

So, if we divide a quantity in the ratio 1:4 what fraction of the original amount is each part?

If we divide a quantity in the ratio 2:3 what fraction is each part?

Example Share 20 marbles in the ratio 2:3.

Solution
Since the ratio is 2:3, one part is $\frac{2}{5}$, the other is $\frac{3}{5}$

$\frac{2}{5}$ of 20 = 20 × $\frac{2}{5}$ = 8 $\frac{\cancel{20}^4 \times 2}{\cancel{5}} = 8$

$\frac{3}{5}$ of 20 = 20 × $\frac{3}{5}$ = 12 $\frac{\cancel{20}^4 \times 3}{\cancel{5}} = 12$

Work out the answers to these word problems. Show all your working.

5. (a) I gave $10 to Ravi and $20 to Ian. What was the ratio of Ravi's share to Ian's?
   (b) What fraction of the whole amount did Ravi receive?
   (c) What fraction did Ian receive?

UNIT 24 Unequal sharing

6. If I share $48 between Glen and Anil in the ratio 3:5 how much will each get?

7. Share $10 between Anette and Mary in the ratio 1:3. How much will each get?

8. Seven thousand litres of water are to be distributed to two schools in the ratio 3:4. How many litres would each school get?

9. Fifty kilograms of cheese have to be shared between two shops in the ratio 5:3. How many kilograms would each shop receive?

25 Circumference and pi

The diagram on the right shows the circle and some more of its parts. An **arc** of a circle is a part of its **circumference**. A **sector** is the region bounded by two radiuses (radii) and an arc. A **chord** is any straight line joining two points on the circumference.

On page 139 we discovered that the circumference of a circle was about three times the diameter, that is,

circumference = diameter × 3

You will need: cans of various sizes, measuring tape and calculator.

- Measure the diameter of different cans and their circumference.
- Measure to the nearest millimetre.
- Tabulate your results.
- Divide the circumference by the diameter in each case.
- Find the average of the quotients to the nearest tenth.

Scientists have calculated this number to be approximately equal to 3·1416 or $3\frac{1}{7}$. This is an important mathematical number. It is called **pi** (a letter of the Greek alphabet) and it is written π.

So we now have circumference = diameter × π, or as you will sometimes see it, circumference = π × diameter (C = πd). Since the diameter is twice the radius the formula is also written

circumference = 2 π × radius (C = 2 πr)

UNIT 25 Circumference and pi

Measure the diameter of each circle.
Calculate the circumference. Use $\pi = 3\frac{1}{7}$

1.
2.
3.

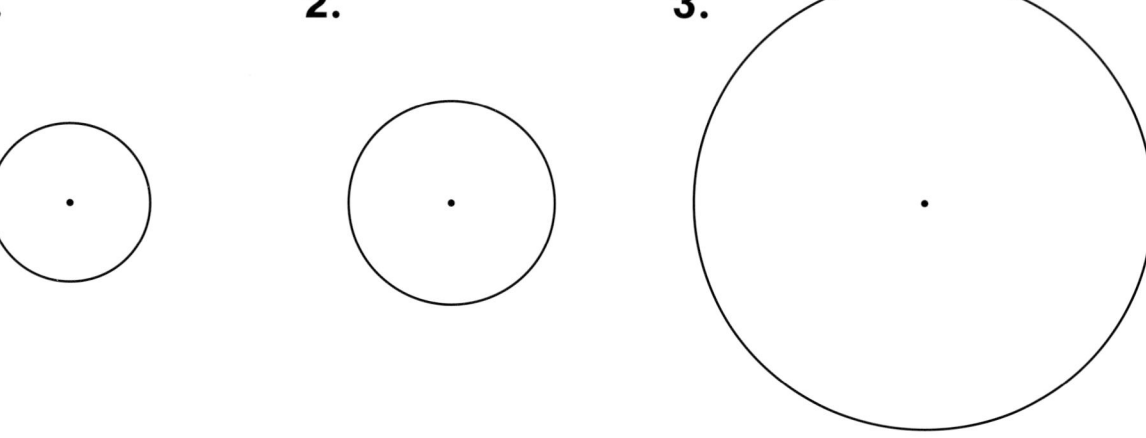

Calculate the circumference of the circles with these diameters:

4. 7 cm   5. 14 cm   6. 21 cm   7. 28 cm

Calculate the circumference of the circles with these radii:

8. 4 cm   9. 6 cm   10. 8 cm   11. 10 cm

12. Which of the shapes below has the greatest perimeter?

13. Which has the smallest perimeter?

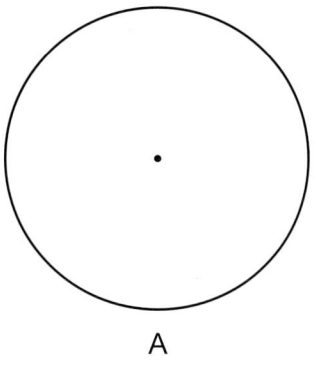   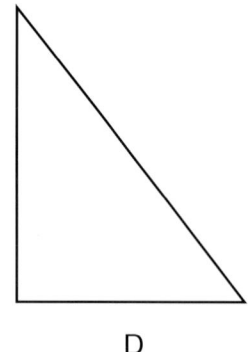

A   B   C   D

14. Arrange the shapes A, B, C, D in order of the length of their perimeter, smallest first.

Circumference and pi UNIT 25

> Since circumference = π × d, diameter = circumference ÷ π
>
> **Problem** Find the diameter and radius of a circle with circumference 154 cm.
>
> **Solution** Diameter = circumference ÷ π
> $= 154 ÷ 3\frac{1}{7} = 154 × \frac{7}{22}$
>
> $\frac{154 × 7}{22} = 49$
>
> = 49 cm
>
> Radius = diameter × $\frac{1}{2}$ = 49 × $\frac{1}{2}$
> = 24·5 cm

Calculate the diameter and radius of the circles whose circumferences are:

15. 22 cm **16.** 44 cm **17.** 66 cm **18.** 88 cm

(You may use your calculator, if you wish.)

In the next four questions give your answers to the nearest cm.

19. 28 cm **20.** 45 cm **21.** 56 cm **22.** 78 cm

Give your answers to these word problems to the nearest whole number.

23. A circular path round the edge of a park measures 400 m. What is the distance across the middle of the park?

24. A bicycle wheel is 45 cm in diameter
   (a) What is its circumference?
   (b) How many revolutions will it make if the cyclist travels 1 km?

25. A motor car wheel is 55 cm in diameter. How many revolutions will it make in $\frac{1}{2}$ hour if it travels at 50 k.p.h. (kilometres per hour)?

245

UNIT 25   Circumference and pi

Perimeter of compound shapes

Work out the perimeter of these shapes.

1.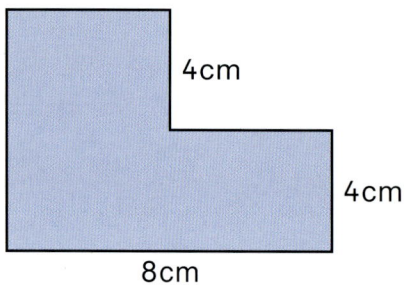

2.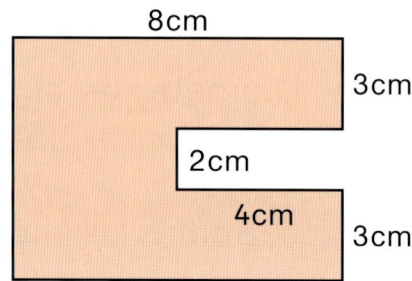

3.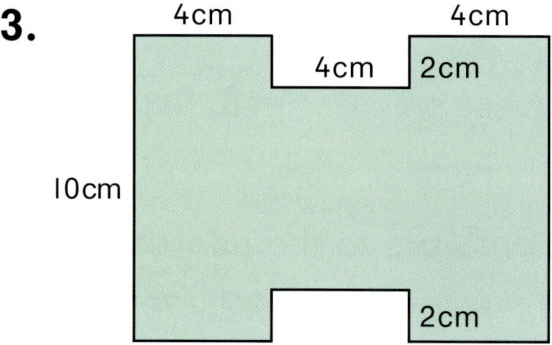

4.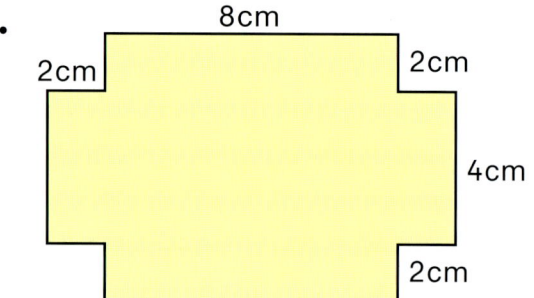

5.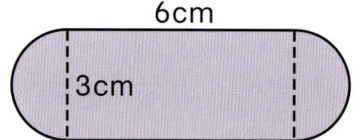

6.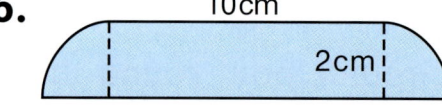

7.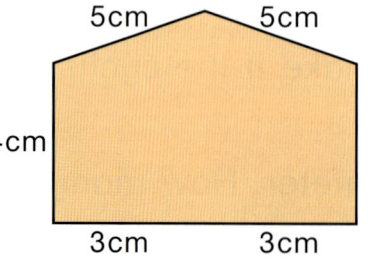

8.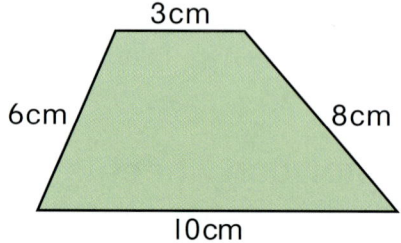

246

Circumference and pi — UNIT 25

Word problems

Work out the answers to these word problems. Show all your working.

1. The perimeter of a square is 1 m 40 cm. What is the length of a side of the square?

2. The perimeter of a rectangle is 4·60 m. If the width is 80 cm what is its length?

3. The perimeter of a triangle is 19 m 10 cm. If one side is 8 m 50 cm, and another is 5 m 60 cm, what is the length of the third side?

4. Fence posts are to be placed 5 m apart around a field 80 m × 60 m. There must be a post at every corner of the field.
   (a) How many posts will be required?
   (b) If a contractor charges $15.00 to supply each post and have it put into the ground, how much will it cost to install all the posts?

5. Wire is sold on rolls of 30 metres. How many rolls must be bought to fence a garden which measures 70 m × 60 m? How much will the wire cost at $535 per roll?

6. A chain is being put around a playing field and 2 m away from the playing area which measures 20 m × 15 m. What would the chain cost at $25 per metre?

7. What would be the length of a side, and the perimeter, of a square which has the same area as a rectangle 16 cm × 4 cm?

26 Area of triangles/Compound shapes/Circles

Area of triangles

Which of these triangles is:

1. (a) an equilateral triangle (b) an isosceles triangle
   (c) a right-angled triangle (d) a scalene triangle?

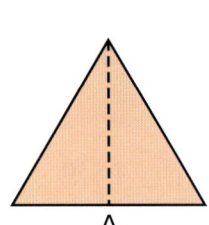
A

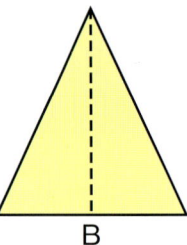
B

C

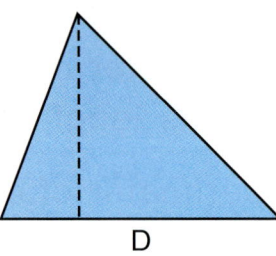
D

Remember: area of a triangle = $\frac{1}{2}$ base × height

2. Measure the height (altitude) and the base of each triangle. Record the measurements in a table.

Triangle	type	height	base	area
A				
B				
C				
D				

Except for triangle C all the triangles above are **acute-angled triangles**. None of the angles in the triangles is an obtuse angle.

The triangle on the right is an obtuse-angled triangle. The height of the triangle is shown by the dotted line.

Area of triangles/Compound shapes/Circles UNIT 26

Area of an obtuse-angled triangle

Problem
The obtuse-angled triangle has a base 3 cm and altitude 3 cm. What is its area?

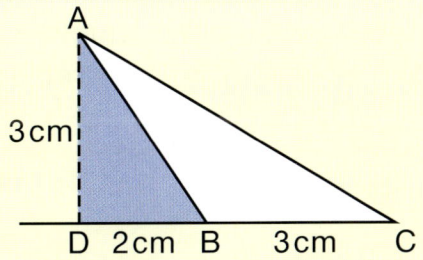

Solution
Let us use the letters at the vertices to name the triangles. If we extend the base of the triangle ABC to meet the line showing the altitude, the extension measures 2 cm.

Area of the large right-angled triangle ADC
$= \frac{1}{2} \times 5 \times 3 = 7\frac{1}{2}$ cm²

Area of the small right-angled triangle ADB
$= \frac{1}{2} \times 2 \times 3 = 3$ cm²

Area of triangle ABC $= 7\frac{1}{2} - 3 = 4\frac{1}{2}$ cm²

$4\frac{1}{2}$ cm² is $\frac{1}{2} \times 3 \times 3$ which is $\frac{1}{2}$ base × height of our triangle ABC.

So, the formula Area $= \frac{1}{2}$ base × height also holds for the obtuse-angled triangle.

Measure the base and heights of the triangles to the nearest cm. Calculate their areas.

1.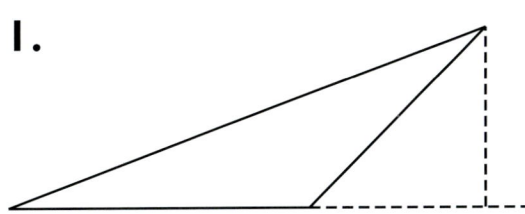

2.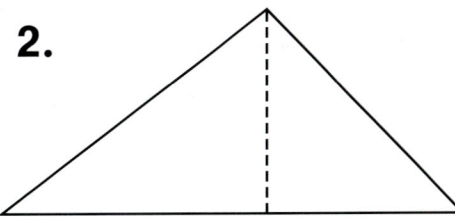

249

UNIT 26 Area of triangles/Compound shapes/Circles

Area of compound shapes

Remember: area of rectangle = length × breadth
A = L × B (A represents area, L length and B breadth)
area of square = side × side or A = S × S = S²

Fig. 1

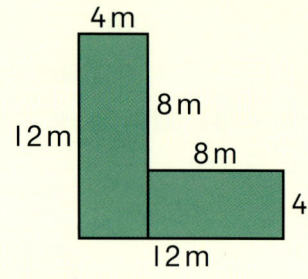

area = area of rectangle (4 × 12)
　　　　+ area of rectangle (4 × 8)
　　 = 48 m² + 32 m² = 80 m²

Fig. 2

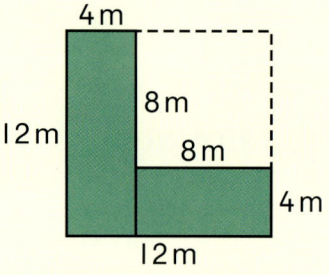

area = area of square (12 × 12)
　　　　− area of square (8 × 8)
　　 = 144 m² − 64 m² = 80 m²

Finding the area of this shape can be done as an addition of two areas (Fig. 1), or as a subtraction from a larger area (Fig. 2).

Work out the areas of these shapes.

1.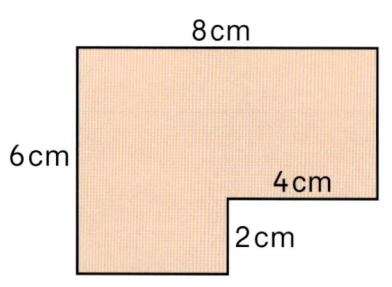

2.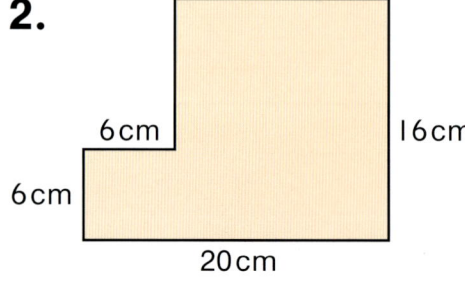

250

Area of triangles/Compound shapes/Circles UNIT 26

3.
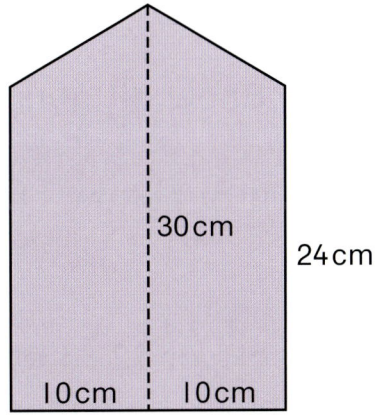

4.
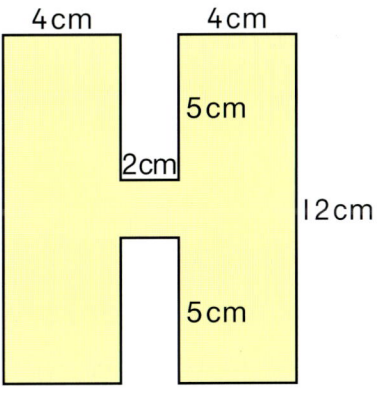

5.
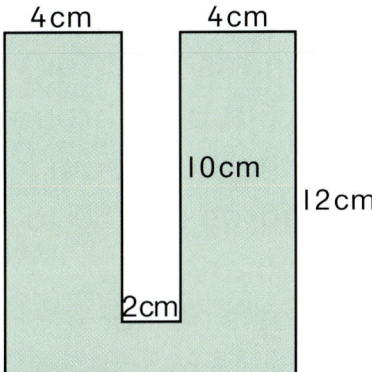

6.
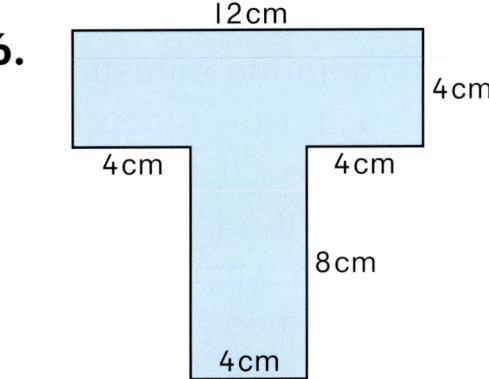

7.
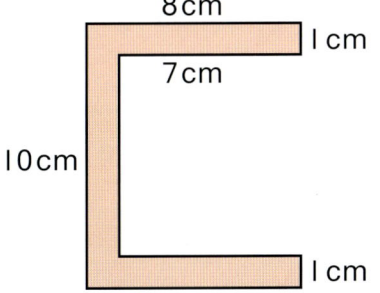

8.
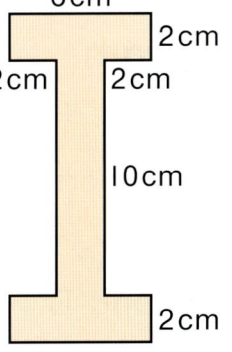

9.
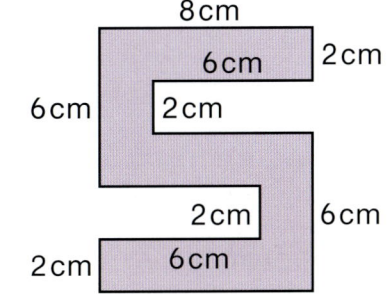

UNIT 26 Area of triangles/Compound shapes/Circles

Word problems

Work out the answers to these word problems. Show all your working.

1. A wall 12 m long and 1·8 m high is to be built of hollow blocks which measure 30 cm × 20 cm.
   (a) How many blocks will be required?
   (b) What would the blocks cost if they are sold at $2.65 each?
   (c) If the builder charges $1.50 to lay each block how much would this cost the owner?

2. A bathroom tile measures 15 cm × 15 cm and is sold for $1.50 each. How many tiles are needed to tile a bathroom 2 m × 3 m to a height of 2 m? The door to the bathroom measures 180 cm × 80 cm. If the builder charges $1.50 to put on each tile what is the total cost to the owner?

3. A floor tile measures 30 cm × 30 cm and costs $7.95. How many tiles are needed to cover a floor 15 m × 10 m and how much will these tiles cost?

The parallelogram

Remember: parallel lines do not meet; they are always the same distance apart.

The rectangle on the right has vertices A, B, C and D.
We can also call the angles at the vertices A, B, C and D.
The sides are then named AB, BC, CD and DA.

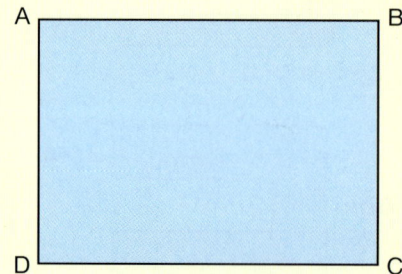

What can you say about the opposite sides of the rectangle?
What can you say about the angles of the rectangle?

Area of triangles/Compound shapes/Circles UNIT 26

You will need: *cardboard sticks, ruler, scissors, drawing pins or similar, protractor.*

Make a rectangular shape from cardboard strips or sticks.
- Fasten the corners with drawing pins (Fig. 1).

Fig. 1   **Fig. 2**

 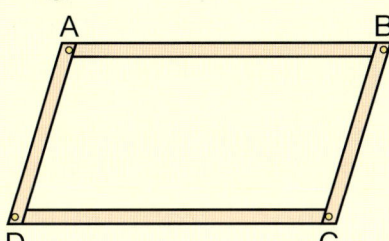

- Hold the bottom stick DC firm and push the rectangle to the right or to the left.
- The shape now becomes a **parallelogram** (Fig. 2).

What can you say about the opposite sides of the parallelogram?

Use the lines in your exercise book as parallel lines and mark off and draw HK and ML 6 cm long.

Join HM and KL.

You have now drawn a parallelogram.

Measure HM and KL and the angles at H, K, M and L.

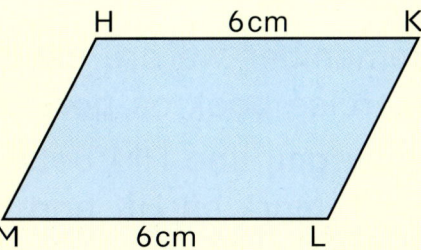

What can you say about the angles of the parallelogram, and the sides HM and KL?

Remember: when two angles add up to 180° they are called **supplementary angles**.

Name the pairs of supplementary angles in the parallelogram.

253

UNIT 26 Area of triangles/Compound shapes/Circles

The rhombus

> **Remember:** A parallelogram is a special quadrilateral; its opposite sides are parallel and equal.
> A rectangle is a special parallelogram; its angles are right angles.

The square is another special parallelogram; all its sides are equal and its angles are right angles.

You will need: cardboard sticks, ruler, scissors, drawing pins or similar.

Fig. 1

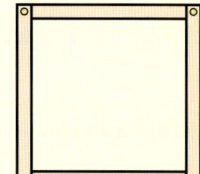

- Make a square shape from your cardboard strips or sticks and fasten the corners with drawing pins (Fig. 1).

Fig. 2

- Hold the bottom side firm and push the top side to the left or to the right.
- You now have a rhombus (Fig. 2). A **rhombus** is a special parallelogram with all its sides equal.

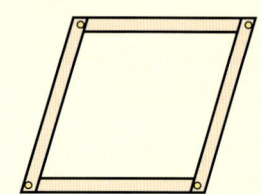

Now draw a rhombus.

Remember we are using the lines in our exercise book as parallel lines.

Draw any line HM between two parallel lines. Mark off HK and ML equal in length to HM. Join KL.

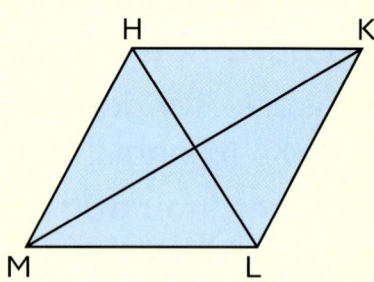

You have now drawn a rhombus.

Measure KL and the angles at H, K, L and M.

Draw the diagonals of the rhombus, HL and KM. What angles do the diagonals make where they intersect or cut each other?

254

Area of triangles/Compound shapes/Circles UNIT 26

Area of a parallelogram

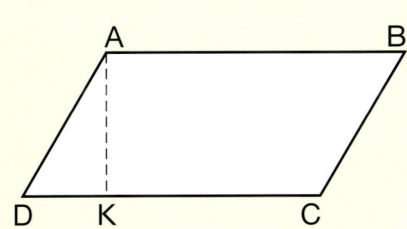 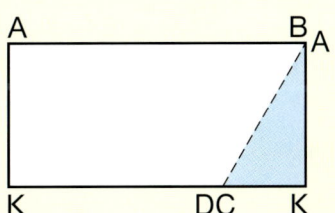

You will need: card, set square, ruler, scissors.

The parallelogram ABCD has sides AB = DC = 6 cm.
- On a sheet of card, draw the parallelogram.
- Use your set square to draw AK perpendicular to DC.
- Call DC the base of the parallelogram and AK the height.
- Cut out this shape and cut along the line AK.

What kind of triangle is the shape ADK?

- Fit the triangle at the other end of the parallelogram. Let AD fall in line with BC.

What shape do you now have?
What can you say about the area of the 'old' parallelogram and the 'new' rectangle?
Which length in the parallelogram is equal to the length of the rectangle and which is equal to the width of the rectangle?
What is the area of the rectangle?
We can say then that the area of a parallelogram
= base × height.

Work out the area of these parallelograms.

1.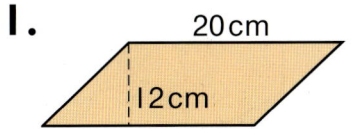
2.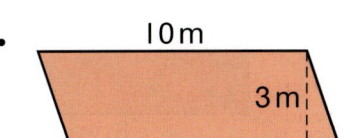
3.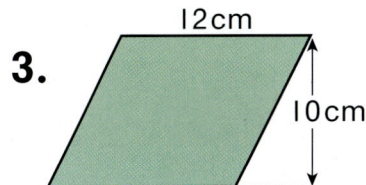

UNIT 26 Area of triangles/Compound shapes/Circles

The trapezium

A **trapezium** is a quadrilateral with one pair of opposite sides parallel.

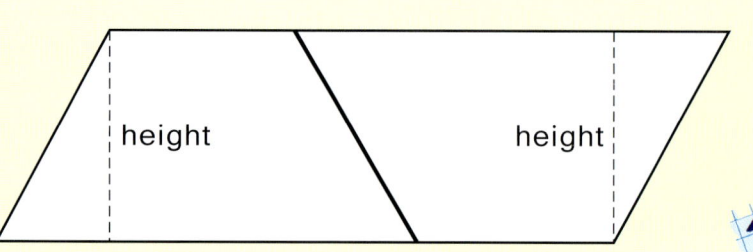

You will need: *card, set square, ruler, scissors, coloured pencils, glue.*

- Cut out two trapeziums of the same size.
- Mark similar edges with similar colours.
- Stick the trapeziums in your exercise book as shown.

What shape do you have?
What is the length of the base? What is the height?
What is the area?

Remember we put two trapeziums together.
Each trapezium = $\frac{1}{2}$ area of the parallelogram
And area of the parallelogram = height × base
= height × (sum of the parallel sides of the trapezium)

Therefore area of the trapezium = $\frac{1}{2}$ height × (sum of the parallel sides)

Work out the area of the following trapeziums.

1.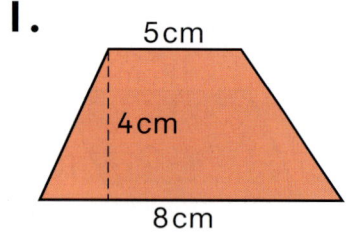

2.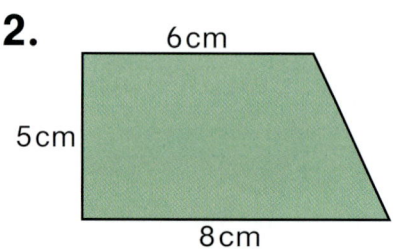

3.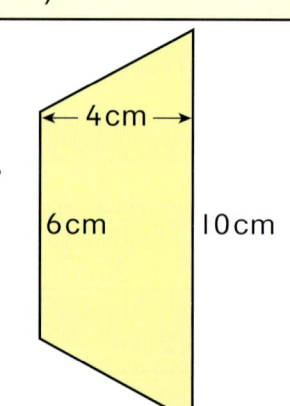

Area of triangles/Compound shapes/Circles UNIT 26

Area of a circle

You will need: *a pair of compasses, ruler.*

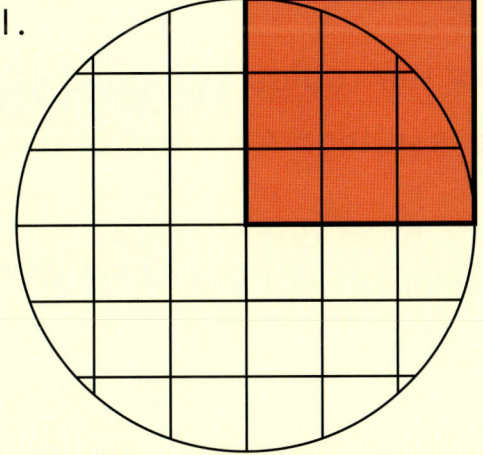

1.
2.

- Measure the radius of each of the circles in cm and enter the measurements in a table like the one below.
- Find the area of each circle by counting square centimetres and enter it on the table. Any area less than $\frac{1}{2}$ cm² should not be counted; any area more than $\frac{1}{2}$ cm² counts as 1 cm².

Draw circles of radii 5 cm and 6 cm on squared paper. Find their areas and complete the table.

Circle	radius	area	(radius)²	area ÷ (radius)²
Circle 1	3 cm	32 cm²	3² = 9	32 ÷ 9 = 3·5̇
Circle 2	4 cm			
Circle 3	5 cm			
Circle 4	6 cm			

257

UNIT 26   Area of triangles/Compound shapes/Circles

There is a relationship between the area of a circle and its radius.
Square the radius in each case and **divide the area** by the **square of the radius**.
Remember we can write the square of the radius as (radius)².

Observe that the area of the circle is less than 4 × area of the small red square.
Complete the table. The first circle has been done for you.
You should find that the area ≈ 3 × (radius)².
Mathematicians have shown that the area of a circle = π × R²

Remember: area of a circle = π × square of the radius
or A = π × R²; A stands for the area, R for radius
and π = 3·14 or $3\frac{1}{7}$.

Take π = 3·14
Calculate the area of the circles with these radii.
(You can use your calculator or you can multiply using factors.)

1. 10 cm   **2.** 5 m   **3.** 7 m   **4.** 20 cm

Calculate the area of the circles with these diameters.

5. 16 m   **6.** 60 m   **7.** 6 cm   **8.** 24 cm

Calculate the area of the coloured portions.

9. 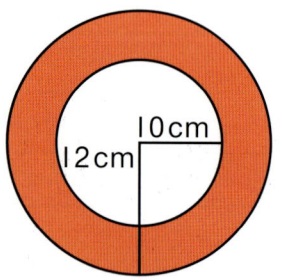   **10.** 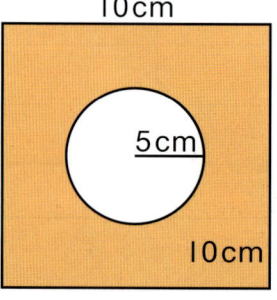   **11.**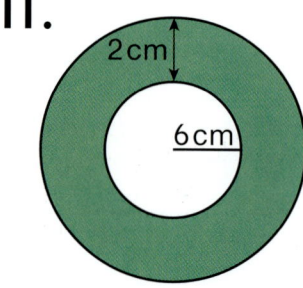

258

Assessment 13

1. Share $20 between Bal and Dave so that Dave will get $2 more than Bal. How much would each get?

2. Divide 40 mangoes into two bags so that one bag has three times as many as the other. How many mangoes will be in each bag?

3. What is the circumference of a circle whose radius is 3·5 cm?

4. A motor car wheel is 56 cm in diameter. How many revolutions will it make after the car has travelled 1 kilometre?

5. How much will the wire cost to fence this field if the wire is sold in rolls of 30 m at $250 per roll?

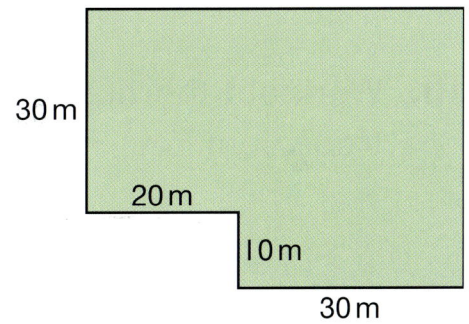

6. Work out the area of the triangle:

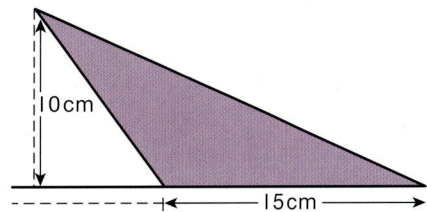

Assessment

7. Work out the area of the shape.

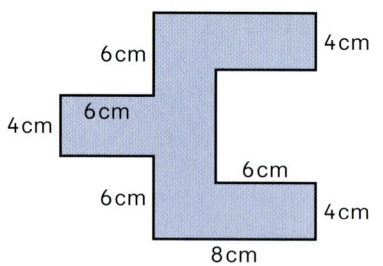

8. A floor tile measures 30 cm × 30 cm. How many tiles will be needed to cover a floor 12 m × 10 m and what will the tiles cost at $11.50 for a tile?

9. Work out the area of the parallelogram.

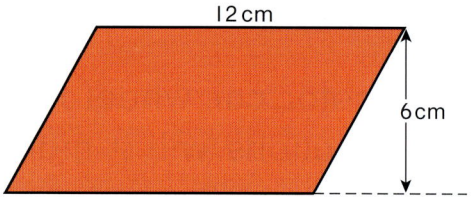

10. Work out the area of this trapezium.

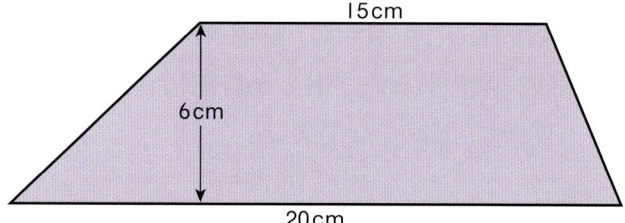

11. Work out the area of this circle.

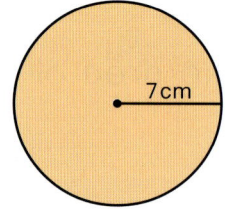

27 Volume and capacity

Litres and millilitres

Say how many millilitres each of these containers hold.

    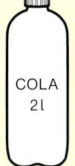 

PAINT 4l — MOTOR OIL 1l — SODA ½l — PUNCH 1l — COLA 2l — ¼l

We can write capacity in litres and millilitres as litres using decimals.

Remember: 1 litre = 1000 ml and 1 ml = $\frac{1}{1000}$ l
 10 ml = $\frac{1}{100}$ l   and 100 ml = $\frac{1}{10}$ l

		1000 ml 1 l	100 ml $\frac{1}{10}$ l	10 ml $\frac{1}{100}$ l	1 ml $\frac{1}{1000}$ l
	5 ml	0 .	0	0	5
45 ml	40 ml + 5 ml	0 .	0	4	5
245 ml	200 ml + 40 ml + 5 ml	0 .	2	4	5
3245 ml	3000 ml + 200 + 40 ml + 5 ml	3 .	2	4	5

3245 ml = 3·245 l

Write as millilitres:

1. 1 l 145 ml
2. 3 l 245 ml
3. 2 l 350 ml
4. 5 l 70 ml
5. 4 l 255 ml
6. 20 l 15 ml
7. 15 l 5 ml
8. 14 l 200 ml
9. 10 l 500 ml
10. 20 l 20 ml

Write as litres and millilitres:

11. 2435 ml
12. 1875 ml
13. 6705 ml
14. 3005 ml
15. 4215 ml
16. 1800 ml
17. 1450 ml
18. 15 030 ml
19. 5260 ml
20. 10 075 ml

UNIT 27 Volume and capacity

Write as litres:
21. 2 l 355 ml   **22.** 3 l 280 ml   **23.** 2 l 85 ml   **24.** 5 l 60 ml
25. 22 l 45 ml **26.** 32 l 308 ml **27.** 12 l 300 ml **28.** 20 l 30 ml

Write as litres:
29. 3155 ml   **30.** 1890 ml   **31.** 2035 ml   **32.** 5005 ml
33. 10 250 ml   **34.** 13 070 ml   **35.** 20 030 ml   **36.** 4040 ml

Remember: when we round off we look at the number to the immediate right to determine how we round off.

Example 3·465 l ≈ 3 l (4, the number to the immediate right of 3 is less than 5)
3·465 ml ≈ 3·5 l or 3·47 l

Round off these quantities (a) to the nearest litre, (b) to the nearest $\frac{1}{10}$ litre and (c) to the nearest $\frac{1}{100}$ litre.
37. 1·535 l   **38.** 4·271 l   **39.** 6·540 l   **40.** 2·925 l
41. 4·320 l   **42.** 6·705 l   **43.** 8·795 l   **44.** 7·895 l
45. 15·020 l   **46.** 13·215 l   **47.** 9·055 l   **48.** 8·008 l

Copy and complete these calculations.

49.
```
    l   ml
    3  175
    5  210
+   2  155
   _____
```

50.
```
    l   ml
    4  205
       975
+   5  100
   _____
```

51.
```
    l   ml
   10  250
    1  475
+   2   65
   _____
```

Volume and capacity UNIT 27

52.
```
    l    ml
    4   100
    5    95
+   3   275
   ─────────
```

53.
```
    l    ml
        735
    5   295
+   4   805
   ─────────
```

54.
```
    l    ml
   14     5
    2    75
+   3   455
   ─────────
```

55.
```
    l    ml
   15   195
    2   675
+   1   700
   ─────────
```

56.
```
    l    ml
    4   250
    5   310
+   1   970
   ─────────
```

57.
```
    l    ml
    2   535
    3   475
+   1   800
   ─────────
```

58.
```
    l    ml
    4   220
    3   105
+   1   695
   ─────────
```

59.
```
    l    ml
    1   612
    3   445
+   1   600
   ─────────
```

60.
```
    l    ml
   15   250
    6   195
+   1   575
   ─────────
```

61.
```
    l    ml
   14   750
−   6   395
   ─────────
```

62.
```
    l    ml
    8   245
−   1   675
   ─────────
```

63.
```
    l    ml
   10     5
−   1    45
   ─────────
```

64.
```
    l    ml
   15    35
−   6   245
   ─────────
```

65.
```
    l    ml
   14     0
−   3   200
   ─────────
```

66.
```
    l    ml
   10   215
−   4   625
   ─────────
```

UNIT 27 Volume and capacity

Reviewing volume

Remember: volume of a cuboid = L × B × H or base area × height.

Calculate the volume of these cuboids.

1.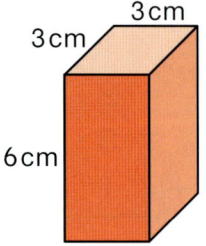

2.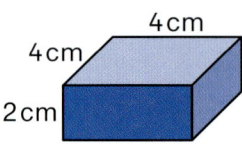

3.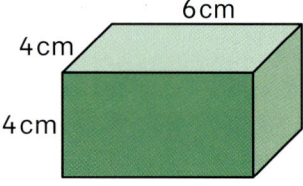

4.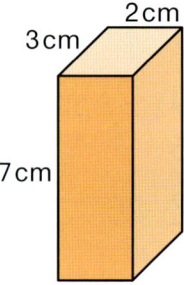

5. Which of the cuboids have the same volume?

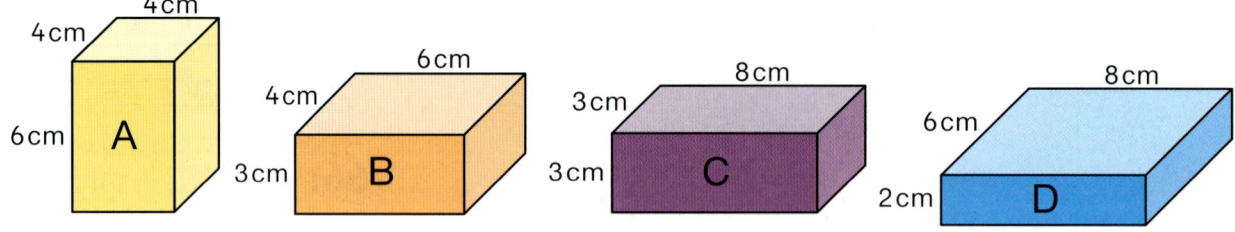

264

Volume and capacity UNIT 27

Calculate the height of each of these cuboids.

6.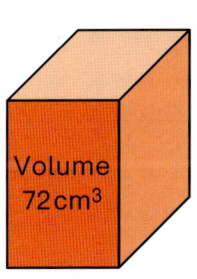
base area
12 cm²

7.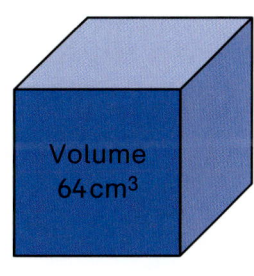
base area
16 cm²

8.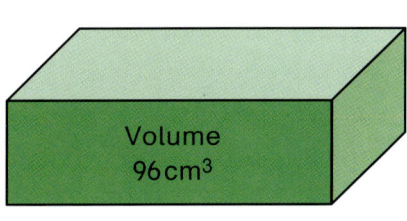
base area
32 cm²

9.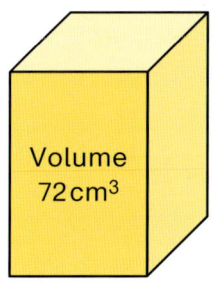
base area
9 cm²

Calculate the base area of these cuboids.

10.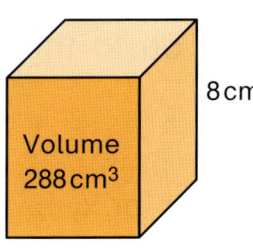

11.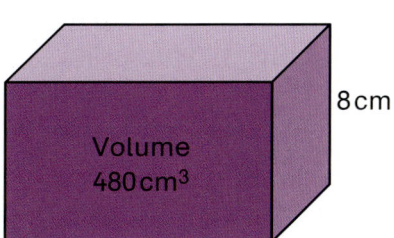

12.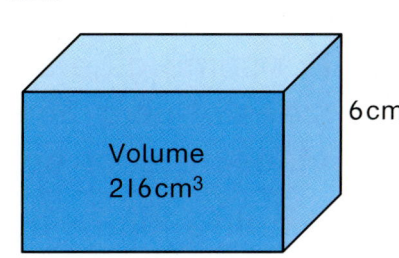

265

UNIT 27   Volume and capacity

Volume and capacity

Making a 1000 cm³ box

Follow the instructions carefully.

You will need:
a large piece of strong cardboard 30 cm x 30 cm, ruler, scissors, glue, litre jug, sand.

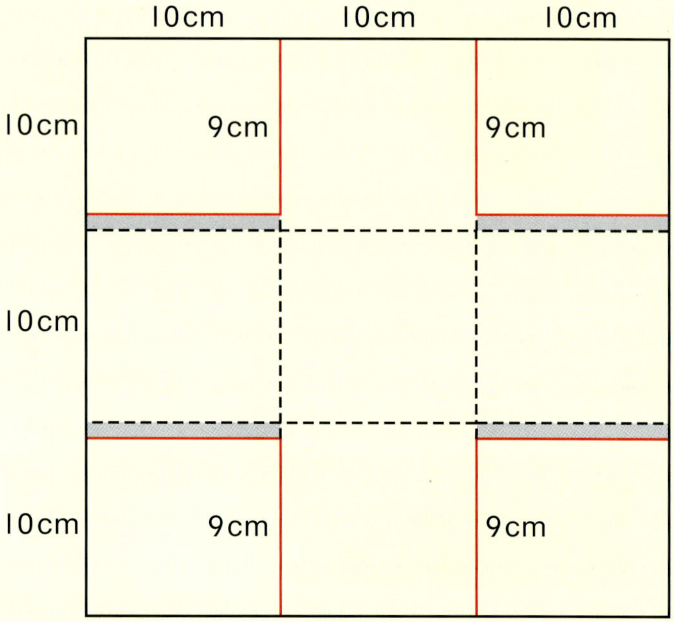

- Measure out squares 10 cm × 10 cm on the cardboard; you should have three rows of three squares each.
- Measure 9 cm as shown above and draw in the red lines.
- Cut along the red lines only and remove the four cut out corners.
- Draw the dotted lines and fold along these lines.
- Put some glue on the shaded flaps and stick them on to the sides of your box.
- Measure your box.

Fill a litre jug or bottle with sand and empty into your box. What do you observe?

How many millilitres in 1 litre? How many cm³ in your box? What can you say about the millilitre and the cm³?

Volume and capacity   UNIT 27

From your experiment with the sand, the 1000 cm³ box, and the litre, you have discovered that 1 litre ≈ 1000 cm³.

If you did the experiment with water, an accurately made 1000 cm³ glass or plastic cube, and a measuring cylinder you would find that

1 litre = 1000 ml = 1000 cm³
so 1 ml = 1 cm³

Problem: A fish tank measuring 50 cm long, 30 cm wide and 25 cm deep is filled with water. How many litres does it hold?

Volume of the tank = 50 × 30 × 25 cm³ = 37 500 cm³
Number of millilitres = 37 500 ml
Number of litres = 37·5 l

How many litres of water do the following rectangular tanks hold?

1. 1 m × 1 m × 1 m
2. 200 cm × 150 cm × 100 cm
3. 1½ m × 1½ m × 2 m
4. 1·5 m × 1·5 m × 1 m

Work out the answers to these word problems. Show all your working.

5. A fish tank holds 40 litres of water. It is 50 cm long and 40 cm wide. How tall is it?

6. A water tank holds 4000 litres of water. It is 2 m square at the base. How tall is it?

7. A fish tank when full of water holds 24 litres. It is 40 cm long and 30 cm wide. How high up the tank will the water reach when the tank is half full?

8. A packing case measures 1 m by 50 cm by 20 cm. How many boxes 10 cm × 10 cm × 20 cm will it hold?

UNIT 27 Volume and capacity

Volume of a cylinder

Most tankers that carry fuel like gasoline, oil and liquefied gas have cylindrical tanks.
Our petrol is stored in huge cylindrical tanks at our refinery.
How much do these tanks hold?

Remember: for a cuboid, volume = L × B × H
or area of base × height

Test the formula: volume = area of base × height for a cylinder.

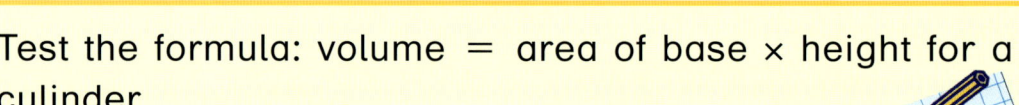

You will need: a cylindrical tin, measuring tape or ruler.

- Fill the tin with water.
- Pour the water carefully into a measuring cylinder and write the volume in ml.
- Write the volume also in cm^3; remember 1 ml = 1 cm^3
- Measure as accurately as you can the radius of your tin.
- Measure the height of the tin.

Remember: area of a circle = π × R^2

Calculate: area of base × height = _____ cm^3

How does this result compare with the volume you measured?
  The true volume of the tin = area of base × height.
  We can write volume of a cylinder V = πR^2 × H

268

Volume and capacity UNIT 27

Find the volumes of the following cylinders.

1. base radius 7 cm, height 10 cm

2. base radius 14 cm, height 15 cm

3. base area 40 m³, height 12 m

4. base area 500 cm³, height 2 m

5. base diameter 14 cm, height 30 cm

6. base diameter 7 cm, height 50 cm

How many litres do these containers hold?

7.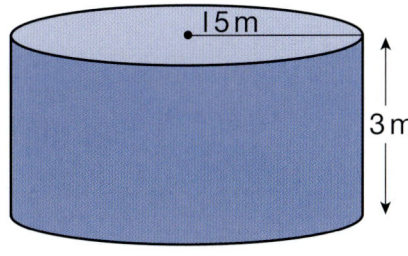

8.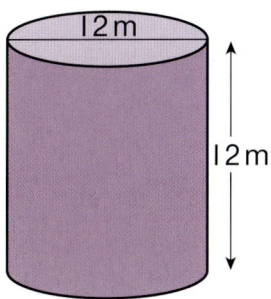

9.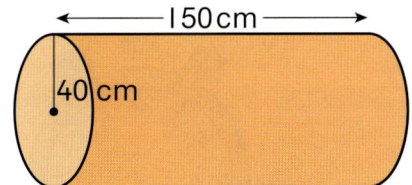

28 Time

Minutes and seconds

Many events are completed in less than a minute.
The 100 m, 200 m and 400 m events at International athletics meetings like the Olympic or World Games take less than a minute.

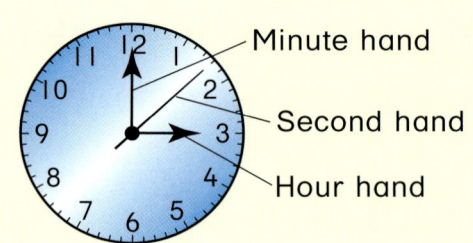

The world record for the 100 m is under 10 seconds, the record for the 200 m is under 20 seconds, and for the 400 m, under 44 seconds.

Many clocks and watches have a second hand that measures seconds.

The second hand takes 60 seconds or 1 minute to go once round the face of the clock.

Remember: the minute hand takes 60 minutes or 1 hour to go once round the clock.
60 seconds = 1 minute and 60 minutes = 1 hour

How long does it take the hour hand to go once round the clock?

Stop watches are made to measure seconds and fractions of a second.

Look at the pictures of the three stop watches below.

(a)    (b)    (c)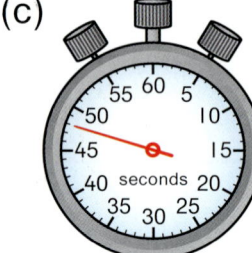

270

Time UNIT 28

1. Which watch shows the longest time?
2. Which watch shows the shortest time?
3. What is the difference between the longest and shortest times?
4. How many more seconds before each watch would record 1 minute?

One commercial break during a TV show lasted 1 minute 35 seconds. The other breaks lasted 1 minute 45 seconds and 1 minute 20 seconds. How much time was spent on the breaks?

Total time was

1 minute 35 seconds + 1 minute 45 seconds + 1 minute 20 seconds

= 4 minutes 40 seconds

	minutes	seconds
	1	35
	1	45
+	1	20
	4	40

In the problem above how much longer was the longest break than the shortest?

Difference = 1 minute 45 seconds − 1 minute 20 seconds

= 25 seconds

	minutes	seconds
	1	45
−	1	20
	0	25

Copy and complete these calculations.

5.   min sec
      2 25
  + 3 30
  ———

6.   min sec
      5 10
  + 3 50
  ———

7.   min sec
      2 40
  − 1 10
  ———

8.   min sec
      4 15
  − 1 40
  ———

UNIT 28 Time

Work out the answers to these word problems. Show all your working.

9. A man exercised for 10 minutes 30 seconds; rested for 3 minutes 20 seconds and exercised again for 5 minutes 10 seconds. How much time did he spend altogether exercising and resting?

10. Ravi won his race in 3 minutes 50 seconds. Mannie came second in 4 minutes 6 seconds. How much more time did Mannie take?

11. Hasley Crawford won the 100 m in 10.06 seconds. Carl Lewis won it later in 9.96 seconds. How many seconds faster was Carl Lewis?

12. The winner of the 100 m sprint was timed in 9.97 seconds. The second placed runner was timed in 10.02 seconds. How much slower was the second runner?

13. Michael Johnson finished the 200 m sprint in 19.95 seconds. Frankie Fredericks was 0.35 seconds slower. How long did Fredericks take?

14. Grace can ride a distance of 5 miles in 20 minutes 25 seconds. How long will it take her to complete a distance of 20 miles if she rides at the same speed?

Time UNIT 28

Speed

> When travelling from one place to another a car will move at different speeds, sometimes faster, sometimes slower.
>
> If you watch the speedometer you will see the pointer changing its position.
>
> If after 1 hour a car has travelled 50 km, we say that the **average** speed was 50 km per hour. **Per hour** means for every hour.
>
> If after 2 hours the car has travelled 100 km, the average speed is still 50 km per hour because in every hour it would travel 50 km if it moved at this speed throughout the journey.

Find these average speeds.

1. 400 km in 5 hours
2. 250 km in 4 hours
3. 300 km in 5 hours
4. 40 km in $\frac{1}{2}$ hour
5. 10 km in $\frac{1}{4}$ hour
6. 15 km in 20 minutes

7. World champions run 100 m in about 10 seconds.
   Measure a distance of 25 m in the playground.
   In groups of 3 or 4, time each other running the distance.
   Make a chart like the one below.

name	time taken to run 25 m	speed	calculated time to run	
			50 m	100 m

UNIT 28 Time

Finding distance and time

> Distance ÷ time = speed
>
> We can write km per hour as **km/hr** and metres per second as **m/sec** (or **m/s**).
>
> If we know the distance travelled and the average speed we can find the time taken.
>
> **Example** A bus travelling at an average speed of 50 km/hr will travel 500 km in
>
> $$500 \div 50 = 10 \text{ hours}$$
> Distance ÷ speed = time

Copy and complete the table below.

distance	300 km	200 m	400 m	50 m	50 m
speed	60 km/hr	80 km/hr	50 m/s	25 m/s	100 m/s
time					

> We can also find the distance travelled if we know the speed and the time taken.
>
> **Example** A car travelling for 2 hours at 100 km/hr would travel
>
> $$100 \times 2 = 200 \text{ km}$$
> Speed × time = distance

Now copy and complete this table.

speed	150 km/hr	40 km/hr	55 m/s	80 m/hr	20 m/s
time	2 hrs	$1\frac{1}{4}$ hrs	10 secs	2 hr 10 mins	10 mins
distance					

Time UNIT 28

The diagram below shows the bus routes and the distances between several places.
All buses travel at an average speed of 50 km/hr.
Answer the questions below.

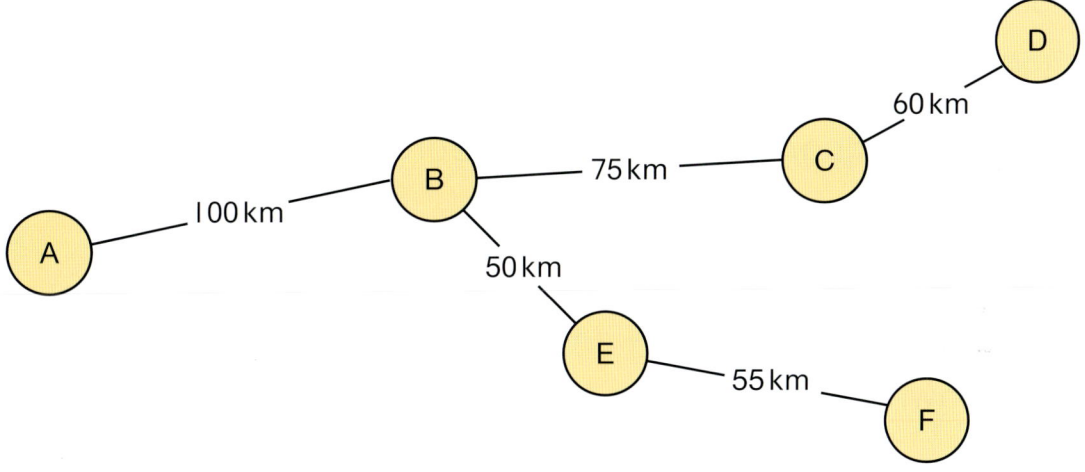

1. (a) How long does a bus take from B to A?
   (b) If a bus leaves B at 7.40 a.m. when does it arrive at A?
   (c) If the bus waits 30 minutes at A before returning, when does it arrive back at B?

2. (a) A non-stop bus leaves B at 8.00 a.m. for D. How long does it take?
   (b) When does it arrive at D?
   (c) On the return journey it stops at C for 15 minutes. If it left D at 12.00 noon when did it return to B?

3. (a) A charter bus on a school outing from A to F must stop at B for 15 minutes for petrol on the outward trip and on the return trip. How long will the trip take both ways?
   (b) If the bus leaves the school at A at 7.00 a.m. and the children spend 4 hours at F at what time do they return to A?

Assessment

Assessment 14

Write answers to the following:

1. $2\frac{3}{4}$ l = _____ ml
2. 1·56 l = _____ ml
3. 3 l 15 ml = _____ l

Round off these quantities (a) to the nearest litre (b) to the nearest $\frac{1}{10}$ litre.

4. 2·545 l
5. 10·905 l

6. From a barrel containing 50 litres of kerosene, 24 l 400 ml was drawn off. How much kerosene was left in the barrel?

7. (a) What is the volume of the metal tank shown on the right?
   (b) How many litres of water does it hold?

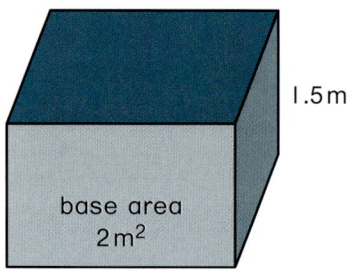

8. A barrel has a circular base of radius 30 cm. How many litres of water will the barrel hold if it is 1.3 m tall?

9. A car travels a distance of 120 km at an average speed of 50 km/hr. How long does the journey take?

10. A bus leaves the terminal at 7.15 a.m. and returns at 3.15 p.m. How much time has elapsed between the departure from and return to the terminus?

29 Statistics

Mean and mode

> **Remember:** the **mean** of a set of numbers is the sum of the numbers divided by the number of numbers in the set. The **mode** is the number occurring most frequently.

1. Look at this set of values:
   15 kg   18 kg   13 kg   17 kg   15 kg   20 kg   14 kg
   (a) Identify the mode.
   (b) Calculate the mean.

2. Ravi achieved the following marks in his term test:
   mathematics 85, language arts 84, social studies 85, science 92.
   What was his average mark?

3. The scores of 20 children in a numbers game were:
   10, 7, 4, 7, 5, 5, 12, 5, 6, 8, 7, 8, 5, 3, 9, 10, 3, 11, 9, 6.
   (a) What was the mean score?
   (b) Which score was the mode?

4. The scores of 24 children in a mathematics test were:
   21   24   20   22   17   19   22   20   214   18   22   23
   23   21   21   23   16   25   25   22   21   23   24   22
   (a) What was the highest score?
   (b) What was the lowest score?
   (c) Prepare a tally chart of the number of students and the scores obtained from the lowest to the highest.
   (d) Which score was the mode?
   (e) Calculate the mean score (use your calculator).

UNIT 29 Statistics

The pictograph

This shows the approximate number of people who attended the movies over a period of a week.

The symbol 😊 represents 20 people.

Monday	😊😊😊😊😊
Tuesday	😊😊😊😊😊😊🙂
Wednesday	😊😊😊😊😊😊😊😊
Thursday	😊😊😊😊😊😊😊🙂
Friday	😊😊😊😊😊😊😊😊
Saturday	😊😊😊😊😊😊😊😊🙂
Sunday	😊😊😊😊😊😊😊😊😊

Use the information in the pictograph above to answer these questions.

1. (a) What was the largest number of people attending the show on any one day?
   (b) On which day did the smallest number of people attend?
   (c) On which days did about the same number of people attend?
   (d) What was the approximate average daily attendance?
   (e) If the true average daily attendance was 154 how many people attended over the period?
   (f) If about 60% of the people attending the show were females, about how many males attended during the week?

278

Statistics UNIT 29

The bar graph

1. The table below shows the approximate number of people who visited the Trade Fair on the days listed.

Fri	Sat	Sun	Mon	Tue
250	350	400	250	200

Draw a bar graph to show this information.

2. The bar graph on the right shows the monthly rainfall of a Caribbean country.

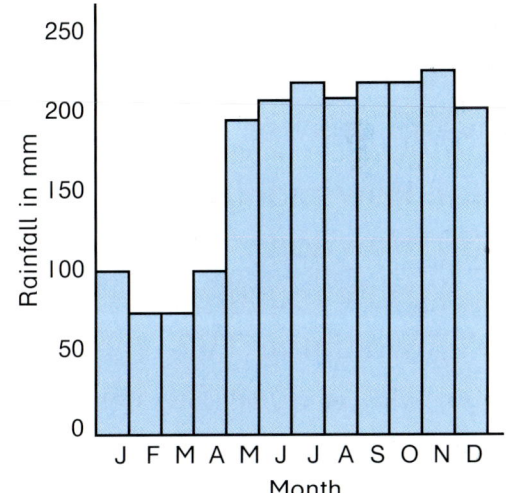

Use the information in the bar graph to answer these questions.
   (a) Which were the driest months of the year?
   (b) Which were the wettest months of the year?
   (c) Which months could you say were in the dry season?
   (d) In which months was there more than 200 mm of rainfall?
   (e) What was the total rainfall for the months in (d)?
   (f) What was the average monthly rainfall?

3. Here are some data for rainfall for another Caribbean country.

Month	J	F	M	A	M	J	J	A	S	O	N	D
Rainfall in mm	165	152	165	140	122	140	119	135	135	137	140	142

Draw a bar graph to show this information.

UNIT 29 Statistics

The pie chart revisited

The pie chart on the right shows how a child spends most of her day. The circle is divided into 12 equal sectors.

How many hours does one sector represent? How much does the angle in a sector measure?

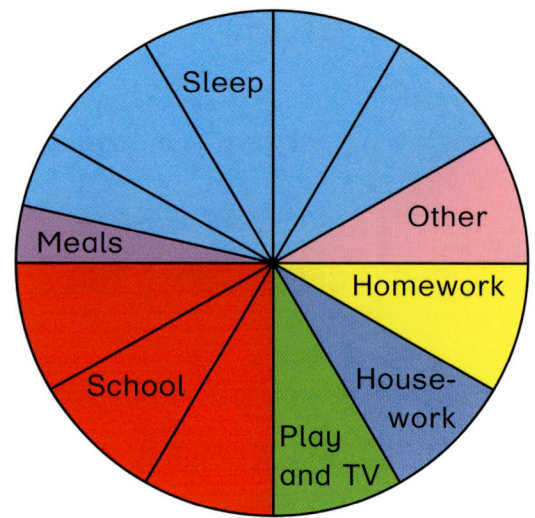

Use the information in the pie chart above to answer these questions.

1. (a) How many hours does the child spend sleeping?
   (b) How long does the child stay in school?
   (c) How much of the day does the child spend playing and watching TV?
   (d) What does the child spend the least time doing?
   (e) How much time does the child spend doing homework?
   (f) What are some of the 'Other' things you think the child might be doing?

2. The information in the pie chart can also be shown on a bar graph. Copy and complete the bar graph on the right to show the information.

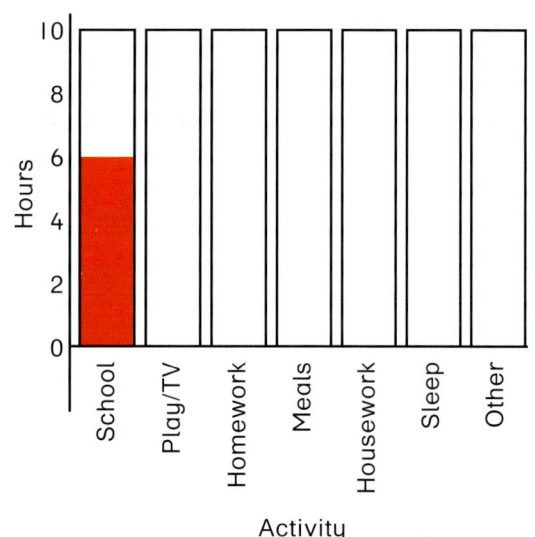

280

Statistics UNIT 29

The bar graph below shows the result of a survey of people's favourite shows.

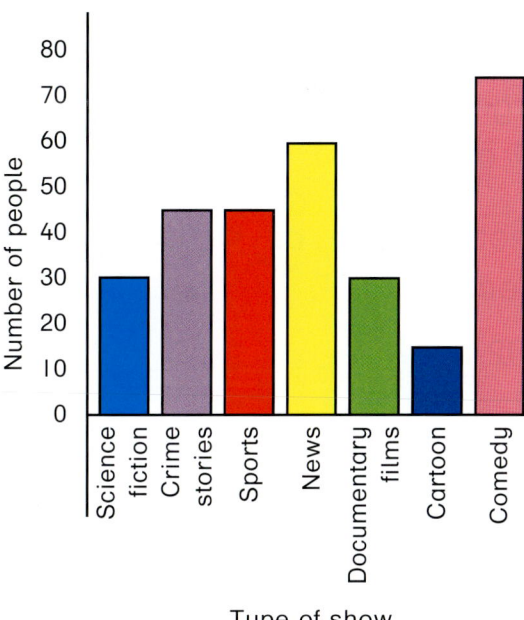

3. Use the information in the bar graph above to answer these questions.
   (a) How many people were in the sample?
   (b) What percentage chose the news as their favourite programme?
   (c) Which was the smallest group?
   (d) What percentage of the total was the smallest group?
   (e) What percentage was the largest group?

4. Work out the percentages for all the other groups and draw a pie chart to show the information.

Remember: 10% on the pie chart means a sector whose angle at the centre of the circle is 36°.

Specimen paper

1. Add together 9703 and 3150.

2. Write in words: 36 019.

3. What is the largest number which can be formed using the digits 0, 6, 2, 9 and 4?

4. Write the correct sign, > or <, in the box to complete the statement correctly.

   3·920 ☐ 3·902

5. $6\frac{1}{2} - 3\frac{3}{4}$

6. What is the area of the shaded part of the grid below?

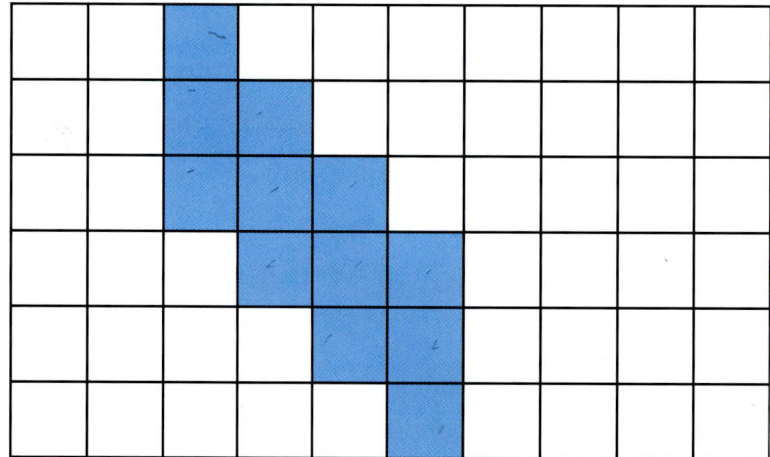

7. The area of the rectangle is 72 cm².

   What is its width?

   9 cm

   Area 72 cm²

Specimen paper

8. What is the length of the pencil?

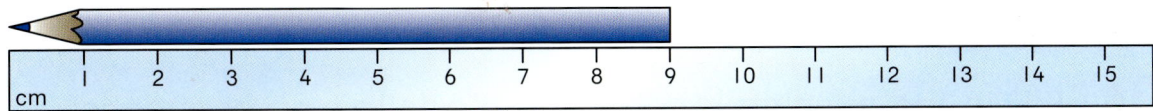

9. Complete the statement below:

   3·25 m = ☐ cm

10. State the time shown on the clock in digital notation.

11. Copy and complete the table below:

Favourite snack	tally	frequency
Pizza	卌	5
Chicken & chips		16
Hot Dog		2

12. From $9\frac{2}{3}$ subtract $4\frac{5}{8}$.

13. In a standard 2 class there are 30 students. If there are 12 boys in the class what decimal fraction of the class are girls?

14. If $\frac{1}{8}$ of a number of marbles is 6, what is the number?

Specimen paper

15. Write the following fractions in order of size, largest first:
$\frac{7}{16}, \frac{3}{8}, \frac{1}{2}, \frac{9}{16}$

16. Fill in the missing numbers in the following sequence:
4, 9, 16, ☐, ☐, 49

17. Andrea had $60.00. She spent 60% on a blouse. How much money did she have left?

18. Two poles A and B are shown below.

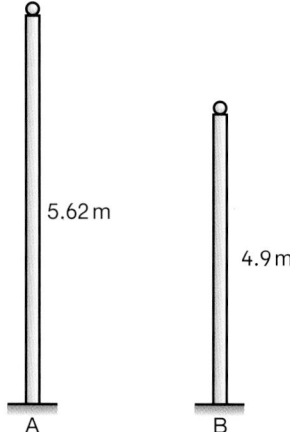

How much taller is A than B?

19. Gail left home at 7.45 a.m. She arrived at school $\frac{3}{4}$ of an hour later. What time did she arrive at school?

20. My younger brother took 10 minutes to eat his breakfast. I took 4 minutes 10 seconds to eat mine. How much more time did my brother take?

284

Specimen paper

21. At a bazaar there were 212 girls; the rest were boys. If 700 people attended the bazaar what fraction of the crowd was boys?

22. The table below shows the method of transportation students use to get to school.

Method of transportation	number of students
Maxi taxis	272
Private cars	124
Bus	
Bicycle	20
None of the above	56

If there are 600 students at the school, what per cent of the students travel by bus?

23. Five boys shared a 2 litre bottle of fruit punch equally among themselves. How much less than $\frac{1}{2}$ a litre would each boy get?

24. Dave's pencil measures 16 cm. Molly's pencil is 6·87 cm longer than Dave's. What is the length of Molly's pencil?

Specimen paper

25. The shaded portion of the floor shown below is carpeted. What decimal fraction is this?

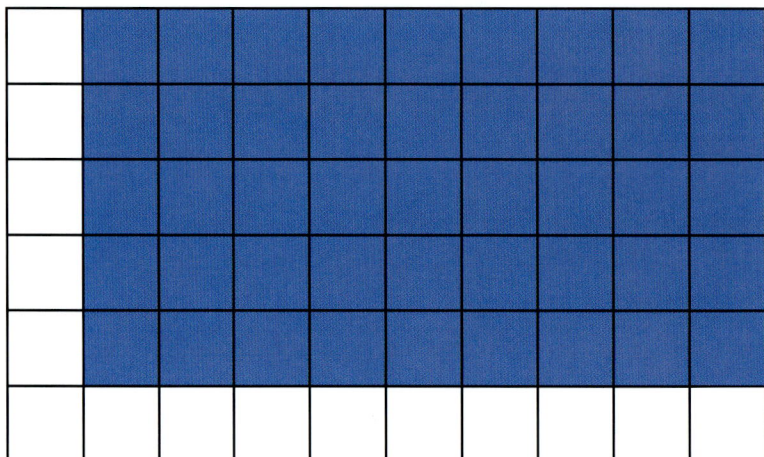

26.
```
    kg    g
     8  3 8 6
  + 1 2  4 0 9
  _____
```

27. Calculate the length of the side of the equilateral triangle if the perimeter is 36 cm.

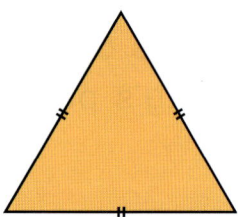

28. A rectangular floor measures 5·2 m in length and is 4 m wide. Calculate its area.

286

Specimen paper

29. Calculate the perimeter of the shape below.

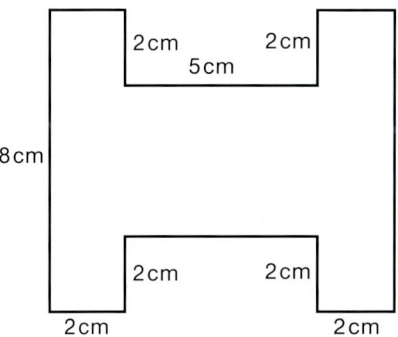

30. What is the volume of the rectangular solid?

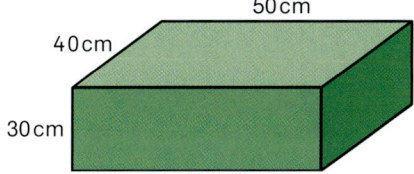

31. Find the area of the shape:

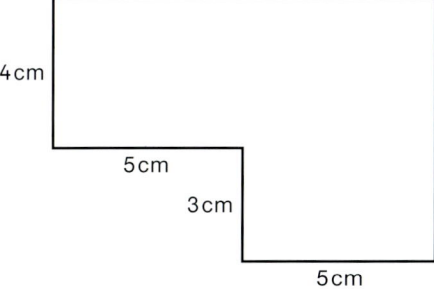

Specimen paper

32. The volume of the cube below is 64 cm³. What is the length of an edge of the cube?

33. O is the centre of the circle below. The line OB measures 7 cm. Calculate the circumference of the circle.

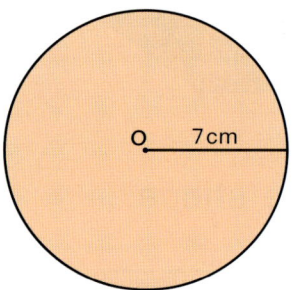

34. The long hand of a clock moved from 2.30 to 3 o'clock.
   (a) Through how many degrees did the long hand turn?
   (b) What fraction of a complete turn did the long hand make?

Specimen paper

35. The diagram below shows the position of triangle A.

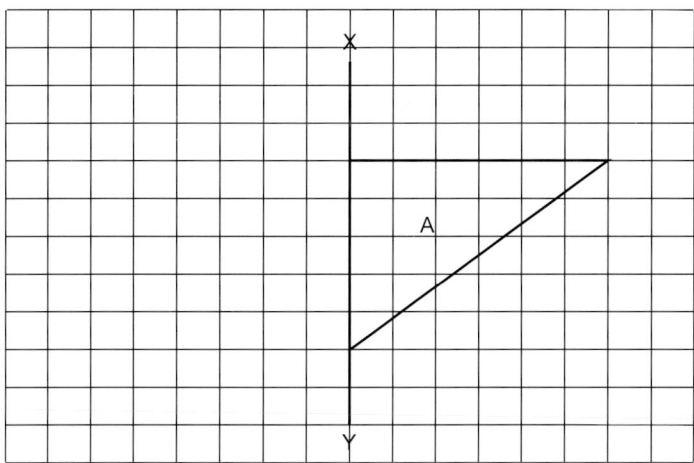

Triangle A is flipped about the line XY. Draw the new position of the triangle.

36. The diagram below shows the movement of the square from position P to position Q.

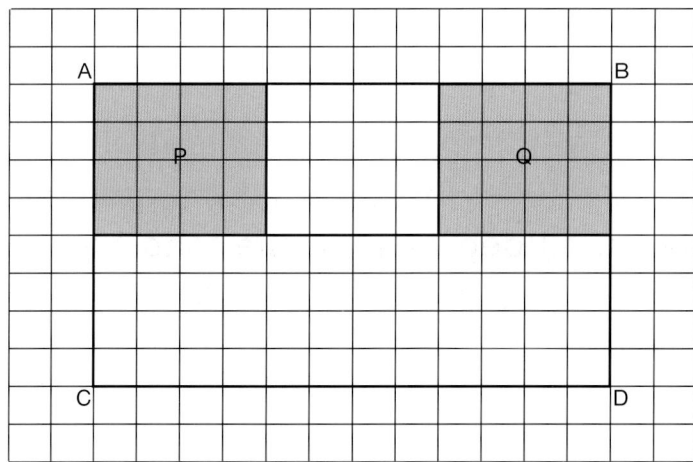

(a) What type of movement was used?
(b) How many such movements are required to cover the rectangle ABCD?

Specimen paper

37. The graph below shows the hobbies of students of several standard 5 classes.

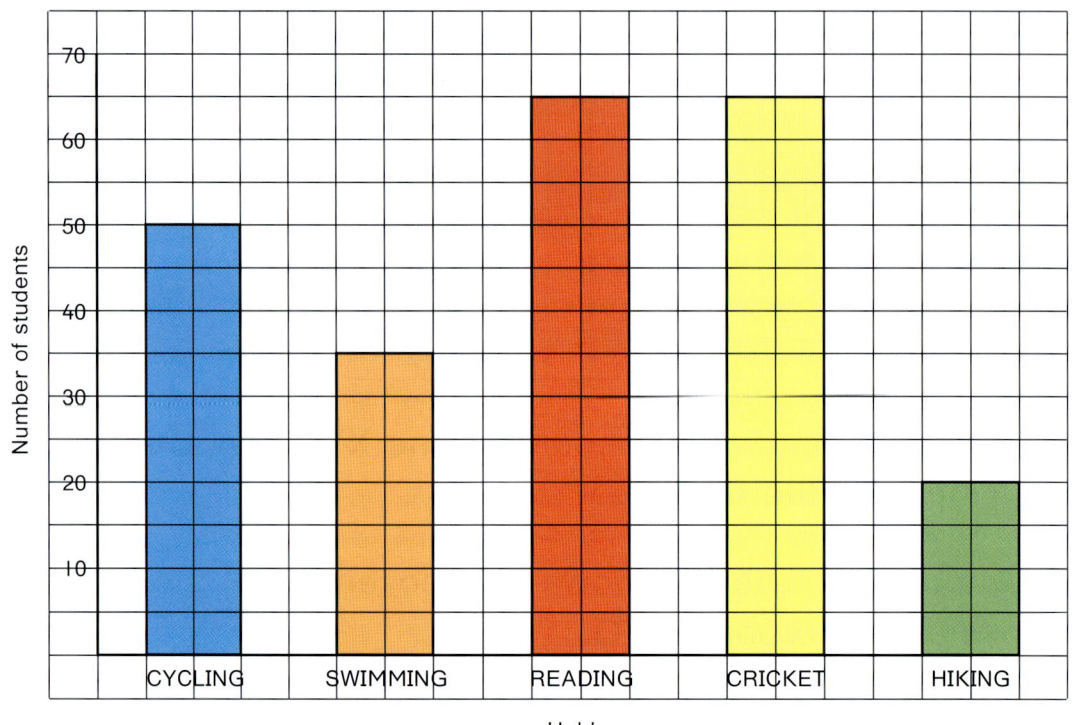

(a) What was the total number of students in the classes?
(b) Which hobby was least favoured by the students?
(c) How many more students preferred reading to swimming?
(d) What per cent of the students enjoy hiking?

38. A man borrowed $5000 for 2 years and paid interest at the rate of 12% per annum.
How much money would he have paid to the bank at the end of that period?

Specimen paper

39. The pie chart below shows Marvin's monthly expenditure. His salary is $4800 per month.
How much does Marvin spend on food?

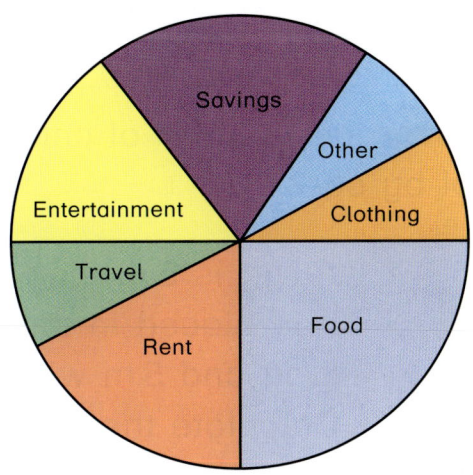

40. Sally bought the following:
   four soft drinks at $1.50 each
   two cakes at $3.25 each
   four packets of biscuits at $9.75 per pkt
How much change did she receive from a $100 bill?

41. In a church hall there are 14 rows of benches with 12 benches in each row.
If each bench can accommodate 10 people, how many people can be seated in the church hall?

42. The regular price on floor tiles is $6.00 each; the tiles are 30 cm × 30 cm. Mr Johnson decided to tile his living room which measures 6 m × 5 m.
What would the tiles cost Mr Johnson if he is given a 20% discount?

Specimen paper

43. The table below shows the number of children in the Standard 5 classes who came to school by car.

Monday	Tuesday	Wednesday	Thursday	Friday
46	52	50	48	44

What was the average number of children per day who came to school by car?

44. 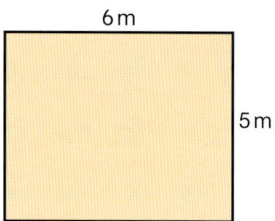 A rug is 5 m long and 4 m wide. It is placed in the centre of a room 6 m long and 5 m wide. Calculate the area of the floor not covered by the rug.

45. The circle is divided into eight equal sectors.
What is the size of the angle labelled A?

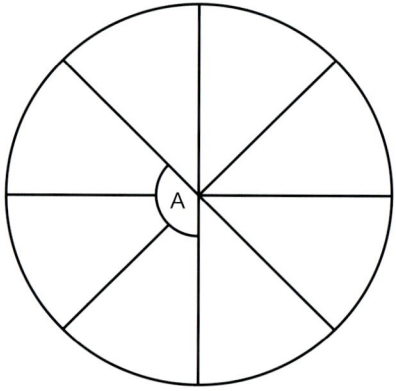

46. Five men working at the same rate built a wall in 4 days. They worked 7 hours a day and were paid at the rate of $20 per hour.
(a) How much money did each worker earn?
(b) If the contractor received $10 000 for the job, what per cent of this money did the contractor earn for himself after paying the wages to his workers?